RETHINKING ISLAM AND MODERNITY

Essays in Honour of Fathi Osman

Edited by
ABDELWAHAB EL-AFFENDI

THE ISLAMIC FOUNDATION
in association with
THE MAGHRIB CENTRE FOR RESEARCH
AND TRANSLATION, LONDON

Published by
THE ISLAMIC FOUNDATION
Markfield Conference Centre, Ratby Lane,
Markfield, Leicester LE67 9SY, United Kingdom
Tel: (01530) 244944; Fax: (01530) 244946
Email: i.foundation@islamic-foundation.org.uk
Web site: www.islamic-foundation.org.uk

The Maghreb Centre for Research & Translation
34 Tyrell Close, London HA1 3UX

Quran House, PO Box 30611, Nairobi, Kenya

PMB 3193, Kano, Nigeria

© The Islamic Foundation 2001/1422 AH

All rights reserved. No part of this publication may be reproduced, stored in a retrieval system, or transmitted in any form or by any means, electronic, mechanical, photocopying, recording, or otherwise, without the prior permission of the copyright owner.

British Library Cataloguing in Publication Data
A catalogue record for this book is available from the British Library

ISBN 0-86037-380-0 PB

Typeset and Cover design by: Sohail Nakhooda

Printed and bound in Great Britain by Antony Rowe Ltd., Chippenham, Wiltshire

Contents

Foreword M. MANAZIR AHSAN		v
Preface		vii
Introduction ABDELWAHAB EL-AFFENDI		ix
1	*Of Darwinian Mice and Pavlovian Dogs: A Critique of Western Modernity* ABDELWAHAB M. ELMESSIRI	1
2	*Secularism, Despotism and Democracy: The Legacy of Imperialism* RAFIK BOUCHLAKA	9
3	*Islam and Human Rights: The Challenge to Muslims and the World* FATHI OSMAN	27
4	*Participation of non-Muslims in Government in Contemporary Muslim Societies* TAREK AL-BECHRI	66
5	*Non-Muslims in Muslim Society* FAHMI HUWEIDI	84
6	*Minorities in the Muslim World and in the West* MUNIR SHAFIQ	92
7	*On the Dilemma of the Islamic Movement: A Political Party or a Reformist Organization?* RASHID AL-GHANNOUSHI	109

8	*The Burden of the Muslim Intellectual: Fathi Osman's Jihād for Human Rights* ABDELWAHAB EL-AFFENDI	123
9	*Summary of the Open Debate* Report by JOHN L. ESPOSITO	144

List of Contributors   183
Index   187

Foreword

WE HAVE GREAT pleasure in bringing out *Rethinking Islam and Modernity* edited by Abdelwahab El-Affendi. This thought-provoking collection of articles by a host of Muslim scholars addresses some issues and concerns which are crucial to the movement of Islamic revival and to the Muslim presence in the West. The discussion on Human Rights, Western modernity, Secularism, Democracy and Gender equality are equally engaging in their approach and depth. Some of the issues in this volume represent new challenges in that these have arisen in the wake of the recent political, historical, social and cultural developments which have hardly any precedent in the history of Islamic thought. Muslim presence in the West serves as an instance in point. Millions of Muslims living as equal citizens in a secular/liberal set-up of Western democratic nation-states is a phenomenon new to Islamic history. More importantly, the Muslims' interaction with the dominant Western thought has given rise to a number of issues which the Muslim community is obliged to resolve at the earliest. The first and foremost issue is obviously the status of Muslims in the West and their discomfort with the prevalent laws. As citizens they are, no doubt, obliged to abide by the law of the land. However, it is their duty both as Muslims and as citizens of the non-Muslim country of their choice, to strive democratically and peacefully for such amendments in the law which may enable them to lead a life as practising Muslims. The nexus between Muslim identity and Islamic law cannot be over-emphasized. What is needed is a meeting of minds both among the members of the Muslim community in the West for evolving a course of action which may ensure the observance of Islamic law in their life and for creating a better awareness among their fellow Western citizens of the importance

Rethinking Islam and Modernity

of the revealed Islamic law for Muslims. A democratic state is bound to respect and accommodate the legitimate demands of people, including those of religious minorities. The volume does a valuable job in drawing attention to this aspect of the Muslim presence in the West.

Another subject which needs our due attention is the issue of gender equation. With the increasing number of working Muslim women in all parts of the world, particularly in the West, the traditional unit of Muslim family life, which has all along been instrumental in infusing and preserving Islamic values, has come under enormous pressure. If we fail to deal attentively with this problematic issue, it will have disastrous consequences for the Muslim identity.

The status of non-Muslims in the Islamic state and the issues of *Dhimmīs* and *jizyah* have been often misrepresented in order to give a bad name to Islam. It goes without saying that Islamic history is well documented and these concepts have been translated into practice for centuries and like other Islamic concepts, these are rooted in the Qur'ān and *Aḥādīth*. Some of the writers in this volume seek to re-assess these in their own ways. We are confident that the debate generated by these contributions, which naturally represent the viewpoint of these scholars, will go a long way in grappling with these issues by way of evoking a range of responses from other Muslim scholars. We look forward to a lively debate on the concerns raised in this volume.

We are indebted to Dr. Abdelwahab El-Affendi for his assiduity and painstaking attention to detail in editing this publication. We would like to thank also colleagues at the Islamic Foundation for their help in the production of this volume.

Rabīʿ al Thānī 1422 AH
July 2001

DR. M. MANAZIR AHSAN
Director General
Islamic Foundation

Preface

THE PRESENT VOLUME has resulted from a conference on 'Islam and Modernity', which was held at the School of Oriental and African Studies in July 1996. The theme of the conference was chosen to honour Dr. Fathi Osman and his enormous contribution to modern Islamic thought. Fathi Osman, historian, writer, academic, Islamic thinker, activist, educational reformer, journalist, teacher, and legal expert, has been at the forefront of modern Islamic reformism for nearly four decades now. His daring innovative thinking on such issues as citizenship rights for non-Muslims, human rights, democracy and Islamic reform has inspired a whole generation of thinkers and writers, and influenced many others well beyond his native Egypt.

The conference in honour of Fathi Osman was organized by the London-based Forum on Islam and Modernity, a platform that brings together a number of groups and intellectuals who had been inspired by his ideas, and the significance of the event again underscored Fathi Osman's reputation and the respect he commands within a broad spectrum of opinion. The organizers and participants in the conference came from as far afield as Malaysia, South Africa, the Middle East and the United States. They included academics, writers, journalists and broadcasters, students and activists, men and women, Muslims and non-Muslims. This capacity for bringing together people from such diverse backgrounds, opinions and traditions sums up Osman's unique contribution: success in appealing to the broadest possible spectrum of views, backgrounds and origins.

The papers presented at the conference, and the lively debate that followed, reflect the deeply-felt concerns of Muslims as they try to come to grips with modernity and its impact on Muslim culture.

Rethinking Islam and Modernity

The presentations at the conference have been supplemented by one new paper by Rafik Bouchlaka, which attempts to trace the philosophical and historical links between secularism and despotism as it has evolved in the Western tradition.

The conference, as well as this volume, were made possible by the contributions of many individuals and groups who cannot all be mentioned here. Sayyid Ferjani, Rafik Bouchlaka and the members of the Islam and Modernity Forum did an excellent job in preparing for the conference and attending to the complex organizational logistics surrounding it. Rafik was a great help in preparing the manuscript. Professor John Esposito was brilliant in chairing the debate, which is summarized in Chapter 9. I am also grateful to the contributors and to the panellists, who have all made this book possible, and also made it unique and interesting.

Introduction

THAT MUSLIMS appear to be still preoccupied with coming to terms with modernity long after this has come to be Europe's past is a revealing fact in itself. Recently, the Iranian President Muhammad Khatami lamented in an essay published in *Time* magazine that Muslims are still forced to repeat questions that should have been answered ages ago. 'Why is it,' he asked, 'that Muslim societies are still stuck with the same questions: What is development and why are we underdeveloped?'[1] Reflections about the confrontation between Islam and modernity have dominated Muslim thinking for nearly two centuries, and they continue to occupy the thoughts of others also. A cursory survey of the literature would reveal scores of titles dealing with 'Islam and Modernity'. If one were to extend the search to all works that deal with the subject, then the list would run into hundreds, if not thousands. Recently, *The American Journal of Islamic Social Sciences* devoted a whole issue (Spring 1997) to the subject of 'Islamic Modernity versus Westernization'. There appears to be no end in sight to this long-running debate. However, even here, there has been some 'progress'. No longer is the topic discussed in the mind-boggling, pseudo-scientific and naïvely patronizing audacity of works such as Daniel Lerner's *The Passing of Traditional Society* (1958). Too much disillusionment has intervened, to say nothing of post-modernist critiques and the collapse of Communism.

Muhammad Arkoun finds even secularist and reformist Muslims who are still prisoners, in their discourse, of the problematics thrown

---

[1] Muhammad Khatami, 'On the Virtues of the West', *Time*, vol. 151, no. 2, 19 January 1998.

up by the Modernity of the Classical Age (1800–1950), 'imposed by the so-called revolutionary civilized Europe until at least 1950.' In order to transcend this impasse, Muslims must undertake a radical double critique: of Western modernity and the Islamic heritage, with the aim of transcending both, instead of just trying to come to terms with European modernity while still prisoner to a heritage that is uncritically re-appropriated.[2]

Part of the problem Muslims have in dealing with modernity is the fact that 'the very term "modernity" has been given a significance both normative and distortive by the myth of progress which has crucially shaped Western thought since the Enlightenment.' Thus modernity is 'understood as intrinsically superior to whatever preceded it – the opposite of being modern is being backward, and it is difficult to entertain the notion that backwardness may have something to say for itself.'[3] Modernity is also equated with 'civilization', 'progress', and 'development'.[4] And this in turn is associated with modern industrialized (predominantly Western) societies. A whole literature in the sub-discipline of 'development studies' has sprung up to explain why non-Western societies are not westernizing far enough, and when will they do so.

Modernity has been defined in terms of many parameters and characteristics. Among the single-parameter definitions we find the Parsonian 'adaptive capacity' to changing environments,[5] or Marion Levy's 'ratio of inanimate to animate sources of power'.[6] One can also look at the Habermasian stipulation that modernization involves the rationalization of the life-world ('the symbolically structured background knowledge on which [the agent] relies in making sense of

[2] M. Arkoun, 'The Concept of "Islamic Reformation"', in Tore Lindholm and Kari Vogt (eds.), *Islamic Law Reform and Human Rights: Challenges and Responses*, Nordic Human Rights Publications, Copenhagen, 1993, pp.11–24.
[3] Peter L. Berger, *Facing up to Modernity*, Penguin Books, Harmondsworth, 1977, p.101.
[4] Helmut Kuzmics, 'The Civilising Process', in John Keane (ed.), *Civil Society and the State: New European Perspectives*, Verso, London, 1988, p.149.
[5] Ibid., pp.149–50.
[6] Berger, *Facing up to Modernity*, p.101.

Introduction

the world, and in practical action' or social life as experienced from the agent's point of view) and the differentiation of two main social subsystems (the market, steered by the medium of money, and the bureaucratic state, steered by the medium of power), which attain a high degree of autonomy from their environment and from the lifeworld. Rationalization means that socialization, social integration and cultural transmission are no longer governed by unproblematic background knowledge determined by myth or religion, but become a 'function of communicative actions aimed at mutual understanding and deliberate consensus formation.'[7]

Berger looks at modernity from the perspective of some of its more problematic aspects, of which he lists five. First among these is abstraction, or 'alienation' which he sees as the fundamental characteristic of modernity, inherent in its underlying processes, such as the capitalist market, the bureaucratic state, urbanization and technologization. It is also present at the level of consciousness in the fragmentation and quantification of knowledge. It is thus destructive of community and of the solidarity and meaning it used to give to human life. The second major aspect of modernity is its 'futurity', where the future becomes the primary orientation of imagination and activity. Allied with this is the subjection of life to the tyranny of the clock and planning. Third, one encounters individuation and the separation of individuals from collective entities. Paradoxically, modernization tends to destroy community and solidarity, while at the same time enhancing the individual's need to belong. The fourth aspect of modernity is liberation of the individual and the multiplication of options. In traditional societies the community for the most part took from the individual the burden of choice by prescribing set paths of action. However, the weakening of tradition in all aspects of life meant that the individual is now 'condemned to choose', with all the anguish and responsibility this tends to cause. The fifth problematic dimension of modernity is secularization, which may not mean the disappearance of religious

---

[7] Harald Grimen, 'Habermas and the Modernization of Japan', in Lars Gule and Oddvar Storebø, *Development and Modernity: Perspectives on Western Theories of Modernization*, Ariadne, Bergen, 1993, pp.200–6.

beliefs and practices, but certainly the 'weakening of the plausibility of religious perceptions of reality among large numbers of people,' and not only in the industrialized West.[8]

The problem with all theories of modernity, as Grimen rightly notes, is that their normative bias is inherent in their very nature, and not incidental to any particular theory. Modernization theory 'is fundamentally a comparative project with a specific aim: In constructing such a theory, one compares a society with its past, with other societies, in order to find what is viable or defensible and what is not in social, cultural and intellectual development.' Such a project is inherently normative and evaluative, because it must compare the reality to some ideal or model. But even here there is a problem. For even the 'modern' industrialized countries vary considerably. Choosing which one to compare others to involves a strong value judgement; not doing so and constructing an 'ideal type' model of a modern country is no less evaluative. In addition, modernization theorists, including Habermas, base their theories on openly evaluative concepts such as 'rationality' or 'progress', which makes such theories intrinsically ethnocentric. Another problem with these theories is their attempt to cover a wide scope of human activities: cultural, political, intellectual, economic, social, etc., which no single model can hope to encompass.[9]

Given this inherent ethnocentric bias in modernization theory, it is inevitable that the discussion of the matter, especially where it is not just a theoretical question but also an actual and pressing practical problem, such as is the case in many Muslim countries, should pose numerous problems. It is not easy to construct a model of modernity that is value-neutral so as to examine the Muslim response to it and add the evaluation afterwards. This problem is compounded by the fact that, unlike the Western and early industrializing countries, which faced the challenges of modernity as an *internal* evolution within those societies, albeit one that had not been devoid of conflict and tensions, the Muslims faced modernity as an *external* challenge. Modernization, whatever else

---

[8] Berger, *Facing up to Modernity*, pp. 102–11.
[9] Grimen, 'Habermas and the Modernization of Japan', pp. 197–200.

Introduction

it might have been, has endowed the West, the historical rival of the Muslim civilization, with an irresistible material advantage that the former used to disrupt the lives of Muslim communities, and later to subdue and control most Muslim societies. This advantage, first felt by Muslims during the Napoleonic incursions into Egypt and the Levant in 1798, continues to the present. To be modern for many Muslims had always meant to be as strong as the West, to be able to stand up to the other and defend oneself. The first field to feel the impact of enthusiastic modernizing reforms in most Muslim countries had therefore been the military, a development that continues to have serious consequences for politics and society in most Muslim countries. As far back as the last century, leading reformists such as Sayyid Jamāl al-Dīn al-Afghānī have pointed out that such superficial reforms were inadequate, arguing instead for a comprehensive cultural, scientific and political renaissance to enable the Muslim community to regain its rightful place in the world.[10] That debate continues today.

The initial spontaneous reaction of the bulk of the Muslim community was to reject modernization. This rejection was an instinctive, pre-theoretical, knee-jerk reaction from the masses. The élite's response, however, had been marked with ambivalence. They wanted the advantages of modernization, but differed about what aspects of it to choose. For the rulers, the advantages of military reform, industry and even education, were quite obvious. For most intellectuals, scientific achievements and democratization were the main attractions. For the public, the exotic goods imported from the West were fascinating for the rich, but detested by the workers and artisans whose livelihoods they destroyed. The whole process thus generated serious conflicts, culminating in a series of revolutions the last of which we do not yet appear to have seen. The last pre-modern revolt in the lands of Islam (if we exclude the Taliban) has been the rise of the Sudanese Mahdī in 1881. Ever since then, the revolts and uprisings the Muslim world has

---

[10] Jamāl al-Dīn al-Afghānī, 'Lecture on Teaching and Learning', in Nikki Keddie, *An Islamic Response to Imperialism*, University of California Press, Berkeley, 1968, pp. 101–8.

Rethinking Islam and Modernity

witnessed have occurred *within* the parameters of modernity. While the Mahdist uprising, given its discourse and methods, could have easily taken place in tenth-century Morocco or eleventh-century Iran, the same could not be said of the Urabi revolution in Egypt, which was separated from the Mahdist rising by only one year. Whether the Muslims like it or not, they have become irrevocably 'modern'. There was no going back to the innocence of pre-modern times.

Even here, though, we meet with some interesting paradoxes. While the instinctive reaction of the pre-modern Muslim masses had been characteristic of a defensive pose seeking to safeguard tradition against perceived threats, the instinctive *anti-modern* reaction of some sections of Western communities had come in turn to influence, even create, an Islamic current that began to feed *intellectual* anti-modernism in the Muslim world. The early generation of prominent European converts to Islam, such as Muhammad Asad, were attracted to Islam precisely because they could find in it the pre-modern spirit of community which the West had lost.[11] Later generations led a fight to safeguard Muslim traditional ways. The Muslim community, which gathered around Shaikh Abdul-Qadir al-Sufi in England in the 1970s, was so anti-modern that members refused to use gas or electricity in their homes, or to send their children to school. The Nation of Islam movement in the United States hearkened to a pre-modern, non-Western, way of life in its own way.

The *intellectual* reaction to modernity did take some time to mature and crystallize. It varied from those who accepted Western influence wholeheartedly, such as the movement of Sayyid Aḥmad Khān in India, and the Kemalist secularizing tendency in Turkey, to outright rejectionists on the fringe. In between, there were modernizing tendencies that emphasized development and change while not opposing tradition, such as the Young Ottomans, and Islamizing trends that insisted on modernizing being strictly filtered through the prism of 'Islamic correctness'. This trend is represented by Afghānī, his main disciple, Muhammad ʿAbduh, and most modern Islamic movements.

[11] See Muhammad Asad, *The Road to Mecca*, Dar al-Andalus, Gibraltar, 1982.

Introduction

The 1979 Islamic Revolution in Iran marked a turning point from the point of view of Islam's interaction with modernity in more than one sense. First, it showed Islam as having transcended its initial defensive posture *vis-à-vis* aggressive westernizing modernity and gone on the offensive. It no longer became a question of Muslims accepting or rejecting modernity, but of Muslims going forth to participate in the modern world on equal terms and even help shape it. Second, the revolution did not represent an isolated development but, like the French revolution before it, reflected the spirit of the times. The 1970s marked what Bernard Lewis called 'The Return of Islam',[12] a phenomenon that reflected itself in numerous shapes and forms, but was hard to miss. Third, and no less important, the oil boom of the 1970s and 1980s, which was in itself a reflection of Muslim self-confidence as displayed in the use of the oil weapon in the 1973 war with Israel, and the subsequent aggressive OPEC policies led by pre-revolutionary Iran, in turn created new conditions for dealing with modernity. The countries which benefited from oil wealth, in particular in the Gulf, were able to make 'post-modernity' an eerie reality, through bypassing the stage of modernity altogether, achieving its material benefits to excess without having to pay any cultural price. Whatever may have been the case, Muslims have now come to modernity just as modernity has in the past come to them.

The conference in which these papers originated is a continuation of this debate. The question that dominated it is the one that has dominated the Muslim discourse on modernization for the last two centuries: How much of modernity is compatible with Islam? Or, put differently, how much of the Islamic tradition can (and deserves) to survive modernity? As mentioned at the beginning of this introduction, the persistence of the question is in itself a symptom of the problem. Arkoun's argument that the question itself is archaic, and his emphasis on the need to transcend both the question and the problematic that created it by engaging in a dual critique of Muslim reality and heritage on the one hand, and of Western modernity on the other, is of course

---

[12] Bernard Lewis, 'The Return of Islam', *Commentary*, vol.61, no.1, 1976, pp.39–49.

Rethinking Islam and Modernity

valid to a great extent. However, the attempts by some Muslims to use the post-modernist critique of modernity as a vindication of pre-modern Islam is, just like the extreme anti-modernism of the European Muslim groups referred to above, at one level no more than an evasion of the issue, and at another level, a self-defeating exercise. Islam, in the end, must come to terms with modernity, *its own* modernity. The 'Return of Islam' to life in the modern world means that Islam must in turn subject itself to the pressures of modernity, and be reshaped by it. A dead religion can afford to be cocooned away as a relic of increasing irrelevance, but it can be kept safe from the ravages of time. A living religion must endure a constant evolution to keep its vigour in changing times.

We need to refer again to Habermas here. He argues that 'modernity is primarily a challenge,' the challenge of discovering one's own norms at a time when 'pre-given models and norms are disintegrating.' Our epoch, he says, is 'essentially characterized by the notion of individual freedoms ... of self-determination – no norm is recognized whose point one cannot see for oneself.' And while it is true that modernity is beset by self-generated dangers and inherent contradictions, its normative content, in particular self-realization and self-determination, remains valid. More important, modernity 'is not something we have chosen, and therefore cannot be shaken off by a decision, by an act of will.'[13]

It is true that, in its non-normative dimension, modernity, the reality of our time and our era, which we choose to call that, is here with us and here to stay. The Muslim community is part and parcel of this modern reality, with its increasing globalization, its struggles, its alienation, its dominant technological and economic processes, its instrumental rationalism and its secularizing pressures. The question is not whether Islam is part of modernity or not, but what part? How are we going to meet that challenge?

The papers in this book (and the debate they evoked) try to address this question in their various ways. Following on Louis Cantori's critique of the secularist dimension of Western modernity (in his contribution to the

---

[13] Jurgen Habermas, *Autonomy and Solidarity*, Verso, London, 1992, pp.225–7.

Introduction

debate – see Chapter 9),[14] Elmessiri finds a more fundamental problem with Western secularism, which he argues presents a moral vacuum filled in turn with 'an implicit structural secularism that is quite comprehensive and covers all aspects of life.' Thus while secularism claims to have separated church and state and abandoned God, it smuggles its values, even its view of God, in by the back door. While this process is initially portrayed as the establishment of man's freedom from God, the affirmation of immanence and the deification of man soon turns out to be the subjection of man to the fickle gods of this world: nature, other men or new invented gods. The 'death of God' soon becomes the death of man, who is first seen to be a mere natural object, and later becomes just a 'trace in the sand' (Foucault). Behind the alleged flux where all are free to do what they want, lurks the Nietzschean logic of power, which divides men into a majority of one-dimensional individuals who care only about the next moment on the one hand, and 'supermen' or leaders who direct the rest to how they should run their life, on the other. This descent of man is mirrored in Western literature, where we observe the decline of the image of the hero from the heroic Prometheus to the one dimensional Sancho Panza of *Don Quixote*. In the end, we are left with the Weberian 'iron cage' of the spiritless modernity, with its one-dimensional man, its 'value-free' world and its illusions about being the greatest civilization that ever lived.

Following on the same theme, Rafik Bouchlaka takes issue in his chapter with the view prevalent in Western political thought with regard to secularism being a precondition for democracy. He finds that secularism has, on the contrary, become a close ally of despotism, especially in the case of Muslim societies. Bouchlaka finds that Western political debate on despotism has, from the beginning, been intimately connected with a decided ethnocentric streak. It regarded first Greeks and then Europeans as the only proper human subjects, while 'other' communities were seen as merely barbarian hordes unworthy of freedom. This conception was revived with vigour in early modernity, with Islam now taking on the role of the 'other', and Muslims seen as

---

[14] Louis Cantori, as his contribution below indicates, takes issue with Western modernity and its Enlightenment roots, with its emphasis on individualism, secularism, a weak state, the fragmentation of power and on confrontation and conflict as a model.

by nature submissive to despotic rule. Bouchlaka, however, finds that modern despotism in Muslim societies has nothing to do with inherent 'Asian' susceptibility to enslavement, and has everything to do with being an imperialist export from the West itself. Imperialism, as Hanna Arendt has convincingly argued, exported to foreign lands a modern state divorced from politics as such and relying solely on naked violence to enforce its writ. The secularizing westernized élite that inherited this disembodied state perpetuated the same models of imperialist domination that rely more on violence and less on persuasion. The modern élite is as alienated from the Muslim societies it governs as its former imperialist masters were, and could only rule by force. The secular order being imposed in Muslim lands can thus only stay in place if the isolated and embattled élite uses naked oppression and relies closely on the support of the old masters, which make this order a very tentative and very shaky one.

Fathi Osman touches on one of the key challenges which modernity poses to Muslims: the question of human rights. An ardent proponent of human rights himself, Osman tries to put forth the argument he has been advocating for over a quarter of a century: that Muslims should join the struggle for international human rights with enthusiasm. In his chapter, Fathi Osman continues his campaign, adducing detailed and meticulously documented arguments based on Islam's basic holy texts and history to show that there are no contradictions between Islam and the advocacy of basic human rights. This approach may appear pedantic to those unaware of the debates going on within the Muslim world on this subject. These debates and conflicts make it necessary to counter anti-human rights arguments, mostly from rulers, which base themselves on (mis)readings of the texts. Osman also surveys the development of the international human rights movements, arguing that it needs to move towards more consistency in upholding human rights for all, broaden the scope of rights it protects and accommodate the cultural diversity of our present world.

In his paper on the challenges facing modernizing Islamic movements, Shaikh Rashid al-Ghannoushi, a seasoned Islamic leader who has already made pioneering contributions to Islamic thought, in

Introduction

particular in the areas of human rights and democracy, offers a radical and very novel critique of modern Islamic activism. Al-Ghannoushi looks at the political dimension of the Islamic mission, and in particular the developments that started in the Umayyad period and continued in our era, leading to a progressive disengagement of religion and politics. Many Islamic groups have sprung up in the past and in the modern era to try to remedy this development, which was seen as an anomaly from the perspective of true Islamic doctrine. Al-Ghannoushi casts a critical look at the endeavour of these groups and attempts to reassess their contribution from the vantage point of a seasoned activist, and also from the perspective of someone who had been reflecting on the issues for quite a long time. He asks whether the Islamic movements should concentrate on work within civil society or insist, as they have done till now, on making the state the focus of their activism. His answers may strike some traditionalists as highly unfamiliar, and they invite fresh rethinking of what an Islamic movement is and what it is for. It should, he argues, reflect the comprehensive spirit of Islam without being itself all encompassing. It should concentrate on the community, rather than on the state, and avoid being confined within the political dimension, or attempting to subsume all other functions in the modern differentiated society under the political.

Judge Tarek al-Bechri looks in his chapter at the concrete application of universal human rights in Muslim societies today. For this purpose, he adopts a novel and very fruitful approach that yields startling insights into both modern human rights norms and Islamic doctrine. Noting that modern human rights conventions base political rights – and most social and economic rights – on citizenship, he argues that there is no real divergence between modern norms and Islamic norms in this area. Islam also assigned rights on the basis of membership in the political community, or citizenship, only the criteria used then were not the territorial-nationalistic criteria of the modern state system. There is nothing, however, which stands against a revision of those criteria if changing political circumstances dictated it. Traditional Islamic jurisprudence did not base the treatment of non-Muslim minorities on religious criteria alone, but political considerations played a major part. The rise of the modern national state in the Muslim world creates a totally new situation, where non-Muslim communities in most Muslim lands played an equal part in liberating the homeland from colonialism, and thus the new polities had automatically been established as a new joint enterprise between Muslims and non-Muslims. It is therefore their earned right to enjoy equal rights, and no basis for discrimination against them can be found.

The same theme of rights of non-Muslims is also pursued by Fahmi Huweidi, who reiterates the themes of his path-breaking book, *Citizens, not Dhimmis*. Huweidi argues that the decline of the status of non-Muslims in Muslim lands was brought about by two major factors: first the general decline in Islamic civilization which ushered in despotism and oppression, affecting both Muslims and non-Muslims; and, second, the Crusades and other Christian incursions into Muslim lands shattered the unity of the allied communities by recruiting non-Muslims, in particular Christians, as allies and agents in the attack on Muslim lands. This is why we find the literature containing detailed treatment of the status of non-Muslims in the Muslim state appearing only after the Crusades, while prior to that no one felt the need to write something in this regard, as no problem existed. Huweidi thus recommends the transcendence of contingent political conditions and going back to the basic sources of Islam to find the values that should govern the dealings between Muslims and non-Muslims. And he tries to demonstrate that, when we do this, we will find the Qur'ān and *Sunnah* affirm the equality and dignity of all human beings, and recommend all deal with each other in equity.

Examining the same theme of rights of minorities, Munir Shafiq looks at the relations between minorities and majorities, both in the lands of Islam and in the West, as determined by the international balance of power. Arguing that the present era is, and has been for the past two centuries, one of Western hegemony, he recommends that we take into account that the Muslims remain, overall, in a very vulnerable position. One method of perpetuating foreign hegemony over Muslim lands is to incite strife between Muslims and the non-Muslim minorities living among them. Unfortunately, some spokesmen for Islam have

Introduction

fallen into this trap of inciting strife by advocating policies that inflame tensions, rather than promote cordial relations between the various communities. This is a disastrous approach, even when advocated in the name of reviving Islam. It is not in the interest of any community or group that this should happen. It is, therefore, incumbent on Muslims not only to advocate policies and approaches which strengthen ties between various religious communities in the region, but also try to promote 'working models' of co-existence and co-operation. Similarly, Muslim minorities in the West and other major countries, such as India, China and Russia, must adopt a realistic attitude towards their problems. Instead of advocating extreme and separatist solutions to the admittedly serious problems they are facing, they should take into account the realities of the local and international situation, and avoid unnecessary strife and conflict. Muslim minorities in the West need to adopt a spirit of cooperation with governments and other groups in their host countries in order to seek solutions for the international and local crises that are causing tensions.

Finally, we pay tribute to Fathi Osman's enormous contributions to the modernization of Muslim thinking by presenting a brief sketch of his long career, which spans four continents, seven decades, numerous countries and contributions to many fields, from education to journalism.

The summary of the debate, which took most of the second day of the conference, completes the picture. As will be seen from the papers and the debate, the views expressed in this volume are diverse. We did not seek to streamline or reconcile them, since we believe they represent genuine voices and strong currents that are influential in the Muslim world today. But the main themes that run through all these contributions are the concern for the revival of Islam, adherence to human rights and commitment to dialogue and cooperation with the other. We hope that the publication of this volume will contribute to all these goals.

July 2000　　　　　　　　　　ABDELWAHAB EL-AFFENDI
　　　　　　　　　　　　　　University of Westminster, London

I

Of Darwinian Mice and Pavlovian Dogs: A Critique of Western Modernity

ABDELWAHAB M. ELMESSIRI

SECULARISM is generally defined as the separation of church and state, which means freeing the state (and some aspects of public life) from religion and religious values supposed to be operative only in the private life of the individual. The definition is quite clear and even sensible, but it leaves too many questions unanswered. Is education part of public or private life? If it is part of public life, run by the state, is it too going to be rid of the burden of religion and religious values? Does the state have a system of values all its own? And what about the leisure industries (television, cinema, sports, etc.), are they too part of that amoral public life? Are we going to ask the state to supervize and censor them according to its value system, or are we going to take matters in our own hands to regulate them and give them shape and direction according to our value system? But then who are 'we', and whence is 'our' value system derived? What about something as public and private as our self-image? Is that going to be left to the state or to the media experts? Do they have a value system at all, and if they do, do we approve of it?

When we ask these questions we discover a vacuum. We will realize that the definition of secularism as the separation of church and state is inadequate because it maintains complete silence regarding the issue of values. What has filled the vacuum is an implicit structural secularism, which is quite comprehensive and covers all aspects of life, both public and private. This comprehensive secularism, as opposed to partial secularism, namely the separation of church and state, has its own epistemology, psychology, view of history; it even has its view of God, man, and nature. Comprehensive, not partial, secularism is the world outlook that underlies Western modernity.

Immanence and the Descent of Man

Comprehensive secularism does not necessarily deny God's existence; it simply marginalizes or reduces Him to irrelevance, claiming to concentrate exclusively on this world (man and nature). Instead of a metaphysics of transcendence, where the universe achieves coherence and meaning through a centre external to it, comprehensive secularism operates in terms of a metaphysics of immanence, where the centre of the universe is immanent (dwelling) in both man and nature, or in either. This results in a violent oscillation between a man-centred outlook and a nature-centred outlook, between extreme individualism and extreme collectivity, between subject and object, between a self-referential human self that considers itself the locus of immanence, and a self-referential physical nature that claims for itself that status. This projects itself as an extreme humanism, that at times negates the natural altogether on the one hand, and on the other, as an extreme naturalism that uniformly negates the human. The fluctuating tension gave rise to what I term 'the heroic age of modernity' or 'heroic materialism'. This is the era of Renaissance Humanism, eighteenth-century rationalism, the Enlightenment, and Romantic Individualism. It generated so much hope, for man deified himself and placed himself at the very centre of the universe, and decided to conquer it.

But after a period of oscillation between man and nature, the tension was gradually resolved in favour of nature. For, within a materialistic frame of reference, and within the context of the metaphysics of immanence, there is nothing outside the realm of matter. In the last analysis, man himself is nothing but an organic part of matter, reducible to nature. This means, in point of fact, the liquidation of all 'unnatural' specificities and transcendental norms, and of the initial dualism of man and nature. It all leads to the primacy of the natural over the human, and the absorption of man into natural processes.

Of Darwinian Mice and Pavlovian Dogs

Rousseau and other simplistic 'Enlighteners' tried to seduce man into believing (without any reference to man's irreducible complexity) that the state of nature, is actually a state of human bliss, a secular garden of Eden, where man can fulfil not only his natural (material), but also spiritual and moral, potential. Hobbes and Machiavelli warned us from the very beginning that man in a state of nature is a wolf or a tiger or a reptile. He is anything but man. For man's whole being, within that frame of reference, is not determined by any human laws, but rather ferocious natural (material) forces and drives, either immanent in his physical being (gene, instincts, *libido*, *Eros*, etc.), or in the physical nature surrounding him (economic or environmental factors). Man's intellectual, moral and emotional universe is fully explained in terms of, and reduced to, the movement of one or more material forces. In other words man, in all his complexity and rich diversity, can be fully accounted for through that which is non-human, namely the general laws of nature. This gives rise to natural man, who is the cornerstone of the modern Western outlook. He translates himself in several forms, the most important being 'economic man' and 'libidinal man'. The first is propelled by the profit motive determined by the means of production, the second by Eros, and the desire for immediate gratification. Television commercials have discovered that simple truth and have tried to merge the two into one: libidinal economic man, where Eros loses his Promethean fire to be harassed in the service of Mammon, and where man's innate sexual desires are fictionalized to turn him into an avid consumer of nature (commodities) and human beings (the opposite or the same sex).

To speak of morality and responsibility within this naturalistic, materialistic frame of reference would be patently absurd. For this natural man is completely determined. He is not the master of his own destiny, nor does he occupy the centre of the universe. The dream of materialistic modernity and secular humanism is frustrated. The heroic age is gone, and we begin to witness the rise of naturalism, bureaucratization, and the atrophy of any sense of human essence. The very concept of human nature and the very idea of totality are considered forms of metaphysics and obscurantism. The 'death of God', we discover, has led to the death of man.

But this annihilation of man had already been foreshadowed in some of the central images of Western philosophy. Spinoza compared man to a piece of stone thrown by a powerful hand, and as it cruises in space, the poor little stone thinks that it is actually moving of its own free-will. Newton compared the whole world to a perfect machine, a clock that keeps on ticking endlessly and uniformly, without any divine or human intervention. The machine without was discovered within, for Locke compared the mind of man to a passive blank sheet, a *tabula rasa*, which indiscriminately registers all sense data that accumulate on it and then mechanically coalesce according to the laws of association. All of this gave rise to Adam Smith's image of man as living in a world regulated by an 'invisible hand': a market regulated by the mechanical laws of supply and demand. The nineteenth century saw a gradual shift from a mechanistic to an organistic world outlook, and therefore organic metaphors replace mechanistic ones. Darwin pointed out that Rousseau's Garden of Eden is not machine-like, it is a jungle that achieves harmony through the 'invisible hand' of the struggle for survival and the survival of the fittest. If Newton had God as a clock maker, in Darwin's world the 'prologue from heaven' is completely erased, and man traces his origins to apes and reptiles. Freud came along and proved 'scientifically and objectively' that the jungle is actually within. Pavlov experimented on dogs, and applied his findings on man. Man and dog are equivalent within his system; they are both completely conditioned by their surroundings. Man, therefore, is completely de-constructed, and the post-modernist promise that man would not worship anything, not even himself, and that man will 'de-divinize' everything including himself, is fulfilled. Foucault celebrates all of this through an image, which is neither mechanical nor organic: man is compared to some traces in the sand washed away by the waves!

De-Devinization and Value-Free Man

'De-divinize' is just one term in a catalogue of terms that have been used to describe Western modernity. They all imply certain negation

Of Darwinian Mice and Pavlovian Dogs

and a definite loss, an absorption of human essence into the non-human. In this catalogue we can include the following terms: 'depersonalize', 'desanctify', 'dehumanize', 'demystify', 'demetaphysicize', as well as 'debunk', 'disenchantment' and, 'disillusionment', and of course the omnipresent and omnivorous 'deconstruct'. These terms are selected because of the common prefixes ('de', 'dis') but there is a whole flood of terms that describe this loss: alienation, anomie, the crisis of man, crisis of meaning, neutralization, isolation, and standardization. One should notice that the terms do not refer only to a loss of essence, but also a process of flattening, of levelling down all complex dimensions and of the emergence of the 'one-dimensional man' (Marcuse).

The process has been described as a process of neutralization, of 'value-free' rationalization. Max Weber predicted that value-free rationalization must penetrate all aspects of life, and result in total enthralment of man. This process of value-free rationalization leads to the rise of neutral, average, elastic men who are willing to change their values at a very short notice (according to one definition of modernity). These simple one-dimensional men are pragmatic realists who have completely abandoned any hope of transcendence, and fully adapted to the status quo, elevating it to the level of the state of nature. They live in an eternal 'here and now', or rather in an ever-fleeting here and now. Therefore, they have mastered the technique of procedural rationalization and operate in terms of instrumental reason. They are capable of performing any act, ranging from building bridges and overpasses in large cities, to concentration camps outside them, no questions asked, as long as it is done efficiently, and as long as means are rationally adapted to ends.

These elastic, neutralized, average sub-men form the vast majority of modern humanity. But they are not the only category. For there is a thinly veiled ethics of power behind the ethics neutrality and value-free universe. Man, according to the ethics of power, is seen as an autonomous self-referential being, standing beyond good and evil, and therefore cannot be judged by any criterion external to him. He is basically Nietzsche's monster of a super-man who knows no boundaries or limits, who imposes his will on other men, and knows only of one absolute value, namely power. The super-man is a category that presupposes the existence of sub-man, just as Nietzscheanism presupposes pragmatism, and just as Hitler presupposes his numerous Eichmanns and his docile masses that cheer and march. But whether a sub-man or a super-man, whether a victim or a victimizer, morality does not come into the picture. Man is either a conqueror or conquered. If a conqueror, then Nietzscheanism (pragmatism of the strong) is his philosophy; if conquered, then his philosophy is pragmatism (the Nietzscheanism of the weak).

From Prometheus to Sancho Panza

As a student of literature, I have always been fascinated by the predominance of the mythic and ironic modes in modernist literature and art. Probably viewing secularization and modernization as a gradual process of desanctification and a receding of the transcendental, might account for the phenomenon. The mythic in modernist literature is a search for a *logos* and *telos* within nature, inside history, in the context of a metaphysics of eminence. It is an expression of man's yearning for transcendence within the limits of the discourse of desanctification and deconstruction. It is a literary expression of the attempt to achieve transcendence through nature, 'natural supernaturalism'. The Ironic is an expression of the hopelessness of the quest. The ironist is a man who still has memories of the heroic age of modernity, but he knows it was a vain dream. Irony is his protest; modernist literature is largely the sad elegy of modernity. When irony gives way to the more fragmented collage, we know that we are in the age of post-modernism, where the flux is all, where alienation and anomie have been normalized. No elegies are written because we no longer have memories of the heroic dream of transcendence.

A similar pattern could be traced in the development of some of the basic images of the hero in modern Western civilization. The first hero of Western modernity is Prometheus who steals the fire from the gods and gives it to man. Fire here stands for knowledge and domination of nature. In that sense, the myth of Prometheus is not unlike the story

Of Darwinian Mice and Pavlovian Dogs

of the fall of man in the Biblical account, where man falls when he eats from the tree of knowledge. But the Promethean Satan, far from being condemned, is actually glorified. The themes of conflict, knowledge as power, the light of reason replacing revelation (the central theme of the Enlightenment), and the limitless boundless autonomous self, are all present in this image. This unity begins to disintegrate with the image of Don Quixote and Sancho Panza. Fact is seen as sterile and arid when divorced from value. Material reality, the only level that Sancho Panza perceives, is seen as half human when divorced from the world of ideals, the only level that Don Quixote knows. With the image of Dr. Faustus, the doubt and scepticism manifest themselves more conspicuously. Faustus, a Promethean figure who sells his soul to the devil in exchange for knowledge, discovers only too late the futility and monstrosity of his bargain. Frankenstein's monster, one of the first fruits of scientific engineering, starts his career by destroying his creator. He is a modern Prometheus (as the subtitle of Mary Shelly's novel indicates). This is followed by Dracula, a vampire that feeds on the blood of its victims, and who has to live in the dark. The contrasting pair of Don Quixote-Sancho Panza resurfaces in Dr. Jekyll and Mr. Hyde, where the scientific imperialist quest results in a dehumanizing dualism. The ball of fire stolen from the gods, which was the source of so much jubilation, is now seen as the source of fear and doubt.

But the fear is normalized, and the doubt is silenced. For the age of post-modernism, given the absence of norms, there is no basis for anger, fear or doubt. Our memory of the past is erased completely. We are Sancho Panza who has never made the acquaintance of the knight. The world is viewed neither as a machine nor an organism; it is simply a game or a collage. In lieu of Michelangelo, we have Michael Jackson, and instead of the Renaissance, we have the porno queens and Madonna. Natural men and women strut on the stage of life with very little knowledge of good and evil, without the ability to distinguish between building bridges and gas chambers. The flux is all, and genes and environment account for everything.

ABDELWAHAB M. ELMESSIRI

One-Dimensional World of Late Modernity

Weber predicted that value-free rationalization would lead to the domestication of man: the condition of society becomes a workshop. This is indeed a very powerful image, but it nevertheless requires some modification. For what emerged was something more composite, a triadic rhythm of production-consumption-pleasure: next to the workshop we have the shopping mall and the night-club (or any variations thereon, such as the tourist agency or the massage parlour). Natural men and women are bombarded with images that seduce them in the belief that life is made up of this highly reductive rhythm and that society is populated with one-dimensional men and women, who move voluntarily and happily from a one-dimensional workshop to a one-dimensional supermarket and hence to a one-dimensional tourist agency that promises them a one-dimensional earthly paradise.

One-dimensional prophets claim either the end of history, and the triumph of liberal democracy, *ergo*, the West and its value-free democracy and technology, or a clash of civilizations, a ferocious struggle against any people which refuses the technological utopia and the value-free paradise, where everything is planned and measured, where all things are instrumentalized, and where human beings are so rationalized, so naturalized, so reutilized, that their conduct is both amoral and predictable, down to the minutest detail. If any unnatural irregularity emerges, they can always consult the experts, the technocrats, and the psychiatrists, namely, the priests of the value-free utopia. Max Weber, in a moment of tragic perception, described this state of affairs as an 'iron cage' run by 'specialists without spirit, sensualists without heart; [and] this nullity imagines that it has attained a level of civilization never before achieved'.

2

Secularism, Despotism and Democracy: The Legacy of Imperialism

RAFIK BOUCHLAKA

THERE IS A GENERAL consensus within modern Western political thought that secularism is a precondition for democracy. This chapter offers a new approach by assessing the possibility of convergence between secularism and despotism. It asks how it can be that secularism is, in certain socio-historical contexts, an ally of despotism in contrast to the habitual claim that secularism supports the values of pluralism and tolerance. This association of secularism and despotism appears to apply especially to the case of secularism in the Middle East region, and there is ample evidence, as we shall demonstrate, to suggest that this situation is a legacy of Western colonialist penetration of this region.

Despotism: The Genealogy of a Concept

The term 'despotism' originated in Greek political thought, and was intimately associated with the distinction Greeks made between themselves as a 'civilized' and fully human race, and 'others' who were seen as 'barbarians' and sub-human. The barbarians were those unfit for self-rule, who needed to be enslaved or ruled by despots. In common Greek usage, the term 'despotism' referred to the relationship of the master to his household. *Despotes* was closely associated with *Oikonomos* (household management) and applied primarily to the role of patriarchs who managed the life of the household, although the patriarch's exercise of his power was seen as despotic only in relation to his slaves, not his wife or children. This mode of relationship was considered from the Greek viewpoint as embedded in human nature. The legitimacy of using others as slaves, Aristotle argues, lies in their lack of full human qualities, having little capacity for judgement, slaves accept their domination by the despot. It is thus self-evident for Aristotle that 'some are by nature free, so others by nature slaves, and for the latter the condition of slavery is both beneficial and just.'[1]

Aristotle distinguishes in his *Politics* between four forms of power: the power of the magistrate, the power of the king, the power of the father of a family and the power of the master. Only the first three may be considered political relationships, since they are exercised between free people. Despotic power, by contrast, is the power of a free man over a human being naturally deprived of his freedom. Aristotle accepted the classical Greek equation of 'despotic rule' and 'arbitrary rule', but extended its application to contexts where political power is analogous to that of a master over his slaves.[2] He treats despotism as a type of kingship where the power of the monarch over his subjects, although indistinguishable from that exercised by a master (*Despotès*) over his slaves, is, nevertheless, seen by the ruled as sanctified by custom, and hence legitimate. This type of rule is characteristic of non-Hellenes or 'barbarians' (whom the Greeks regarded as slaves by nature).[3] Just government, according to the Greeks, is that which seeks the common interests of the governed. Conversely, despotic authority exercised itself in the interest of the master and only by accident to the advantage of the slave. This is a matter of natural necessity, where certain beings are created to command, and others to obey.

Aristotle thus employs the term 'despotic government' by analogy to designate a deviation in governments that no longer conformed to the principle of 'absolute justice'. He regards tyranny as a deviation

---

[1] Aristotle, *Politics*, ed. and trans. by Ernest Barker, Book II, 1255a, p.14. See also Christopher Stephen Sparks, 'Montesquieu's Vision: The Spirit of Uncertainty and the Haunting of Modernity', unpublished Ph.D Thesis, University of Westminster, June 1995, pp.182–3.

[2] R. Koebner, 'Despot and Despotism: Vicissitudes of a Political Term', *Journal of Warburg and Courtauld Institutes*, vol. 4, 1951, p.275.

[3] Melvin Richter, *The Political Theory of Montesquieu*, Cambridge, 1977, p.45.

Secularism, Despotism and Democracy

from kingship, oligarchy from aristocracy and democracy from republican government. All these types of government are deemed despotic because their rulers seek their own interests, though they may accidentally benefit their subjects. Tyranny 'has no regard for any public interest which does not also serve the tyrant's own advantage. The aim of the tyrant is his own pleasure.'[4]

During the Greek-Persian wars, 'despotism' was extended in its use to designate the political conditions of Persia and other Asian peoples as 'Barbarians', with no potential for reasoned public debate and, hence may legitimately be treated as slaves.[5] Despotism among Asiatics (i.e. barbarians) is despotism in the proper sense, not by analogy as is the case among the Greeks. Asiatics are incapable of constructing a public sphere and must remain eternally in domestic relations.[6] Their destiny must naturally be in the hands of the Greek master. Barbarians are only in their proper place in slavery and 'should be governed by the Greeks'.[7]

'Asiatic Despotism' and Modern European Discourse

Modern Europe reinvented the old fiction of 'Asiatic despotism' in a European/Other dichotomy recreated after Aristotle. From the sixteenth century with Jean Bodin, and the eighteenth century with Montesquieu, despotic power came to be identified with what Bodin referred to as '*la monarchie tyrannique*', the extreme form of a corrupted regime where the monarch abrogates the laws of nature and treats his subjects as slaves.[8] Further, from the Renaissance onwards, European

---

[4] Aristotle, *Politics*, Book V, 1311a.
[5] Aristotle notes, 'Another type of kingship is the sort which is to be found among some uncivilized [i.e. non-Hellenic] peoples. All Kingships of this sort possess an authority similar to that of tyrannies, but are nonetheless constitutional and descend from father to son. The reason is that these uncivilized peoples are more servile in character than Greeks and will, therefore, tolerate despotic rule without complaint. Kingships among uncivilized people are, thus, of the nature of tyrannies, but being constitutional and hereditary they are at the same time legitimate.' Ibid., Book III, 1285a.
[6] Alain Grosrichard, *Structure de Srail, la fiction du despotism Asiatique dan l'Occident Classique*, Seil, Paris, 1979, p.23.
[7] Aristotle, *Politics*, Book I, 1252b.
[8] Grosrichard, *Structure de Srail*, pp.24–5.

political thinkers and philosophers tended to define the character of their political and cultural world by contrasting it with that of the Turkish order, so geographically close, yet infinitely remote. Machiavelli (in early sixteenth-century Italy) was the first theorist to use the Ottoman State as the antithesis of European monarchy. In the two central passages of *The Prince*, he saw the autocratic bureaucracy of the Ottoman Porte as an institutional order that was distinct from all the states of Europe.[9]

> The entire Turkish Empire is ruled by one master and all other men are his servants, he divides his kingdom into Sandjaks and dispatches various administrators to govern them, whom he transfers and changes at his pleasure. They are all slaves bounded to him.[10]

Bodin also developed a political contrast between monarchies bound by respect for the persons and goods of their subjects, and empires unrestricted in their dominance over them. The first represented the 'royal sovereignty' of the European state. The second was the 'lordly' power of despotism eventually alien to modern Europe but encountered in such states as the Ottoman. With Montesquieu in the eighteenth century, the concept of despotism gained immense significance in Western political discourse, replacing the concept of tyranny as the term most often used to denote a system of total domination, as opposed to the exceptional abuse of power by an individual ruler. Despotism, according to Montesquieu, is the rule of a single person subject to no restraint, constitutional or moral, but revolves around the ruler's caprice and passions. Unlike legitimate rulers, the despot is forced to resort to terror as the guiding principle in the governance of the state's affairs.[11]

The affinity between Aristotle and Montesquieu can be detected in two points. First, the term 'despotism', which was used by Greek thinkers only figuratively, was now given primary political significance.

---

[9] Perry Anderson, *Lineage of the Absolutist State*, London and New York, 1993.
[10] Machiavelli, *The Prince*, London, 1979, pp.26–7.
[11] Richter, *Political Theory of Montesquieu*, p.46.

Secularism, Despotism and Democracy

The 'semantic reversal' begun in the sixteenth century achieved its advanced form in the eighteenth century with Montesquieu. This heralded the 'politicization of the domestic'. It was not the domestic category that provided the model of thinking of the political sphere, rather the reverse. Rousseau, for instance, spoke of the 'unique despotism of fathers', but he used the political concept in the figurative sense. Conversely, Aristotle has used the term despot and its derivatives essentially in the domestic sphere. His centre of reference remained the domestic, even when he treated the political. The perspective from which Montesquieu considered the political was the public sphere, even when reflecting on domestic relations.[12] A case can be made for reading his definition of despotism as an attempt to articulate the aspects of absolutist power which threatened to reduce public life to the domain of private power. The political thought of Montesquieu can be understood not as a radical shift from Aristotle, but rather as a kind of revival and inversion of it.

Second, for Montesquieu, despotism indicates a discursive order of power relevant to Asiatic society. This corresponds exactly to both the ethnic geographical and conceptual conditions of Aristotle's 'other'. With the fall of Byzantium into the hands of Muslims in the fifteenth century, and the installation of the Ottoman Empire at the gates of Christian Europe, the 'Turk' became the living embodiment of the 'other' in European thought. By the eighteenth century, however, the geographical reference of ideas initially conceived in contact with the Ottoman domain spread steadily further East in the wake of colonial exploration and expansion to include Persia, then India and finally China. Prompted by the proximity of Ottoman power, the confrontation with Islam became coeval with the new birth of political theory in the Renaissance, and thereafter accompanied its development through the Enlightenment.[13] The revival and new currency of the term despotism in modern Western discourse went side by side in parallel with the construction

---

[12] Bassam Tibi, *The Crisis of Modern Islam*, trans. by Judith von Sivers, Salt Lake City, 1988, pp.10–11.
[13] Anderson, *Lineage of the Absolutist State*, p.262.

of a geographical fiction of a 'despotic Orient' and more particularly a 'despotic Islam'. The secret chain which provided the communication between Paris and Isphahan in Montesquieu's *Les Lettres Persanes* recovered the myth traceable back to Aristotle, of a 'despotic Asia' confronting a 'monarchic Europe'. The Persian figures in the *Lettres* are closer to fiction than they are to reality, and are more European than Persian. Through them, Montesquieu represented his fantastic Oriental 'other', thus conceptualizing the old Western fiction of a despotic Orient. He considered despotism as contradictory to human nature: 'after all we have just said, it would seem that human nature would rebel relentlessly against despotic government.'[14]

The paradox remained that 'in spite of the love of men of freedom, in spite of their hatred for violence, the majority of people submit to it.'[15] How could this paradox be accounted for? Montesquieu does so by contending that in certain parts of the world, particularly in Asia, nature produces human beings against its very self, human beings that are slaves by nature, and for this reason have a tendency to support this strange form of government. 'As all men are born equal, slavery must be contrary to nature, though in certain countries, it is founded on a natural reason, and we must distinguish these countries from those where even natural reasons reject it such as European countries, where it has fortunately been abolished.'[16]

Montesquieu clearly subscribes to Aristotle's views regarding the political nature of Asiatic people, differing only on the point that, while the latter deems slavery to be a natural phenomenon, he condemns all forms of slavery in the name of nature, except in the case of Asiatic societies, societies where 'physical nature' itself is appealed to in justification of the very slavery phenomenon that had been dismissed as unnatural and excessively unjust to European man.[17]

Tocqueville and 'Democractic' Despotism
With Alexis de Tocqueville, this age-old dichotomy of freedom/ despotism, Europe/Asia, loses its central position. In Tocqueville's

[14] Montesquieu, *L'Esprit des Lois*, p.52. [15] Ibid. [16] Ibid., Chap. 7.
[17] Tibi, *Crisis of Modern Islam*, pp.52 and 53.

Secularism, Despotism and Democracy

conception of despotism and its relation to modern democracy we find a powerful challenge to the notion that the imagined alternative to modern democracy was embodied in an external 'Other'. Tocqueville foresaw the possibility of modern democracy turning into a system of oppression without a historical precedent and to which he could not assign a proper name: 'I seek in vain, for an expression that will accurately convey the whole of the idea I have formed of it. The old words despotism and tyranny are inappropriate. The thing itself is new, and since I cannot name it, I must attempt to describe it.'[18] Modern democratic societies no longer feel threatened by despotism because the domination of that old form of government over its subjects is in the process of being broken.[19]

Tocqueville argues that the new form of despotism is different in quality from the 'ancient regimes'. Contrary to its forerunners, it is soft and invisible. Despotism in modern democracy degrades its subjects without tormenting them.[20] The hands and eyes of the state infiltrate more and more in daily life and 'in the name of democratic equality, government becomes regulator, inspector, advisor, educator and punisher of social life.'[21] In that sense the nation becomes nothing but a herd of timid and industrial animals of which the government is the shepherd.

The establishment of the democratic system, according to Tocqueville, has a dual effect. On the one hand, there is the full affirmation of the individual, which is bound up to 'the wish to remain free,' and on the other, the subjugation of the individual to a sovereign power which he calls 'social power' and associates with the need to be led.[22] The main paradox of modern democracy lies in the double psychological tension between the need to be strongly governed and at the same time the wish to remain free. Individuals believe in a strong

---

[18] Tocqueville, *De la democratie en Amérique*, Algeria, 1991, vol.2, p.415.
[19] John Keane (ed.), *Civil Society and the State: New European Perspectives*, Verso, London, 1988, p.55.
[20] Tocqueville, *De la democratie en Amérique*, pp.414–16.
[21] Keane, *Civil Society*, p.58.
[22] Claud Lefort, *Democracy & Political Theory*, trans. David Mary, London, 1988, p.26.

unified power, but one that is controlled and directed by free citizens. This paradox can be summarized in the combination between centralization and sovereignty of the people.

Tocqueville maintains that the ideals of equality and social justice are not synonymous with that of liberty, but can contradict it, and so the two should be carefully distinguished. He argues that the people tend, in a modern democracy, to replace the ideal of liberty with the goal of state-secured equality.[23] In an egalitarian society, every individual is naturally isolated, thus enjoying no protection from relatives or social class. 'The individual is easily cast aside, and tread on mercilessly.'[24] It is, indeed, an irony that democratic societies which, for the first time in history, introduced the value and ideal of freedom into political discourse, are also the very ones that opened the gate to a new form of despotism.

Despotism in the Tocquevillian discourse is not treated in its traditional form of a political system of naked power depriving subjects of their rights and individuality, but as a micro-physical and invisible body. That is because it evolves from within the democratic system itself. It is nevertheless, reasonable to seek a new terminology to designate this despotism and to seek a new remedy: 'the political world changes, we must necessarily seek new remedies and new words.'[25]

Imperialism, Secularism and Despotism

The genealogy of secularization in the Middle East region can be traced to European imperial expansion in the region. Imperialism in this context does not only denote military expansion but all the forms of hegemony, political, economic and cultural. It was the German political philosopher Hannah Arendt who advanced a new approach to the affinities between despotism and imperialist expansion. Arendt's analysis will only prove valid to our present purposes if we reverse its context. What we are concerned with is not imperialism in itself, its internal impulses and strategies, or its impact on its producers and

[23] Keane, *Civil Society*, p.57.
[24] Tocqueville, *De la democratie en Amérique*, p.424.
[25] Ibid., p.249.

Secularism, Despotism and Democracy

exporters. We are concerned, rather, with its effects on its victims and subjects in foreign lands. To be more explicit, we are preoccupied with the traces of the 'Great Game' more than the game itself.

The main characteristic of imperialism, as illustrated by Arendt, is its drive towards expansion for its own sake, expansion as a permanent and supreme goal in itself. This characteristic is the natural outcome of the introduction of economic purposes concerned with profit and investment in the political field through the late marriage between national state and bourgeoisie. Expansion as an end in itself and as an ultimate aim of politics is a new concept in the history of political thought. The novelty stems from the realm of business speculation 'where expansion meant the permanent broadening of industrial production and economic transactions characteristic of the nineteenth century.'[26]

Since the imperialist conception of power is one of expansion as an end in itself and not as a means, there was no attempt to found new political bodies in overseas possessions. Imperialists, Arendt argues, tended to 'assimilate rather than integrate, to enforce consent rather than justice, that is, to degenerate into tyranny.'[27] The natural results of imperialist strategy were summarized by Arendt in two points:

1. The export of means of power without political institutions and regulations. The instruments of state violence (the police and the army in particular) were the main priority in the list of external exports. Violence has always been seen as the 'ultimo ratio' in political action, and power has always been conceived as the visible expression of rule and government.

2. The separation between political means and institutions. In the movement of expansion, imperialism transforms the state into a productive machine of violence and coercion in occupied lands. The state's instruments of violence, which in the

---

[26] Hannah Arendt, *The Origins of Totalitarianism*, Everyman's University Library, London, 1967, p.137.
[27] Ibid.

'mother' countries exist beside with the national institutions and are controlled by, and separated from, them, are freed from any similar encumbrances. In that sense violence was 'given more latitude than in any Western country.'[28]

Arendt states that imperialism deployed two instruments for the political control of foreign peoples. The first was the use of race as an ideological basis of politics, the second was the deployment of bureaucracy as a device for foreign domination. Racism, as the deep ground of imperialistic policies, has certainly absorbed and revived the old Western tradition of racialist attitudes.[29] Racialist thinking denotes a lack of any basis for community other than that of blood alliance. The European adventurer who had ceased to belong to an 'artificial community' founded on concessions and regulations, had become like the native populations in occupied lands. Arendt predominantly perceives these as uncivilized people, in the sense that they live like animals at the impulse of nature, instead of founding a human order upon it.[30]

Arendt saw bureaucracy as the key element in the organization of the 'Great Game' of expansion. Bureaucracy here signifies lawless and arbitrary rule, for anonymous agents of expansion felt no obligation to man-made laws. The only mechanism they used was the issuing of decrees through the vehicle of bureaucratic hierarchy. Her view of bureaucracy contrasts radically with Weber's definition of it as a highly rationalized and responsible form of government that works according to rules. This difference may be explained by the vantage points from

---

[28] Ibid., p.137. Arendt contrasts power with violence since power in her view corresponds to the human ability to act correctly and communally. Power is never the property of an individual, it belongs to a group and remains in existence only so long as the group keeps together.

[29] Arendt refers to Degobineau in France (1853) in his *Essai sur l'Inegalite' des Races Humaines* and to Edmund Burke in *Reflections on the Revolution in France* (1790) as two theorists of race-thinking in Europe. The first elaborated the idea of 'race aristocrats' against a 'nation' of citizens, the second that of the 'rights of Englishmen' against the rights of men.

[30] See Margaret Canovan, *The Political Thought of Hannah Arendt*, Everyman's University Press, London, p.39.

which each considered the issue. Weber looked at bureaucracy from its internal logic and mechanism, from the point of view of the official, whereas Arendt saw it from the point of view of the subject, observed from a distance.[31]

The horizons revealed by Arendt's elaboration of the subject of imperialism, may be summed up in two points relevant to our discussion:

1. With the separation between the political body and the institution of violence in overseas territories, the state became little more than a machine of violence and punishment. The state came to be identified with the official institutions of force, especially the military and police. It follows that the object of politics became merely to adjust and distribute the means of coercion and manipulation over the social texture. The genealogy of this phenomenon is traceable to the mode of governance established by imperialist conquest, where 'the state-employed administrators were nothing but functionaries of violence and they could only think in terms of power politics.'[32]

2. The alienation of the political structure from its social base was the natural consequence of the absence of a common language and vehicle of communication between the political élite and the wider population. Administration, as Arendt demonstrates, played a key role in this process of 'externalization' between governor and governed. Bureaucracy here is not rationalization in the Weberian sense but is a mere tool for domination. As Arendt puts it, 'bureaucracy was the organization of the great game of expansion in which every area was considered as a stepping-stone to further involvement and every people an instrument for further conquest.'[33]

In the imperialist project, if we are to make sense of the Arendtian terminology, aloofness becomes the only attitude of governing, since the subjects are considered as a mere field of power and the recipients

[31] Ibid., p.33.   [32] Arendt, *Origins of Totalitarianism*, p.137.   [33] Ibid., p.186.

of politics rather than its producers.[34] In the post-colonial era this mode of relationship between the political élite and its social base did not undergo any radical change. The only difference was the replacement of foreign administrators by native ones. The process of modernization and secularization, on which the imperialist state and its successor, the independent national state, were based, meant nothing more than the stifling of society by bureaucracy and military/police institutions. Secularization, thus, signified a project for the complete destruction of the infrastructure and mechanisms of social cohesion, in the interest of the monopoly and accumulation of the power of an over-centralized state. Hannah Arendt observes that in 'the imperialist epoch, a philosophy of power became the philosophy of the élite who quickly discovered and was quite ready to admit that the thirst for power quenched only through destruction.'[35]

The problem with Arendt's position is that it preserved the classical Orientalist dividing line between civilized Europe and uncivilized indigenous peoples who 'live like animals' at the mercy of nature instead of imposing a human order upon it. When the civilized degenerate, they degenerate into the condition of the natives, yet still remain distinct from them. Arendt points to the Boers, the bearers of the imperialist project to South Africa, who had become, like the native population, a rootless herd of wandering people bound together by blood as a tribe and not by location as a nation. But this similarity brought about by the deformation and evils of imperialism does not weaken the typological distinction drawn by Arendt between an 'original civilized nation' and 'an uncivilized native people.'[36]

What Arendt neglected was the fact that the imperialist project in its

---

[34] Arendt insists, that every political order that isolates its citizens from one another, becoming separate from the political community, degenerates into a domination based on violence because it destroys the communicative structure without which power cannot emerge.

[35] Ibid., p.144.

[36] Arendt preserved the traditional classification of a despotic Orient, as we can see from the following quote: 'The very integrity of the British administration made despotic governments more inhuman and inaccessible to its subjects than Asiatic rulers.' Ibid., p.112.

geographical expansion did not confront peoples bereft of history. On the contrary, imperialism extended to great centres of civilization possessing a rich symbolic heritage deeper than that of the imperialists themselves. This is the case in the Middle East, the cradle of human civilization and heir to long traditions of political institutions and mechanisms of self-regulation. Indeed, the shift of the 'world centres' from the eastern and southern Mediterranean shores (in Cairo, Baghdad, Damascus and Istanbul) to London, Paris and Vienna, for instance, did not signify that the latter were more civilized than the former, only that they have become more powerful and more capable of controlling strategic geopolitics. Early turning points in the balance of power were the defeat of the Ottoman army at the gates of Vienna in the fifteenth century, as well as the discovery of the new American continent and the control of international trade routes.

Secularization in the Muslim World

The project of secularization in the Islamic world, due to its dependence on imperial penetration, was associated with the emergence of a restricted élite uprooted from its social base. In the post-colonial era, this élite was reproduced by a Westernized education system and through the international economic system, characterized by the division into a periphery and a centre. The relationship between periphery and centre is one based on power. This asymmetrical, or shall we say 'vertical', interaction can be detected not only on the economic level, but also in the field of 'culture and symbols'. The centre consolidates its centrality through its own accumulation of the means of power and manipulation, thus relegating the periphery into a 'marginal position' by depriving it of power and wealth, and even from its own 'language'.

Bassam Tibi borrowed John Galtung's term 'bridgehead élite' in order to explain how structural dependence can be maintained today without the need for military presence.[37] The élite, in the course of the westernization they tend to undergo, adopt the norms and values of the foreign dominant culture, and defend the interests of foreign powers

---

37 John Galtung, 'A structural theory of imperialism', *Journal of Peace Research*, vol.13, no.2, 1971. See also Tibi, *Crisis of Modern Islam*.

rather than those of their own societies. Galtung maintains that 'the center of the principal nation has a bridgehead in the periphery and it is to be sure a well-chosen one: namely in the center of the peripheral nation. This bridgehead is established in the center of the peripheral nation, such as that the center of the periphery is bound to the center of the center, the bond being a harmony of interests.'[38]

To extend this analysis one can say that the project of secularization, the close ally of Westernization, is essentially the emergence of a new hermeneutic discourse through Western invasion, a communication channel to the foreign powers, one incapable of relating to the main body of the indigenous population. If there is any adequate definition of culture, it is that it is a symbolically mediated communicative system. In this sense, culture is dependent on mechanisms of correspondence, but it also has an inherent performative dimension. Culture is fundamentally a symbolic system, functioning as a medium of communication between members of a society. The elementary function of a symbol is to allow a sender to communicate with a receiver. But as Armando Salvator puts it: 'to convey a meaning is also to perform an act which modifies the consciousness of the receiver and also his behaviour, so expanding or limiting the abilities of both the receiver and the sender.'[39]

One can, indeed, refer to Islam as a 'symbolic communicative system' and a medium of collective identity revolving around its internal hermeneutics. Secularism, on the other hand, is a child of colonization, which has created its own hermeneutical system connected to Western hermeneutics. It remains confined within the boundaries of a limited élite, with little resonance within the wider society. Nevertheless, if we contemplate the general cultural scene in the land of modern Islam, we are confronted with the existence of conflicting 'symbolic communicative systems'. One of these is very restricted in its extension, moving within the narrow circle of the élite. It emerged in the context of imperialism and the pseudo-modernization of the last two centuries. It is

[38] Galtung, 'A structural theory of imperialism'.
[39] Armando Salvator, *Islam and Political Discourse of Modernity,* Ithaca Press, Reading, 1997.

Secularism, Despotism and Democracy

true that this communicative system is active, and even dominant, especially in official institutions. Nevertheless, it remains isolated from the deeper currents of society. The other symbolic communicative system is, on account of its indigenous character, entrenched within the profound movement of society, revolving around the hermeneutics of Islam. For that reason, it can be seen as the linking bridge between an important section of the élite and the masses.

With only a very narrow area of overlap, we can see that these two communicative systems are expressive of two wholly distinct societies on a conflicting course. I term these a 'surface society' and 'an in-depth society', which are parallel and asymmetrical in their movement, rhythms as well as their strategies.[40] A similar point is made by Albert Hourani. 'In trying to explain the history of the Middle East in modern times,' he argues, 'we should always be aware of two interlocking rhythms of change: that which reforming governments and thinkers and external forces tried to impose upon society, and that which a great stable society with a long and continuous tradition of thought and of life in common that was producing from within itself, partly by its own internal movement, and partly in reaction to forces coming from outside.'[41]

While the secular élite sought to achieve a radical rupture with the socio-cultural traditions of Islamic society, finding their model in Kemalist radical secularism in Turkey, the reality in the depths of Turkish society as a whole was one unexpected by the secularists. It is quite misleading to attempt a reading of modern Islamic society on the basis of the movement of the élites and their strategies without contemplating the rhythm and language of their society as a whole. There are admittedly many expressions of rupture and discontinuity in modern Islamic history, but these must not obscure us from the chain of continuity and self-accumulation of Islamic culture in modern times.

Indeed, we ought not to stumble into simplistic views, such as that peddled by traditional Orientalism, which opposes an enlightened and

---

[40] Jaques Berques, *L'Egypte, Imperialism et Revolution*, Paris, 1979.
[41] Albert Hourani, 'How Should We Write the History of the Middle East', *International Journal of Middle East Studies*, vol. 23, p.129.

dynamic élite in Muslim communities to a 'stagnant' and 'backward' society encumbered by religious traditions, values and symbols. There exist, as we have indicated above, two different modes of movement and change. One is the movement of the secular élite, the other is that of society with its own rhythms and intellectual resources. The indigenous social and intellectual forces are in a state of renewal originating from their very own references, resources and strategies. This is not to say that modern Islam is a completely indigenous phenomenon. Indeed, there has been, since the last century a movement of 'acculturation' to and interaction with the modern West, which can express itself in implicit or explicit configurations. Islamic reformism since Sayyid Jamāl al-Dīn al-Afghānī (d.1897) and Muhammad ʿAbduh (d.1905) in the 19th/20th century, offers a telling indication of Islam's internal vitality as well as its acculturation with the West. We must not overlook the fact pointed out by Gibb, who argued that even though the emergence of thought processes operating within the Muslim community has been influenced by the impact of the West, yet the ideas and cultural forces active within the Muslim world and the norms to which they appeal, originate primarily in the internal intellectual and historical Islamic context.[42]

It is generally true that the reaction to external challenges varies from one culture to another due to its inherent abilities and energies. In the case of Islam, one may say that the Western challenge, which was associated with military invasion, did not lead to the dissolution of the high culture of Islam but rather to its activation and renewal. Strong as the impact of Western invasion on Islamic thought and society had been, it ought not to obscure from us Islam's continued vitality.

As pointed out by Gibb, no movement of thought can take place in a void. Shaken by foreign invasion, Muslim society and culture found ways of incorporating the new reality within its system. Muslims had inherited a rich order of symbols that remained active and intensely vibrant in their hearts and minds, in their consciousness and subconscious. Modern Islamic culture possessed its own methods of selection and adaptation of foreign elements in a movement of interiorization and reinterpretation.

[42] H.A.R. Gibb, *Modern Trends in Islam*, New York, 1972, p.109.

Secularism, Despotism and Democracy

The political discourse of secularism has not been the product of an internal movement within Arab-Islamic history, nor has it been one of peaceful acculturation between the 'world of Islam' and that of the West. Secularism was the child of imperial expansion which brought about a new balance of power in the interest of external forces and their 'bridgehead élite', eventually leading to the marginalization of the mass population. As such, the process of secularization was a project of a tiny élite that was not unrepresentative of society as a whole. Not only is this minority alienated from its social milieu, but it finds itself in permanent confrontation with it. The state and its official institutions are used as tools for the manipulation and targeting of the masses. It is, therefore, difficult to conceive of the persistence and continuity of secularism in isolation from the state as a tool of coercion and organized violence. This contention is further substantiated by the recent experiences of Turkey and Algeria. There, when the secular élite ventures into tentative democratization, it appears to discover how infinitely marginal it is, cast adrift and isolated from the mass population, and thus forced to submit itself entirely to the hands of the military.

Conclusion

In Western political and sociological discourse, the emergence of secularism is associated with what John Rawls describes as the setting-up of 'overlapping consensus'.[43] Secularism is linked, according to Sandel, to the neutrality of the state, its isolation from religious sectarianism and the establishment of political consensus amongst the various religious and political forces.[44] This leads to the proposition that links secularism to political pluralism and democracy. Perhaps one of the most sacrilized equations in Western academic discourse is the necessity of this connection between secularism and democracy. As John Keane put it, ' "no secularism no democracy" is the sacred slogan' of the modern Western

---

43 John Rawls, 'The Domain of the Political and Overlapping Consensus', in Robert M. Stewart (ed.), *Readings in Social and Political Philosophy*, Oxford University Press, Oxford, 1996.
44 Michael Sandel, 'Religious Liberty: Freedom of Choice or Freedom of Conscience', in Rajeev Bhargava (ed.), *Secularism and its Critics*, Oxford University Press, Delhi, 1998.

élite.[45] What Rawls, Sandel and others overlooked was the fact that, under certain historical and cultural circumstances, secularism can be productive and supportive of despotism, not democratic change. This was and is still the case in the Middle East. Also secularism can generate socio-political fragmentation, not rational and civil consensus as Rawls thought. Indeed, secular governance is just as complicated as religious governance.

In a final irony, the entrenched idea in Western political discourse linking despotism and 'Asian barbarians' finds its ultimate refutation in the fact that it was Western imperialism, and the 'barbarism' it bequeathed to the East, which generated a particularly vicious form of despotism under which many modern Muslim societies languish. This is indeed a very important point to ponder.

---

[45] John Keane, 'After Secularism: A Proposal', an unpublished paper presented at the Centre for the Study of Democracy seminar, University of Westminster, January 2000, p.2.

3

Islam and Human Rights: The Challenge to Muslims and the World

FATHI OSMAN

THE MODERN DRIVE to ensure wider respect for basic human rights has been dominated by Western-led initiatives. This has posed problems concerning how Muslims should react to such initiatives and what Islam dictates with regard to them. This chapter attempts to trace the questions posed by the discourse on human rights to Muslims in particular and the world in general. For Muslims, there are questions of doctrine and interpretation, as well as practical problems regarding selective enforcement. For the world as a whole, there are questions regarding clarification of concepts, universal application and the development of a truly universal consensus on human rights.

The Origin of Modern Human Rights Concepts

Since the signing of the Magna Carta in England in June 1215 and the promulgation of the Bill of Rights there in 1689, several national documents have been issued in the West to spell out provisions for the protection of human rights, most significant among which were the human rights provisions in the 'Declaration of Independence of the United States' in July 1776 and in the first ten amendments of the US Constitution. These amendments became known as the Bill of Rights, adopting the name of the English Bill. The 'Declaration of the Rights of Man and the Citizen' in France in August 1789 followed shortly afterwards.

Other national documents or provisions followed in this direction, until an international effort could be made to bring about the 'Universal

Declaration of Human Rights' issued by the General Assembly of the United Nations in December 1948. Meanwhile, the socialist thought in general, and the Marxist thought in particular, has been stressing the centrality of social justice for a genuine democracy, a trend that was crowned by the Russian Revolution and the establishment of the Soviet Union in 1917. The Soviet Union fought on the side of the Western Allies in the last World War and occupied a distinguished place in the United Nations, supported by other socialist states in Eastern Europe, as well as China and other socialist states in other countries. In response to this trend, other international documents from the United Nations followed, such as the 'International Covenant on Civil and Political Rights' and the 'International Covenant on Economic, Social and Cultural Rights', which were both approved by the General Assembly of the United Nations in December 1966 and made effective from July 15, 1967. Most Muslim countries became signatories of the Declaration of Human Rights, with the exception of Saudi Arabia which expressed its reservations about the Declaration, arguing that its own full commitment to the rules of Islam does guarantee rights ordained by the highest authority in the world: the Creator and Lord Supreme of all humanity.[1]

A 'Declaration of the Rights of the Child' was issued by the General Assembly of the United Nations on November 20, 1959. The Assembly chose 1978 to be the 'Year of Human Rights', then it selected the next year, 1979, to be the 'International Year of the Child'. Then regional cooperation in some parts of the world produced such documents as the 'European Conventions on the Rights of Man', issued by the European Council in its meeting in Rome in 1950. In September 1968 the Council of the League of Arab States decided to form a 'Permanent Regional Arab Committee for Human Rights' which held regular meetings and submitted its resolutions to the Council. The legal committee of the Organization of Islamic Conference drafted a 'Document of Human Rights in Islam' in September 1987, a pioneering effort in its emphasis on significant Islamic points.

---

[1] See *Conferences on Moslem Doctrine and Human Rights,* Ministry of Justice, Riyadh and Dar al-Kitab al-Lubnani, Beirut, n.d.

Islam and Human Rights

In addition, international non-governmental organizations have been formed to monitor the observance of human rights in different parts of the world, and to report and campaign on any grave violations in any country. One such organization is the London-based Amnesty International, which was established in 1961 and extended its offices in different countries, especially the United States and Western Europe. Later on, similar organizations followed, such as the New York-based Human Rights Watch, which has a similar scope. A London-based group, 'Article 19', campaigns in the areas of press freedoms and freedom of expression.

Throughout the second half of the twentieth century, these international documents and instruments issued by the General Assembly of the United Nations have raised many problems. These have been difficult to solve or decide upon by consensus or a considerable majority of all the countries of the world, or even within the UN, an organization with its own problems in its charter and structure. The resolutions of the General Assembly are not binding on members, and the resolutions of the Security Council – the highest body of the international organization – can be paralyzed by the veto of any of its five privileged permanent members. Even if such a resolution were to be passed without a veto, it can be without effect if any one or more of these privileged states decide to ignore it or to veto any sanctions based on it. However, such organizational and procedural handicaps have not been the only source of problems, although they did represent a major one. There are many other problems about the theory of human rights protection as well as the practice; some of these have been faced by Muslims in particular, while others confront the whole world.

1. Problems on the Muslim Side

Muslims have no problem with human rights in principle. The Qur'ān addresses in many verses, the 'children of Adam' in their totality and 'human beings' as such, while it addresses, in many other verses, those 'who have attained to faith' or the 'believers'. God has conferred 'dignity' on the children of Adam, whatever their innate and acquired differences may be (Qur'ān 17:70). The universality of the human being is stressed in this verse by underlining that God has enabled human beings to move through land and sea, and the economic development within social justice is stressed by underlining that God has 'provided for them the sustenance out of the good things in life.'

From the Qur'ānic perspective, the human being is not merely supposed to 'survive' at the lowest level of biological survival, but to enjoy the 'dignity', 'universality', and 'good life' conferred on him/her by God, and to develop all his human potential, spiritually and morally, psychologically and intellectually, as well as physically. Thus the human species can achieve its potential, God-given advantage over many of God's creation, as the Qur'ānic verse stresses, while the human responsibility of maintaining and developing the universe is carried out at the same time: 'He (God) brought you into being out of the earth, and charged you with developing it, and made you thrive thereon' (Qur'ān 11:61).

According to the Qur'ān, the ruler is one of the people who is entrusted with authority by the people, and thus is responsible before them (Qur'ān 4:59). The caliphate is a contract of mutual obligations between the rulers and the ruled, and it was historically an actual and real contract, not a fictitious or presumed one as the social contract of John Locke (d.1704) or Jean-Jacques Rousseau (d.1778). Islam teaches Muslims that God only is the One who has no equal or like (Qur'ān 42:11, 112:1–4). He is the One who cannot be questioned, while all humans are equal and should be questioned. The principle of *Sharīʿah* secures the participation of the people in policy-making and decision-making processes. Divine law has supremacy over the rulers and the ruled, the influential and the weak, men and women, adults and children, Muslims and non-Muslims. It applies within the Muslim state, as well as governing relations between Muslim states and others. All of humanity has to fulfil the two-fold responsibility of human and universal development through getting together and knowing the common grounds and the particulars of each human society (Qur'ān 49:13), complementing each other and cooperating and competing in this two-fold development peacefully and virtuously.

Muslim peoples have to present a model in this respect (Qur'ān

2:143, 3:104), but within the global humankind, not separated or isolated from it. Muslim unity and solidarity should not imply a new ethnocentrism based on chauvinism or material exploitation and aggression, but should mean cooperation in securing peace and development, and furthering morality and God-consciousness (Qur'ān 5:12). Muslims are always ready to listen and learn from any human experience (Qur'ān 39:17–18), since they are taught in the Qur'ān that the human merits are conferred by God on humankind in its totality. The believer has to seriously and honestly search for wisdom, and wherever it is found, the believer is the most deserving of it whatever its source may be, as the Prophet's tradition teaches.[2] When he was young, before receiving the Divine Message, the Prophet of Islam attended with his clan chieftain a tribal pact that aimed to secure justice and defend anyone who suffered injustice, which became known as the 'Pact of the Nobles' (Ḥilf al-Fuḍūl). Later on, the Prophet reaffirmed his commitment to that pact, saying that if he were called upon to honour it in Islam, he would not hesitate to do so. And this in spite of the parties to that pre-Islamic pact being naturally non-Muslims.

The Muslim intellectual, jurisprudential and political heritage has included much positive evidence of such an Islamic humanistic and universalistic perspective.[3] We need not dwell on these here, but to be

---

[2] Reported by al-Tirmidhī.

[3] A few examples of this are:
  a) the Caliph ʿUmar's rebuke to the governor of Egypt: 'Since when have you turned people into slaves while they were born free?' The occasion was ʿUmar's ruling against the governor's son and in favour of a Copt who was hit by him after the Copt overtook him in a race. See Ibn ʿAbd al-Ḥakam, Futūḥ Miṣr wa-l Maghrib, ed. Abdel-Munʿim Amer, Cairo, 1961, pp.224–6;
  b) the Caliph ʿUmar's affirmation of the right of all the people in the public treasury and responsibility of the ruler to ensure they receive their dues wherever they may be. See Ibn al-Jarīr al-Ṭabarī, Ta'rīkh al-Rusul wa'l-Mulūk;
  c) the Caliph ʿUmar's decision to secure the needs of a destitute Jew from the public treasury. See Abū Yūsuf, Kitāb al-Kharāj, Cairo, 1392 AH, p.136;
  d) the agreement between Khālid Ibn al-Walīd with the people of Ḥirah, where he undertook to provide from the public treasury for the needs of all old, sick, or poor persons. See Abū Yūsuf, Kitāb al-Kharāj, p.156;
  e) the statement of Rabīʿ ibn ʿĀmir in front of the Persian leader Rustam, where

honest and objective, we should not ignore the fact that the Muslim heritage has also had its negative side, and it is intellectually and morally essential to nurture a critical attitude among the Muslims, especially their younger generations. We are to insist only on judging according to the criteria of Islam, even against parents, kinsfolk, and co-believers, and to ensure that such an intellectual and ethical honesty replace both extremes of an apologetic defensive attitude and a rejectionist one, which has dominated our generations in modern times.

Muslims then can and must endorse and support, as a result of their faith in One God and in the accountability of every human being, any national or universal effort that aims to ensure that no human individual, group or power (be it political, economic, or social within the country, or be it the whole world) can oppress or subjugate others. The problems Muslims face with universal human rights are basically related to certain general conceptual matters that have not been quite settled in the Muslim mind, and which may have their implications not only in the area of human rights, but in other areas as well. A few specific details in the Universal Declaration of Human Rights issued by the General Assembly of the United Nations in December 1948 have raised controversy among Muslims; top of the list has been freedom

he summed up the objective of the Muslim community as being 'to bring people out from the narrowness of life to its spaciousness and from injustice to justice'. See al-Ṭabarī, the reports on the year 14 AH;

f) the opposition of the jurist al-Awzāʿī for the Abbasid ruler's decision to move all of the non-Muslim community from a certain strategic area in Lebanon when some of them were accused of collaborating with Byzantine enemies on the grounds that the responsibility should be precisely restricted to those who might be guilty in a fair inquiry and trial and not generalized to the whole community without evidence. Al-Awzāʿī argued that non-Muslims 'were not slaves but free people who Muslims have promised protection'. See al-Qāsim Ibn Sallām, al-Amwāl, ed. Muhammad Khalil Harras, Cairo, 1975, pp.221–2;

g) the order of the Caliph ʿUmar ibn ʿAbd al-ʿAzīz to withdraw from Samarqand after his judge reached the decision that the Muslim army under Qutaybah ibn Muslim had entered the city by deception. See al-Balādhurī, Futūḥ al-Buldān, ed. Radwan Muhammad Radwan, Cairo, 1959, p.411; see the book of this author in Arabic, Ḥuqūq al-Insān Bayna al-Sharīʿah al-Islāmiyyah wa al-Fikr al-Gharbī, 1st ed., Cairo, 1982, 2nd edition [in print], Lexington, NY, 1996.

of changing one's beliefs (Article 18 of the Declaration). In what follows, we touch on some of the main problems of human rights from the Muslim perspective.

1.1 *The Basic Sources*

Since Islam provides, in its divine sources (the Qur'ān and the Prophet's traditions, the *Sunnah*), broad legal principles and some specific rules in the various arenas of human life, Muslims in modern times, especially those who are committed to the Islamic perspective on the wholeness of the human being and life, which has to be conducted in accordance with God's comprehensive guidance and law, often find it problematic to follow man-made laws. This problem becomes more serious when there is a partial and total contradiction between these laws and *Sharī'ah*. This problem presented itself in the past only with regard to certain agreements between a Muslim country and a non-Muslim one. In modern times, however, it was posed with regard to the national laws adapted from secular Western legal practice as well, in addition to international agreements and treaties such as the Universal Declaration of Human Rights. Muslims constitute a considerable proportion of the world's population but they are by no means the majority. Within Muslim minorities in different countries, many Muslims feel uncomfortable with prevalent laws, especially in family matters where the laws may be completely different from, or even contradictory to, Islamic law. They may not be fully aware that permanently living in a country, and in many cases acquiring its citizenship, implies a commitment to observing its laws and caring for its interest and that fulfilling this commitment is a moral and legal obligation in Islam (Qur'ān 5:1, 16:91–6, 17:34). However, Islamic law has been accepted as an inseparable part from the Qur'ān and the *Sunnah*, and the enforcement of this law by successive Muslim states (at least nominally) for centuries until recently, when Western domination abolished it or restricted it to family matters. This long experience had resulted in an intimate connection in the Muslim mind and psyche between Islamic law and Muslim identity. The situation becomes more complicated in the case of international law. The latter are not the outcome of agreements between identifiable parties that Muslims chose to deal with, but represents a process involving all the countries of the world, international organizations that claim to represent the whole world. Muslims may also have difficulties with the way the organization is run or with the role of some of its key members. We have to realize however, that God's law is not an alternative to human reason, nor is it supposed to put it out of action.

Human reason is the invaluable favour of God to mankind. By the same token, the fruits of the human experience are a similar favour that must be valued. Early Muslims did not hesitate to benefit from the Byzantine and Sassanid expertise in administration and taxation, and many wise sayings referred to as *Naṣā'iḥ al-Mulūk* (advice to kings) attributed to various pre-Islamic leaders and learned men were quoted in Muslim works written to advize rulers. Muslims in this contemporary world would have to get familiar and feel comfortable with globalization and pluralism in this era in which diversity in views has become inevitable. Openness is life, while being closed off and isolated is suicidal. Accordingly, they have to accept relativity in making choices and decisions. Any matter often cannot be purely in one's interest or purely against it, let alone be purely good or purely evil, and global pluralism makes relativity inevitable since various contradictory factors in the countries of the world contribute to the final outcome. Looking at such complex matters as either black or white is unrealistic, oversimplified and wishful thinking in our contemporary era of globalism and pluralism. We should recall that most considerations in *Sharīʿah* are based on the best possible human thinking, not on certainty. The Caliph ʿUmar demonstrated his outstanding statesmanship and his penetrating juristic intellect when he said, 'A sensible person is not the one who is able to know good from evil, but the one who is able to discern the lesser of two evils.'

1.2 *Terminology and Semantics*
We have become used to certain terms from our Muslim heritage, and we do not realize that language and culture are human and thus open to change. Since the Qur'ān is the permanent word of God, we may be

inclined to think that our entire intellectual and religious heritage, in which the Qur'ān has always been central, should have the same sacredness and permanence. Consequently, we feel uncomfortable with the word 'freedom', since the Qur'ān only speaks about liberating or setting free the slave. The Arabs before Islam did not suffer from despotism of monarchs or clergy, but from conflicts of egoism and tribalism. As a result, the use of the word 'freedom' literally in the Muslim heritage was restricted to describing a state that was parallel to slavery.

However, this cannot mean that the concept of freedom in its broader sense did not exist, since the Qur'ān uses words like dignity (*karāmah*) (Qur'ān 17:70) and self-esteem (*'izzah*) (Qur'ān 63:8), in conjunction with the exhortation to faith in God and the eternal life to come. Such a concept of human freedom and even the term itself used by ʿUmar in addressing the Muslim governor of Egypt: 'Since when have you enslaved people who are born free by their mothers?' The prominent jurist al-Awzāʿī also used the term in his remarks to the governor of Syria, where he described the non-Muslim people there as 'free people for whom the Muslims promised protection.'

The concept of freedom, in its broader sense, was thus very well understood, and used often, appearing in scattered theological and juristic works. This contradicts the claim of the well-known American scholar, Franz Rosenthal, who said that he could not find a 'definition' for the word 'freedom' in such a broad sense in the Muslim heritage, and engaged himself in tracing the word in its limited uses in relation to areas such as slavery, imprisonment and forced labour, in addition to the theological discourse about human free-will and predestination. It is probably due to the association of the use of the term with Europe and the West, from which the freedom of the Muslim people suffered for the last successive centuries, and which has been blamed for spreading individualistic and materialistic tendencies, not to mention ethical and behavioural permissiveness, many Muslims have become sensitive to, or uncomfortable with, the word. Fewer Muslims feel uncomfortable with the word 'rights', as the term obligations (*takālīf*) is more widely used in Muslim terminology. Modern debates often overlook the frequent use of terms such as 'right of God' and 'right of the human being' in Islamic jurisprudence (*Uṣūl al-Fiqh*). Rights may be considered religious obligations with regard to those who have the rights, and should demand them and struggle in a legitimate way to acquire them, and those who should secure the rights of others.

It could be argued that the term 'justice', which is used frequently in the Qur'ān (Qur'ān 4:58, 135, 5:9, 42, 7:29, 16:90, 49:9, 57:25, 60:8) is more suitable and preferable, and probably more comprehensive and accurate than words such as 'freedom' and 'equality'. One has to bear in mind, however, that equality is connected with freedom in the Western conception of human rights, since equality in oppression or deprivation of freedom or rights is not considered genuine. Besides, broad concepts may require specification, and the umbrella concept of justice, for example, has required an emphasis on social justice to avoid ambiguity or administrative and/or judicial limitations. We have to seriously consider the sociological development of language and conceptual and functional needs, and to strive to go beyond the strict literal application of terms to comprehend their wider meaning. Our theologians, jurists, philosophers and thinkers in general have, over the centuries, developed a wealth of new terms that did not exist before, and were not in use in the early times of the Companions and their successors. Language is a living and growing structure that is by nature changing, as are all living beings.

1.3 *Change*

The problems we have discussed with regard to 'sources' and 'terminology and semantics' may have an epistemological and ontological root, closely related to the concept of 'change' in this world and in life. All creation, be it material or living beings, undergoes continuous change. This includes individuals and societies, and accordingly their needs, since God is the only Eternal Being (Qur'ān 28:88, 52:26–7, 57:3, 112:1–2). There are certain moral values which are assented to by all human beings, or most of them, in different times and places, and which have been called 'common sense', but which may be understood and practised in different ways. Since Islam is the last of God's messages to humankind, it provides permanent principles, as well as the dynamics for responding to human change. Change follows the general natural laws, or God's *Sunan* (Qur'ān 3:137, 4:26, 33:38, 62, 35:43, 48:23). Human societies have their own natural laws, and social or political developments follow certain laws, like the succession of day and night (Qur'ān 3:26-7). God does not treat Muslim individuals or societies with regard to the general natural laws exceptionally or with favouritism: '... and had God so willed, He could have indeed put them down (those who stubbornly denied the truth) Himself: but He willed to test you all through one another' (Qur'ān, 47:4). Muslims have to struggle, suffer and persevere according to the natural laws (Qur'ān 3:140–2, 165). Their piety and sincerity will be rewarded in the life to come, but in this world they obtain the best through individual and social commitment to peace, balance and steadfastness as a result of their belief in the One God and the life to come (Qur'ān 3:140, 4:104).

The modern Muslim thinker and poet Muhammad Iqbal (1873–1938) underscored 'the principle of movement in the structures of Islam,' and stressed the essential place of *ijtihād* in this respect.[4] The dynamism that Iqbal pointed out, and for which he campaigned, contrasts with what the other prominent name in modern Muslim thought in India, Abu'l-Kalam Azad (1888–1958) called reconsolidation, (*ta'ṣīl*) of the fundamental verities of Islam. Azad argued for presenting Islam's inherent merits, as he was not inclined to reopening the door of *ijtihād* anew.[5]

While the modern West has concentrated on change in this world, many Muslims have tended to emphasize permanence and ignore change, its effects, and its implications in human life in different times and places. They tend to believe that opposition to diversity and variation in Muslim thinking and society is a natural and essential consequence of the belief in the One God and in Muslim unity. Such a

---

[4] See Muhammad Iqbal, *The Reconstruction of Religious Thought in Islam*, New Delhi, 1984, pp.146–80.
[5] John Obert Voll, *Islam: Continuity & Change in the Modern World*, Boulder, Colorado, US, 1982, p.225.

fundamental misconception has developed other distortions about human nature, the message of Islam, and Muslim history. A static understanding of the Islamic model has led to ignoring human diversity. The flourishing civilization under the Umayyads and Abbasids has been simply considered a deviation from the right path, since the pattern of that lifestyle was different from what had existed at the time of the early caliphate in Madinah.

Naturally not every difference is deviation, and all of Muslim life cannot be restricted to the political system and the rulers. Magnificent material and intellectual developments in Muslim civilization that were contributed to by all the people, whatever the rulers' behaviour may have been, cannot be denied, and they had their impact on non-Muslim countries at the time. Hereditary monarchy and absolute authority characterized the Umayyad and Abbasid dynasties, but during that period fascinating developments took place in the exegesis of the Qur'ān, the examination and collection of *Sunnah* and the commentary on it, jurisprudence, theology, logic and philosophy, linguistics and literature, science in its various fields, medicine with its various areas, architecture, art, agriculture, industry, trade, transportation, etc. Can we ignore such total distinguished civilizational developments produced by all the people because of the negatives of palace life?

An important fruit of that civilization, which had its variations in different times and places, was the success of Muslim thinking in general, and Islamic jurisprudence in particular, demonstrating vitality and dynamism. Through the mechanisms of *ijtihād*, it managed to cope with change and to respond to emerging problems. These mechanisms included analogy (*qiyās*), preference (*istiḥsān*), consideration of unspecified common benefit (*al-maṣlaḥah al-mursalah*), goals and general principles and objectives of *Sharīʿah* (*maqāṣid*), and implementation of *Sharīʿah* in government policies (*al-siyāsah al-sharʿiyyah*). Different views appeared, and various schools developed, and each school had its differences among its own prominent jurists. Schools also displayed regional differences, while positions within them changed from one generation to the next. One reads more than one view attributed to the same jurist in his limited individual life, expressed in response to a certain development in his thinking, in the social circumstances, or in the particular cases he dealt with.

The leading jurist al-Shāfiʿī (150–205 AH/767–820) developed two different sets of jurisprudential works during his lifetime: an earlier one when he lived in Iraq, and a later one when he came to Egypt, where he lived until his death, and where he is buried. If such a distinctive change occurred in one individual's life, and was connected with his movement between two contemporary Muslim societies, one can conceive of how change is inseparable from humanity, and how dynamic Islamic law is in coping with human change. Unfortunately, Muslim legal and juristic history does not enjoy the importance that it deserves in the courses studied at the educational institutions of *Shariʿah* in different Muslim countries, and are not put into perspective through the universal legal development, and in relation to the social developments in the various Muslim societies throughout history. Muslims may have the advantage of available rich sources in their social history, represented in their voluminous heritage in the areas of general, regional, and city histories, biographies and autobiographies.

Westerners, who are fully aware of the qualitative changes humanity has passed through in the last two centuries, and even in the last decades of the last century, cannot understand at all how our model of fourteen centuries ago may be applied now. This is especially so when such zeal for restoring the past is connected in some views with condemning, or at least disregarding or undervaluing, the flourishing civilization in Damascus, Baghdad, Cairo, Qayrawan, Fez, Cordova, Samarqand, Bukhara, etc. In our fondness for 'oneness' and 'permanence', we may be tempted to impose Islam from above by force or otherwise. This inclination towards totalitarian and authoritarian tendencies may lead to a conscious or unconscious assimilation of the influence of fascist views or Marxist ones.

1.4 *Formulation and Codification*

The problems faced by Muslims with regard to sources of legislation, terminology and the challenge of adapting to change, have in turn created a technical problem related to the formulation and articulation of modern laws. Many Muslims believe that our heritage is sufficient for the legal needs of all Muslim societies in all times and places. They like to continue in the same way as the previous Muslim generations, with no distinction between jurisprudence and legislation. The decision on any option from among the different views offered by one juristic school or more is left to the judge. They may not be aware that as early as the time of Ibn al-Muqaffaʿ (140 AH/757), the writer complained to the Abbasid Caliph about the sharp divergence in the rulings of the judges of neighbouring courts in cases similar to one another in all respects, because of their different juristic views. They may also not be aware that Muslims started an experience of legislation and codification in modern times through the legal opinions (*fatwās*) issued by Shaikh al-Islām in the Ottoman Empire, and this developed into the issuing of *Majallat al-Aḥkām al-ʿAdliyya* (published and put into effect 1870–77). In the same period, Qadri Pasha codified family and civil laws in *Sharīʿah* according to the Ḥanafī school for the Egyptian government. Given this background, Muslim resentment against Western-inspired legal formulations in national and international fields, especially with regard to such documents as the Universal Declaration of Human Rights. We may recall here that giving up *Sharīʿah* as the law of the land in Muslim countries was connected with imported Western laws to substitute for it.

However, we should admit that Muslims have been influenced for a long time by traditional jurisprudence (*uṣūl al-fiqh*) and its emphasis on disjointed detail. Accordingly, we care more about tracing the details of a particular rule in civil or penal law, than dealing with state obligations, contract, criminal action or penal philosophy, or with presenting the general concepts and principles of the civil or commercial law, etc. Therefore many principles and procedural questions remain neglected in Islamic thought, even though the resolutions of different international legal conferences about the merits of *Sharīʿah* enlightened many people in this respect. We thus hear little discussion of the need to discourage conviction, the dropping of a charge in case of any reasonable doubt, the basic requirement of social justice and education for punishment, the observation of the rights of both the defendant and the victim, social rehabilitation for offenders and the great variety of discretionary penalties, (taʿzīr). The latter issue is especially important, given that the restrictions on the implementation of fixed penalties (ḥudūd), which make taʿzīr the flexible and efficient source of penal law that responds to changing social needs, instead of always concentrating on ḥudūd when discussing Sharīʿah. All these and other principles have to be presented and elaborated on, so that no misunderstanding takes place.

Islamic civil law and its general principles, may be better conceived through general concise Qur'ānic principles, such as stipulating the consent of concerned parties in contracts, the justifiable claim in securing any profit or gain (Qur'ān 4:29), evidence and securities in civil and commercial transactions and the rights and obligations of witnesses (Qur'ān 2:282–3). Related to this is also the requirement that family matters ought to be run by the mutual consultation and consent of both spouses (Qur'ān 2:233), and that women and men are both mutually responsible for caring for each other and for the whole society through enjoining the doing of what is good and forbidding the doing of what is wrong.

If we understand Sharīʿah in its totality, its general concepts and principles, and its dynamism, and devote due effort to studying the general goals and objectives of Sharīʿah to illuminate our understanding, development, and implementation of our Islamic laws in our contemporary circumstances, we shall be more receptive and will benefit more from modern legal thinking in the field of human rights as well as in other fields. I believe that in the School of Judiciary Training for Sharīʿah Courts in Egypt, where both Sharīʿah and modern legal experiences are taught side by side, the interaction between Sharīʿah professors and their colleagues who teach modern secular law with its various branches in the faculties of law in Egypt has resulted in mutual benefits on both sides. Recently, scholars of modern Western laws have become more aware of the merits and richness of Sharīʿah. This constructive interaction has been reflected in the articles published in the journals of these faculties as well as in the doctoral dissertations and other academic work combining Western Islamic jurisprudential sources through collaboration of scholars from both disciplines.

1.5 *Equality and the 'Other'*

Human rights are universal, and they apply equally to all human beings whatever their inborn or acquired differences may be. Through such a universal human perspective, the 'other' is as equally human as you, be he/she of another gender, race or ethnicity, faith, age, or ideology. The Qur'ān emphasizes that all humankind was created from one couple: a male and a female, in spite of all their diversification into various peoples and tribes. They are meant to develop knowing and complementing one another through the diversity of human qualities and the diversity of the natural resources distributed among them in their homelands (Qur'ān 49:13). The first human couple, the two mates, were created from a single living entity 'and out of the two spread out a multitude of men and women' (Qur'ān 4:1, see also 16:72, 30:21, 39:6, 42:11), and two mates who have the same origin and are of the same kind are inclined towards one another, and affection and tenderness are engendered between them by God (Qur'ān 30:21). When they form a family together, they have to run its affairs with mutual consultation and consent (Qur'ān 2:233), and in the society both men and women are equally in charge of, and responsible for, one another, and both 'enjoin the doing of what is right and forbid the doing of what is wrong' (Qur'ān 9:71).

Muslims have to deal with non-Muslims with justice, fairness, and kindness, as long as the non-Muslims do not initiate aggression or hostilities and seem inclined to peaceful actions and relations, 'for verily, God loves those who act justly' (Qur'ān 60:8). In many verses the Qur'ān addresses the 'children of Adam' in all their plurality, and in more verses 'human beings' in their totality, as well as addressing in others 'those who have attained to faith' in the One God, the life to come, the Qur'ān, and the Prophet to whom it was revealed. Yet many Muslims may accept being kind to the other, but not being 'equal' to him/her. They may think that the two attitudes are the same, or that kindness may suffice or substitute for equality. Here again we come to the problem of terminology and semantics. 'Nicety' is essential for human relations, and 'equality' may be a legal and outward formality if it is not based on 'moral' conviction and virtuousness. Nevertheless, nicety consciously or unconsciously implies a feeling of superiority; one feels that he/she is superior to the other but he/she ought to be nice in dealing with him/her. We talk two different languages with those who believe in the universal human rights, when we insist on speaking about our belief in, and practise of, kind-ness, while they need an explicit and clear commitment to 'equality' of the 'other' to 'us', in spite of whatever the differences between the 'other' and 'us'.

1.5.1 *Equality for Women*

Unless we change our terminology, and talk the common language of the world, our exchanges with advocates of universal human rights will always be 'the dialogue of the deaf'. The main areas about which we have to be clear and articulate are: the relations between men and women and between Muslims and non-Muslims. We have been used to thinking that women have been created for family life and for raising children, and thus their natural place is in the home. Nothing in the Qur'ān or the *Sunnah* clearly supports such a claim or assumption. Such a division of labour between the husband who earns the living of the family and the wife who stays at home doing housework had existed throughout history in most societies, including the Arab society at the time of Islam, and the subsequent Muslim as well as other societies in modern times. However, such a very long experience in so many countries does not necessarily mean that it is an eternal natural law, nor can it be proved to be God's law in Islam.

While different words are used in English for 'husband' and 'wife', and the root of the word 'husband' means the master and manager of the house, this may be merely the reflection of a sociological tradition that has existed throughout history. Arabic, however, uses the same word, *zawj*, meaning mate or companion, for both husband and wife. Some may add the suffix 'ah' to *zawj* to indicate that the word in a particular context means wife, but this is not a linguistic rule or obligation, and the Qur'ān uses the word *zawj* and its plural *azwāj* to mean wife and wives respectively (Qur'ān, 2:35, 4:12, 20, 6:139, 7:19, 33:4, 6, 50, 59, 60:11), as well as husband and its plural (Qur'ān 2:230, 232, 58:1). One may argue whether this may be better for the family or not, and I may go further to say that some Muslim and non-Muslim women may prefer to stay in the home, but this does not mean that this is God's law that is explicitly spelt out in the Qur'ān and the *Sunnah*. The discussion has to be moved from theology to sociology, or from the divine revelation to the human intellect and discretion.

The Arabic word *qawwāmūn*, with its proposition ʿalā, which describes the relation of men to women, does not imply any superiority; it simply means 'taking full care of'. The verse reads: 'Men, take full care of women, for what God has granted some of them distinctively from the other, and what they may spend out of their possessions' (Qur'ān 4:34). The distinctiveness between men and women is related to the woman's pregnancy, delivery, and nursing, which make it necessary that the man should have the responsibility to provide for her needs and the needs of the children, at least when she is hindered with such a distinctive function, that of reproduction. This hindrance is not permanent, and it cannot be a reason to keep the women at home all their life, and neither does it hinder their intellectual and psychological capacities. A woman will not be bearing children or raising children all her life, and at a certain age, children have to go to school and study when they get home, in this way remaining occupied most of their day. Besides, suppose that a woman did not marry or bear children, what, then, should keep her at home? It is time to look at the woman as an equal human being, not just a bearer and a raiser of children, a cook, a home-cleaner, a dishes and dirty-laundry washer, etc. The family and children require a joint-effort of both man and woman. Since the woman has her right and obligation in obtaining an education according to the guidance of Islam, it is good for her personality and the society, just as it may be good for the family as a whole, and so her right to work should be secured. This means that the husband has to share the housework, since it is not fair for the wife to have to still do it all as was customary before, while she is also working. It was reported that the Prophet used to help with the housework when he came home.

As mentioned above, family affairs should be run by mutual consultation and consent of both spouses (Qur'ān 2:233), and the children should be raised and trained to always use their minds and speak up when they see something wrong, even in the family, but at all times decently and politely. The woman's right to inheritance is stated in the Qur'ān, and an addition can be supplemented by writing a will that has priority over the mandatory distribution of inheritance stated in the Qur'ān (Qur'ān 4:11–12). The (voluntary) will ought to take priority, and a Muslim should feel his/her responsibility to write his/her will as the Qur'ān urges, even when he/she becomes suddenly on the brink of death without having been prepared (Qur'ān, 2:180, 240, 5:109–11). In society, men and women are equally and jointly in charge and responsible for one another in fulfilling their collective obligations towards the public as a whole (Qur'ān 9:71). A woman has the right to vote, to be a member of parliament, a minister, a judge, and even an officer in the army. Which jobs may or may not be convenient should be decided by women themselves – not imposed on them – according to their own conviction and based on their own interests. In a modern state, it is institutions that rule, not individuals. Women, whatever their number in executive, legislative or judiciary positions are included in bodies and are subject to a system. Laws are codified, and discretionary decisions are subject to be reviewed by those who have higher positions or by the courts. No single man or woman can maintain absolute power in a modern state.

Considering the testimony of two women equal to that of one man in witnessing the documentation of a credit is connected with a certain practical consideration that is explicitly mentioned in the Qur'ānic text: 'so that if one of them [the two women] might make a mistake, the other could remind her' (Qur'ān 2:282). Women might not, in general, have been familiar with business matters and their financial and legal requirements, especially in Arabia in the time of the Prophet's message. But this does not mean that a woman that has had the necessary education or business experience cannot be equal to a man in this respect. Classical jurists pointed out that this was not a general rule on the testimony of a woman, and that the testimony of one woman is sufficient if she knows what she is witnessing and is reliable.[6] In our times, should not a woman who may be a lawyer or an accountant be equal to a man in witnessing the documentation of a transaction? How can some jurists allow a woman to judge with full jurisdiction on all matters, if she cannot be a full witness in the first place? Is it not obvious that the limitation regarding her witnessing a document of credit is understood as only conditional and exceptional in relation to certain cases?

In a report of the 'Muslim Women's League' of Los Angeles, California, USA on the United Nations Fourth World Conference on Women, in Beijing, China in September 1995, these lines among the highlights of the 'Impact of the Conference' are very significant:

> The role of women in society is continuously changing and becoming complex ... Although the conference did not focus directly on religion, Islam did figure prominently in a number of debates. In general, Muslims were perceived by others to be opposed to the equality of women, against the complete human rights of women, and afraid to discuss any issue relating to sexuality that did not fit their value system. The environment at this Conference did not provide an effective opportunity to present a balanced picture of Islam, nor any other major philosophy for that matter. But for Muslims, this inadequate forum was especially frustrating because it helped to reinforce *negative stereotypes* about Islam that continue to exist throughout the world. *The obvious counter to these stereotypes, then, is for Muslims to discredit them through action rather than idealized speechmaking.* Such action would entail responding pro-actively to problems of health, poverty, education, and violence against women extant among Muslim communities all over the world ...
>
> [T]his conference will serve as a catalyst for such debates among Muslims, as they examine *interpretations* of Islamic laws that discriminate against women. This calls for *discussion of issues Muslims prefer to avoid that have serious ramifications, especially where Islamic law is legislated and*

---

[6] See by this author, *The Rights of Muslim Women in the Family and the Society*, Los Angeles, California, 1988.

Islam and Human Rights

enforced ... Although Islam was sometimes viewed in a negative light by the other delegates, the behaviour of some of the individuals from different countries provided an image that challenged the stereotypes ... [On the other hand,] many Muslims who attended felt that the reality faced by women raising families by themselves, being subject to violence and violations of their rights, forced into exploitative relationships, and so on means that *the ideals of Islam are far from being implemented, even in countries governed by Sharīʿah*.[7]

1.5.2 *Relations with non-Muslims*

As for the Muslim/non-Muslim relations within countries and globally, Muslims have to be fully aware of the era of globalization, achieved through the revolution of transportation and communication that all of mankind is undergoing. This situation does not allow any country or human group left alone to manage its own affairs separately from the whole world. Even countries like Nepal and Myanmar (Burma) have been exposed to the present global communications revolution. The Internet has speeded up world communications and removed barriers between countries in a way that would have been beyond imagination only a few decades ago.

Global pluralism is a solid reality that cannot be escaped, and national pluralism will always be what the majority of the world persistently requires. Besides, Muslims cannot demand justice for their minorities all over the world unless they secure it for non-Muslim minorities living among Muslim majorities. Isolation in such an era of globalism could not be afforded by China, for example, where almost a billion people live, since isolation from the economical and technological developments that are continuously taking place throughout the whole world would simply mean death.

Islam teaches justice, understanding, cooperation, and kindness in dealing with non-Muslims and all 'others' at country and international levels (Qur'ān 49:13, 60:7-8). Muslims should be honestly keen to maintain peace with others in their country and in the whole world,

---

[7] Muslim Women's League, *Report on the United Nations 4th World Conference on Women and Non-Governmental Organization Forum in Beijing, China, September 1995*, Los Angeles California, pp. 13–14. The emphases in the passage are the author's.

cooperating in furthering virtue and righteousness, not fostering evil and aggression (Qur'ān 5:3). They should promote reconciliation and defend the wronged party against injustice, and vie with others in doing good (Qur'ān 5:48). Diversity is a natural law for humankind, and no conformity or domination of one single way of thinking or way of life can be expected. People are different in their various abilities so as to be tested with how they deal with their differences and constructively interact, benefiting from God's gracious guidance in their efforts (Qur'ān 5:48, 11:118-19, 49:13). It is the real challenge to the human 'ego' to deal with the other, and even with the enemy, justly and kindly, since the human being is inclined to deal nicely with his/her own people.

Here again, what is required in universal human rights is 'equality', not merely nicety. Muslims and non-Muslims should be equal in rights and obligations in a Muslim country, which should mean that a non-Muslim can vote, be a member of parliament, a minister, a judge, an officer in the army, and may reach the top in any position. They should enjoy their basic rights of belief, expression, and assembly. The general principle in Islam is that 'there should not be any coercion in matters of faith' (Qur'ān 2:256, also 10:99, 11:28). Non-Muslims can have their organizations and their institutions protected. Their religious processions with their prominent religious symbols have been secured in early conquests. They could obtain equal access to the state public services, especially in the field of public safety, health, education, economic development and social security, which has to be provided to them from the *zakāt* revenues or from other state revenues.[8] Churches and synagogues ought to be protected in the same way as mosques, and their protection is a legitimate obligation (Qur'ān 22:40). They should be equal to Muslims in obligations such as taxation and military service.

I do not think Muslims have any legal problem with regard to full equality with non-Muslims in rights and obligations. What emerged as

---

[8] See Abū Yūsuf, *Kitāb al-Kharāj*, Cairo, 1392 AH, pp.136, 155–6; Abū ʿUbayd al-Qāsim ibn Sallām, *al-Amwāl*, pp.803–5.

Islam and Human Rights

the status of *dhimmīs* (non-Muslims within the Muslim state) was historically developed rather than built in the permanent laws of the Qur'ān and the *Sunnah*. Many scholars, including Westerners, admit that the status of non-Muslims in the Muslim world during the Middle Ages, was better than what the Jews or other religious minorities received in the Christian countries in those ages. The important question is: Are Muslims now ready to go further to secure and sanction full equality for non-Muslims in a contemporary Islamic state? When reservations and 'ifs' and 'buts' are raised, how can Muslims expect that non-Muslims will be convinced of, or loyal to, the concept of an Islamic state while they are offered full equality without reservations in a secular democracy?

A majority cannot deny a minority its rights, on the grounds that a minority has to respect the rights of the majority to have their state system. Unless the state system secures human rights for all citizens without discrimination, it would encourage contradictions and disputes within the country and would lose world support. Furthermore, any discrimination against a Muslim minority in a non-Muslim country cannot be strongly opposed universally if a similar injustice is committed by Muslims against non-Muslim minorities. Whatever the 'nicety' in human relations may be in daily life, 'equality' has to be secured and sanctioned by law.

In a modern state, as we have stressed before, no single person rules, but institutions are in charge and laws are codified. Non-Muslims, whatever their number in a certain body may be, would be part of a system. If the Shāfiʿī jurist al-Māwardī (d.450 AH/1058) allows a *dhimmī* to be an executive minister beside the Muslim Caliph, every public official now may be considered to be merely 'executive' in a sense, since no one, not even the head of the state, has absolute power or can rule as a single person. Even as a judge, the non-Muslim applies *Sharīʿah* as the codified state law, whatever his/her beliefs regarding Islam may be.

Matters that are considered very close to the faith, such as family matters, and matters of a purely religious character such as those related to *zakāt*, *waqf*, or mosques, can be assigned to Muslim judges who share the litigants' faith. The military service may have some religious character for Muslims, but it meanwhile signifies national defence for non-Muslims. Non-Muslims were allowed to share with Muslims the responsibility of defending Madinah in the Prophet's Constitutional document, which he drew up just after his migration there. This did not particularly work, but it cannot affect the validity of the principle. Non-Muslims became involved in defending certain strategic areas in the conquests of Syria, Persia and Iraq.[9] It has been well established that the payment of the head-tax (*jizyah*) was a substitute for military service, and those who were charged with military responsibilities were exempt from its payment. Modern juristic authorities have argued for equal citizenship for all in a contemporary Muslim state, which ought to be a substitute and development of the *dhimmī* status which we have used in our juristic heritage.[10]

Religious and political pluralism has to be maintained within the country, and the right to form political parties and different kinds of organizations and associations, including labour and professional unions and philanthropic associations should be secured for all citizens of the Islamic state. Muslims can have several Islamic parties if they have differences regarding the concepts, or strategy, or even the structure and the leadership with which they feel comfortable. Several political groups appeared in the earliest Muslim political assembly in Madinah following the death of the Prophet: the *muhājirūn* (immigrants from Makkah), the *anṣār* ('supporters', Muslim residents of Madinah), and those who had their inclinations towards the family of the Prophet, and believed that the Caliph should be from his descendants, beginning with his cousin, ʿAlī ibn Abī Ṭālib. Later theological views were in many cases connected with political ideas, as represented

---

[9] See al-Balādhurī, *op. cit.*, in his section on al-Samira, p.162, and al-Jarājimah, p.164. In his chapter on the conquest of Syria (al-Shām), Ibn Jarīr al-Ṭabarī, *op. cit.*, reports on the participation of al-Asāwirah and al-Ḥamrāʾ in the Muslim conquest of the non-Muslim lands.

[10] See for example Abdul Karim Zaidan, *Aḥkām al-Dhimmiyyin wa'l Musta'minīn*, Beirut (n.d.), pp.53–5, 61–125, and Rashid al-Ghannoushi, *Ḥuqūq al-Muwaṭṭanah*, Herndon, VA, 1993.

in the views of the Shīʿah (who called for a Caliph from the Prophet's descendants), *al-Khawārij* (who emerged in their opposition of the Caliph ʿAlī), *al-Murji'ah* (who supported the status quo under the Umayyads), and the *Muʿtazilah* (who appeared under the Abbasids). Islam has never forbidden differences which are simply natural as a result of the human intellect and the human free-will, but Islam only guides the Muslims on how to settle their differences methodically and ethically (Qur'ān 4:59, 83, 16:125, 49:6-13). Non-Muslims also can have their political parties, since the People of the Book have to enjoin the doing of what is right and forbid the doing of what is wrong (Qur'ān 3:114). Secularists should be allowed to express their opinion and organize their parties, since all parties are required to practise their activities peacefully, without provoking hostilities and confrontations.

The freedom of expression in a modern state cannot be separated from the right of association and assembly, whether temporarily for a casual expression of opinion, or permanently in an organization, since the individual expression of opinion is without effect for a government that enjoys a huge majority and possesses organizational, material, and technological superiority, in addition to monopoly of certain oppressive measures.

In universal relations, Muslims and non-Muslims have to deal with each other fairly and cooperatively. Muslim universal solidarity is not meant to be a new bloc that threatens or disturbs world peace, since Muslims have to cooperate only to promote virtue and righteousness, not evil and aggression (Qur'ān 5:2). Muslims have to support universal peace based on justice (Qur'ān 2:208, 8:61), be a positive factor in developing understanding cooperation and reconciliation, and in preventing and terminating aggression and securing universal justice (Qur'ān 49:9, 13). They can join regional and universal organizations for economic and cultural cooperation, as well as hold an agreement with one or a few states. They have to always keep their promises and fulfil their obligations (Qur'ān 6:152, 13:20, 16:91–6, 17:34). It may be better for them to be always present and constructive in universal organizations and forums, and air their grievances and criticism from within. We have to be realistic about universal justice, and realize that each member state in a multi-state organization cares only, or more about its interests, rather than about the common benefits or universal justice. We have to always develop ourselves and cooperate together, and thus we let others realize that we are needed, and that observing mutual interests is a more secure constant for all parties than exploitation and subordination.[11]

Pluralism within a Muslim country and within its regional or global milieu, does not entail a compromise with regard to the Muslim faith in any way. Nor does it signify scepticism or indifference among the believers. As it was well put by Nicholas Rescher:

> The fact that others may think differently from ourselves does nothing as such to preclude us from warranted confidence in the appropriateness and correctness of our own views. The idea that pluralism's recognition of the existence of other alternatives entails a sceptical suspension of opinion on the grounds of our being obliged to see the existence of other opinions as annihilating the tenability of our own is, to put it mildly, far-fetched. Pluralism holds that it is rationally intelligible and acceptable that others can hold positions at variance with one's own. But it does not maintain that a given individual need endorse a plurality of positions – that the fact that others hold a certain position somehow constitutes a reason for doing so oneself. Any viable proceeding in this range of discussion must distinguish between the standpoint of the individual and the standpoint of the group. Pluralism is a feature of the collective group: it turns on the fact that different experiences engender different views. But from the standpoint of the individual this cuts no ice. We have no alternative to proceeding as best we can on the basis of what is available to us.[12]

This reminds me of the splendid wise saying attributed to Imām al-Shāfiʿī: 'Our view – as we believe it to be – is right, but it could be later proved to be wrong, and the view of others – as we believe it to be – is wrong, but it could probably be later proved to be right.'

[11] See by this author, *Children of Adam: An Islamic Perspective On Pluralism*, Georgetown University Press, Washington, DC, 1996.

[12] Nicholas Rescher, *Pluralism: Against the Demand of Consensus*, Oxford, 1993, p.88–9.

1.6 Conceptual and Practical Strategy

The way the questions raised above is settled will affect the Muslim conceptual and practical strategy in our era of globalism and pluralism. Muslims have to think and plan as part of the contemporary universality and plurality, not as a dominating or isolated entity. The designation of *Dār al-Islām* as an entity apart from the rest of the world, whether this world is hostile and belligerent to the Muslims, or has peaceful relations with them, was historical and theoretical. Muslims actually had relations with the whole world, and their travellers and merchants reached Scandinavia, the Volga basin, the heart of Africa beyond the Sahara, China, and South-East Asia. Muslim geographers and travellers mentioned 'the Muslim lands' in their fascinating works, but they never mentioned the term 'land of war' (*Dār al-Ḥarb*) that was coined by some Muslim jurists. Even with regard to the Byzantine Empire, with which the Muslims had continuous border disputes, the geographers simply refer to it as 'the kingdom or land of the Byzantines, "*Rūm*".' The Muslim *Ummah* is not a new bloc that adds to world splits and conflicts, but rather a restrictive element for peace and cooperation. The universality of Islam is not restricted to the Muslims in their *Ummah*, but represents the grace of the 'Lord of all being' (*Rabb al-ʿālamīn*) (Qur'ān 21:4).

Besides, a Muslim organization or movement cannot claim to represent all Muslims in any country, let alone in the whole world. It needs to communicate with the masses and interact with them, without seeking to impose its ideas and policies. It should not take for granted the support of the people just for being Muslim. Furthermore, Muslims should act and think within the country as part of people in its totality: Muslims and non-Muslims. They have to strongly resist being authority-oriented, and stop thinking that reform for them can only be imposed from above, since this may lead them to believe that they have either to rule or lose.

If Islamic movements are one day to rule efficiently, they need to be thoroughly familiar with the conditions in which people live and evaluate government efforts to tackle the problems facing them. We have to realize that any steps taken to improve things in the fields of public health, education, economic development, civil services, defence and international relations, will be in line with Islamic values. Any achievements in these areas by Islamic movements will have a direct effect on the people and their perception of, and readiness for, the Islamic comprehensive way of life. They could also be seen as a testimony to the movement's experience and capability.

To reach an accurate evaluation of conditions in the country and in the world, it is necessary to coordinate all possible efforts and capabilities within the Islamic organization, in other Islamic organizations and all organizations which are committed to and work for justice and morality. We should be realistic in working for our ideals, realizing that a comprehensive Islamic way of life cannot be achieved instantly. Neither can international relations turn instantly towards justice, peace and cooperation.

We ought to make a distinction between ideals and principles, strategy and tactics and long-term, medium-term, and short-term plans. We should also be clear in our minds about priorities and alternatives. This has to be decided dynamically, and to cope continuously with the changing circumstances.

The *Shūrā*-democracy polemics have to be settled once and for all. Until we have a real efficient concretization and methodologization of the concept of *Shūrā*, we have no equal or parallel to the existing developed mechanisms of democracy. These remain the best available means for the implementation of the concept of *Shūrā* in spite of all its shortcomings which are widely recognized and strongly criticized in democratic countries themselves, another point for democracy. The ways of selecting the early caliphs, or the juristic theory of 'the people of binding and dissolving,' (*ahl al-ḥall wa'l-ʿaqd*) had never been applied in the past, and cannot be workable today. Fortunately, such fondness for everything related to the past, even words and forms which cannot be by nature or according to *Sharīʿah* be eternal since they emerge through changing circumstances and by *ijtihād*, is retrogressive. Moreover, democracy has been increasingly, albeit uneasily, accepted in theory and in practice in the contemporary Islamic thinking, although the polemics still survive here and there.[13]

Muslim organizations would have to prove the truth of the statement by a senior fellow at the Center for Strategic and International Studies in Washington, DC, Edward N. Luttwak, who said: 'In (most) Arab states the Islamists are *the only* functioning opposition to anti-democratic governments.'[14] It is their chance, then, to deeply root this in their concepts and actions, and to reach and mobilize the broadest possible mass support, and through such an interaction they would then be addressing their understanding of the Islamic comprehensive way of life.

Furthermore, Muslim activists have to make clear for themselves, for the Muslim masses and for non-Muslims, the means that they intend to use to achieve their goals and implement *Sharī'ah*. Would this be gradual, or should it be done in one go? Should it begin from below or from above? Should Islamists accept sharing power with others? How would they react towards possible opposition from the authorities or oppressive measures from them? One should not wait until such answers emerge through practice in order to always secure consistency, and to avoid perplexing their supporters and the masses, and avoid any chance of being accused of conceptual or strategic ambiguity and contradictions. Such uncertainties could permit violence and its supporters to try to exploit the vagueness and push the movement into an unknown wilderness.

2. Problems for the Wider World

Dealing with the problems of human rights on the Muslim side at some length does not mean that the problems facing the whole world in this respect are less important. They are very important, and their effect naturally reaches all, including the Muslims. Here are some of the

---

[13] For more elaboration on the conceptual and practical strategy of the contemporary Islamic movement see the Arabic book of the author *Fi al-Tajribah al-Siyāsīyah Lil Ḥarakah al-Islāmiyyah al-Muʿāṣirah*, Lexington, Kentucky, 1991.

[14] Luttwak, Edward, 'The Answer to Islamic Violence is Democracy', in *Los Angeles Times*, 11 April 1996.

main serious problems that have been facing the world as a whole in this field.

2.1 *Conceptual Issues*

There are first some questions regarding whether the concept of human rights has been comprehensively expressed and well articulated in the Universal Declaration of Human Rights of 1948. It is obvious that rights are inseparable from duties. That had been the problem faced by the French Declaration of the Rights of Man and the Citizen of 4th August 1789, and an attempt of balancing the rights and duties followed in the declaration that preceded the French Constitution of 24th June 1793. The Qur'ān uses the word 'dignity' which has been conferred by God on all the Children of Adam (17:70), and which comprises enjoining the rights and fulfilling the duties together as well as the various dimensions of human life, including the spiritual-moral ones.

The General Assembly of the United Nations realized the socio-economic gap in the Declaration of December 1948, and was most likely influenced by the Marxist viewpoint that political rights can never exist without securing socio-economic rights. Thus the International Covenant on Economic, Social and Cultural Rights came out on 16th December 1966, and became effective from 15th July 1976, at the same time as the International Covenant on Civil and Political Rights. Later, the 'Vienna Declaration and Program of Action' followed on 25th June 1993, trying to show 'the profound relationship between human rights, democracy and development' – as John Shattuck, US Assistant Secretary of State for human rights and humanitarian affairs stated.[15]

The Vienna conference also tried to secure more rights for women and children, calling for ending sexual harassment and gender-based violence, and setting a target date of 1995 for the universal ratification of the UN Convention on the Rights of the Child. In September 1995, another United Nations effort occurred in Beijing: 'UN Fourth World

---

[15] *Los Angeles Times*, 26 June, 1993.

Conference on Women and Non-Governmental Organizations Forum.' The point of all these efforts is that neglect of a clear definition and articulation of the rights of women and children would be a serious legal and moral offence against a huge part of humanity that needs protection and suffers torture and suppression.

There is generally a need to move beyond 'traditional' formal equality and seriously consider genuine equality of opportunity. Rights have to be multi-dimensional, including development accompanied by justice in the distribution of economic and social opportunities on the one side, and civil and political rights on the other, since both are inseparable and mutually reinforcing. Development may raise threats for natural resources and the environment, and short-term policies for economic growth could cause long-term damage to the environment, which would affect all of life on the planet, including human life. Islam has offered eye-opening teachings on economic and sanitary use of water resources, and preservation of plant and animal life, even during war. A balance between economic growth and preservation has to be struck and indicated.

In such a complex equation, 'affirmative action' and its balance with human rights ought to be discussed and underscored. In society there may be groups that have for a long time been deprived, and will never be able to compete fairly with others for the available chances unless they are supported for some appointed time by additional assistance and protection. This could include the assignment of certain quotas for such deprived groups to be admitted to schools, appointed to jobs in the public and private sectors, in addition to welfare benefits. This may affect the individual human rights of those who have not suffered from such deprivation, and the conflict between the two sides has never been settled in the United States or elsewhere. A universal approach is required in this respect.

Demands for rights to equal opportunities, development and social justice have not been limited within the borders of each country, but there has been a serious deprivation and exploitation of a great part of the world population for the benefit of the more prosperous part during the colonial era and until the present time. The collective right of deprived peoples and groups in development have to be recognized and articulated, as the Vienna Conference recently tried to do. However, the logistics and measures for securing such a right have to be underlined. Loans from developing countries or international agencies to poor countries are overloaded with burdensome conditions and loan-servicing charges. These burdens cannot allow any considerable development, and they reduce the purchasing power and productive capacity of the borrowing country to just paying back the loan-servicing charges and buying food or some consumer goods for the people. Vast sectors of the population in these countries live from hand to mouth, and may be forced to borrow more to buy the essentials they require. The lending countries, directly or via international financial agencies, exploit the debtors through loan servicing and the sale of consumer goods, and sometimes the sale of surplus military equipment.

Moreover, developed countries always argue that they cannot, and should not, help countries in which human rights are not secured. Such an argument is often influenced by the Western classical concept of human rights. To what extent can we mark out what ought to be universal, and what may be an acceptable margin for cultural differences? For example, recently, China has been charged with child-abuse in the orphanages. Men related to cultures other than the American have been indicted, by Americans, of woman- or child-abuse for some actions to which they are used in their culture (these actions do not include beatings, the use of which should be completely out of the question and are blameworthy in any case). Animal slaughter, according to the Muslim practice, has been sometimes considered cruel; Koreans, for example, have been condemned for slaughtering dogs for food. In cases such as these, I believe that it is not only universal human rights that ought to be observed, but also the law and culture of the land in which a person of different origin lives. This should by no means be taken as defending the abuse of women, children or animals.

What I would like to stress here is the need for a comprehensive and accurate articulation of what has to be 'universal' human rights, which must be secured at all levels in the whole world, as opposed to the law and culture of any particular country which have to be observed by its citizens and residents only. In addition, it should be required that state authorities highlight for visitors or foreign residents the specific norms and laws where these are different from international standards, as does Malaysian Airlines in announcing on its flights that its law imposes the death penalty for drug trafficking.

One must also remark that an important moral dimension is missing in the Universal Declaration of Human Rights, and has to be incorporated in the concept of comprehensive human rights. This has become a serious issue after the flood of sex and violence on television, and has been aggravated by the rise of the global communications networks such as the Internet. The United States is in the process of rating television shows and enabling viewers to block what is not suitable for children using remote control. Even Walt Disney products that specifically address children have recently shown female characters in what seems to be sexually suggestive scenes, raising parents' complaints. As for the Internet, Germany has practised censorship in certain cases, but a panel of three federal judges in the United States has considered as a violation of freedom of expression, the restrictions and sanctions of the Communications Decency Act of 1995 against indecent and patently offensive words and images. The Malaysian Prime Minister, Dr. Mahathir Mohammed, has suggested that a code of ethics for the Internet should be drawn up by the United Nations to check any abuse.

But a comprehensive and truly universal approach to human rights would be ineffective without sanctions. How can these comprehensive human rights be observed throughout the whole world? Should they be incorporated in every national state constitution according to a United Nations resolution that would require these actions? How can this be sanctioned, and what would be the requital for a violation, especially when we bear in mind the limitations in the United Nations charter, structure, and operational capabilities? It may seem that a better formulated declaration with an obligation to incorporate it in the constitution of member states may be the possible approach, in connection with a serious effort to reform the United

Nations and its supervision of human rights. Programmes of education and mass media campaigns to raise public awareness of human rights and the available means for defending them nationally and universally are essential in this respect. United Nations agencies and private organizations that monitor the situation of human rights in all countries ought to be encouraged and supported.

2.2 *Obstacles for Implementation*
As justice is indivisible and may be obstructed under certain circumstances, human rights cannot be maintained where civil or regional war is putting human life itself at risk in a certain land. Raping women, and massacring them along with men and children, has recently become among the most vicious atrocities of war. Starvation has become an evil and damaging weapon, which hits mainly the non-combatants – the elderly, disabled, women, and children – who cannot defend themselves or escape danger. War crimes should be traced, investigated and tried efficiently, so that they would not be repeated, at least on the massive scale that we have been witnessing in the last few years. Oppressive regimes, which sometimes enjoy Western support, can be as harmful to their people as any evil and destructive military assault. A psychological 'feeling of security' is a basic human right that is as essential as satisfying basic material needs, and the Qur'ān significantly connects both as significant divine favours or tests (Qur'ān 106:4, 2:155). Where minorities are subjected to economic and cultural deprivation, in addition to crushing political and psychological intimidation, there is naturally no place for individual human rights. Dominant illiteracy, ignorance and backwardness add to the suffering of the people, making them even more vulnerable to abuse. All these unfavourable circumstances cannot provide a suitable climate for securing human rights, nor for monitoring them and trying to defend the wronged party.

Of course, a declaration of human rights, however comprehensively and perfectly it may be articulated, cannot on its own solve all the world's problems. It needs serious efforts on many fronts, and patience and persistence in its implementation. Gaining footholds for democracy in some developing countries will naturally help to secure human rights in those countries, and will enable these countries to develop an awareness of the centrality of human rights in other countries and in the whole world. There is a mutually reinforcing dynamic between the situation of human rights in a certain country and international concern and support for them through the United Nations and its affiliated bodies and agencies.

Essential also is the role of developed countries, which lecture on human rights, but need also to resist the temptation of exploitation and its short-term benefits to extend a hand for real development to those who need it, a move that will bring long-term rewards for the whole world. At the very least, they need to abandon their short-term and short-sighted strategic and economic policies of supporting the undemocratic regimes. The United Nations and all its affiliated bodies and agencies need also to be made more efficient in serving the member states equally without being captive to certain great powers. And, finally, Muslims need to work intelligently, constructively and cooperatively to bring about reform in their countries and in the whole world.

2.3 Immigrants and Asylum-Seekers

The Universal Declaration of Human Rights affirms the right of every human being to leave his/her home country and to seek political asylum in another country if he/she wishes, providing that the person has not been tried for non-political crimes or what contradicts the purposes of the United Nations and its principles (Article 13). The Declaration does not refer to the responsibly of other countries to secure the rights of the immigrants and the seekers of political asylum, and to facilitate the process of accepting their request, and does not put some reasonable limits on the discretion of the country in rejecting or accepting such requests, a discretion which is natural but should not be abused in an arbitrary or unfair manner.

In our era of globalism, moving from one country to another for economic or political reasons ought to be facilitated. Among the significant aspects of human dignity, the Qur'ān emphasizes 'being borne over land and sea' (Qur'ān 17:70), just as it emphasizes that the earth has been made 'wide-open' for people to move through so as to earn their living or secure freedom (Qur'ān 4:97, 100, 29:56, 39:10, 67:15), and blames those who succumb to oppression instead of emigrating to where they could escape persecution. Muslims are under an obligation, according to the Qur'ān, to accept the request of any combatant from the enemy's army who seeks shelter with them, and they have to offer this person safe passage to the place in which he feels secure (Qur'ān 9:6). Such freedom of movement throughout the world will enable all people in the world to complement each other and cooperate for the benefit of humankind in its entirety.

Many immigrants have to undergo unimaginable risks to cross their country's borders into those of another country without a visa, because of the impossible restrictions for obtaining one, and they lose their possessions, and sometimes their lives. If they manage to enter the country they have to face harsh treatment from the police when they are discovered, or exploitation when they try to find work. Although businesses need the immigrants and benefit from them in their farms and factories, they do not like to support any increase in legal immigration so that they may continue to pressure the illegal immigrants to work for them under the most exploitative and severe conditions.

There should be reasonable obligations on the countries to which immigrants come, and there should be a role for the United Nations to observe the rights and obligations related to immigration throughout the world. Immigrants usually bear all risks to escape poverty, earning their living where there is affluence, and it is the responsibility of the wealthy to offer chances for residence and work in their countries for the mutual benefit of both parties. As for the seekers of political asylum, they should also have certain responsibilities towards the country offering asylum, and reasonable limits should be put on the country's discretion in this respect. One cannot accept the rejection of asylum requests from individuals who may lose their life without a trial, while offering it to less vulnerable groups. Some do not consider the pressures and threats faced by some Islamist activists to be sufficient 'political' justification for seeking asylum in another country, while such 'activism', in the view of some governments, is seen as beyond the pale.

In addition, the UN ought to have a role in observing matters related to seeking political asylum, facilitating its processes, and suggesting alternatives for asylum seekers. It should use its influence to secure temporary residence for refugees until asylum is granted. It is also time for the universal organization to use its influence to defend the rights of the 'opposition' in any country. A special body or agency may be needed for observing the rights of the opposition and political asylum, since the two are connected. The universal organization is often accused of mismanagement and duplication of functions by some agencies and budgetary waste in some areas, while there is a complete absence of the organization in some crucial fields.

2.4 The United Nations and Human Rights Enforcement

A more positive and constructive role for the UN is needed, and there was no shortage of advice on reforming and restructuring the international organization, especially on the occasion of its 50th anniversary in 1998. However, the problems do persist in spite of attempted reforms. The Universal Declaration of Human Rights did not include sanctions or procedures to secure human rights or to stop a violation of these rights. According to the International Covenant on Civil and Political Rights of 1966, a committee for human rights was formed to discuss the reports of the states which joined the Covenant regarding their efforts to secure the rights stated in the Covenant. It is required to receive the notifications which may be submitted by one state against another concerning failure to fulfil certain obligations stated in the Covenant, and it offers its good offices to the concerned parties so as to reach a settlement, as it can refer the matter to a special committee for conciliation with the consent of the concerned parties. In an annexed optional protocol, the state, which chooses to join it, agrees to the jurisdiction of the Committee of Human Rights to receive the notifications submitted by its citizens who may claim that their human rights have been violated by another state. The Committee then merely sends its views to the state and the notifying persons, and refers to its efforts in response to such notifications in its annual report.

It is obvious that this whole approach is basically optional and limited to states accepting the Protocol, and it ends with the Committee's views, which are neither binding nor enforceable. Securing international justice for all those who claim violations of their human rights by their own states or by another means that all such claims must be fairly investigated and settled. An international tribunal that inquires, indicts, and tries human rights offenders and a UN High Commissioner with an effective apparatus are imperative in this respect.

Conclusion

Whatever the conceptual and practical problems facing Muslims and the whole world with regard to human rights, it has been of great benefit for all humankind that this concept has been stressed and clarified universally and debated continuously for almost half a century. Muslims and others should not become frustrated by the shortcomings in implementing these principles, and the resultant human rights violations that they may have suffered through this period. They must not also be become frustrated by the UN, its charter, structure and performance, but they ought to look with hope to the future.

Muslims have to bring back the productive interaction between the permanent divine guidance and the changing human living and thinking circumstances through the effective dynamics of *ijtihād* and the essential consideration of the goals and objectives of *Sharīʿah* and its general principles. They ought to figure out what is divine and permanent and what is human and changeable in our juristic heritage, and this may not always be easy, since jurists were not often used to make their human understanding and inference distinctive from the direct meaning of any text of the Qur'ān and the *Sunnah*. We ought to release ourselves from being enclosed and exhausted in the juristic details, and we have to enjoy the full, healthy and rich life in the ever-productive divine guidance in its width and depth. We should also be the honest and courageous advocates and defenders of human dignity of all human beings: men, women or children, Muslim or non-Muslim, related to any land, race or ethnicity. We have to present to the whole world (and reflect in our thinking and behaviour) the universality of Islam, and the grace of the Lord to all beings through His message. Through such a universalistic and humanistic presentation of Islam, we can prove that it copes with our age of globalism and pluralism, which it had actually pioneered over fourteen centuries ago. We could also demonstrate that Islam provides the moral depth which humanity has been missing and badly needs. Muslims can help themselves and help all of humanity realize that human dignity is the cornerstone of God's message to all mankind in all generations, since He is in no need of being acknowledged or worshipped; He wants us to worship Him alone so as to be liberated from worshipping tyrants and fallacies. The believers in the One God and morality and the supporters of human rights ought to adhere firmly and persistently to working together to prove to the whole world that what they call for is needed and is beneficial for all individuals and societies.

The international community, especially the developed countries, has to realize that there is a responsibility to cooperate constructively, not to merely lecture others or condemn them. Humankind is in no need of much talk about 'globalism' and 'post-modernism', but it badly needs 'qualitative' change in its thinking and practices to cope with the changes that we have all been talking about. We are now in one boat and we have to prove our intellectual and behavioural vitality and initiative in facing the new rigorous winds of change. Otherwise, if we merely carry on what we have always been used to thinking or doing, we will all be drowned, the strong and the weak, the rich and the poor, men and women, believers and atheists.

> Verily, God does not change people's conditions unless they change their own selves... (Qur'ān 13:11).
>
> And beware of a temptation to evil which does not only befall those among you who are bent on evil doing... (Qur'ān 8:25).
>
> And rather help one another in furthering virtue and righteousness, but never help one another in furthering evil and aggression... (Qur'ān 9:2)

4

Participation of non-Muslims in Government in Contemporary Muslim Societies

TAREK AL-BECHRI

THE UNIVERSAL DECLARATION of Human Rights adopted by the United Nations General Assembly on 10th December 1948, remains today one of the most distinguished political documents in the world. This important declaration was not formulated in a vacuum, but epitomized the essence of several centuries of enlightened thinking in the West. It was preceded by two other instruments: the American Declaration of Independence in July 1776, following the American war of independence from Britain, which declared that: 'All men are born equal' and emphasized the right of man to life, freedom and equality; and the *declaration des droit de l'homme et du citoyen*, issued during the French Revolution in August 1789, which stated that: 'all human beings are born with equal rights.' The latter declaration was soon to gain fame and wide acceptance, and its principles are considered the basis of modern Western political thinking.

The 1948 Universal Declaration of Human Rights has influenced constitutions and national laws in several countries. Following its adoption, the UN had to deal with the more arduous task of incorporating the principles of the Declaration into an international convention legally binding for UN Member States. The United Nations Commission on Human Rights proceeded with the drafting of two covenants: one dealing with civil and political rights, while the other dealt with economic, social and cultural rights. These were adopted by the UN General Assembly on 16th December 1966, but for them to be binding, ratification by at least 35 members was required. It took a further ten years

Participation of non-Muslims in Government

before the International Covenant on Economic, Social and Cultural Rights and the International Covenant on Civil and Political Rights came into force on 23rd March 1976 and 3rd January 1976, respectively.

The International Covenant on Civil and Political Rights affirms the right of every human being to life, freedom, security and privacy; the right to fair trial and protection against slavery and detention; the right to freedom of thought, conscience, religion, opinion and expression; the right to freedom of movement and assembly. The International Covenant on Economic, Social and Cultural Rights affirms, among other things, the guarantee of a decent standard of living; the right to work and to a fair wage; to health and education; to the formation and membership of associations. What immediately interests us with respect to minorities is the issue of human equality. Minorities in modern times are usually discussed within the framework of equality as defined in the above human rights instruments, which have come to assume international status in today's world.

It is not difficult to claim that Islam had presaged these international instruments in setting forth certain principles, which they have incorporated, aimed at the protection of man's right to a free and decent living by virtue of his humanity. The most fundamental of these principles is the equality of man, and this is a fact of history. This universal principle is contained in all relevant instruments, and is stated in Article 1 of the UDHR which says: 'All human beings are born free and equal in dignity and rights.' Its essence is conveyed in the statement by ʿUmar ibn al-Khaṭṭāb, the second *Khalīfah*, when he said: 'Since when have you enslaved human beings when they were born free?' The statement is lent greater weight by the fact that it had come from a ruler at the pinnacle of his authority. He was not a mere intellectual or a philosopher, and did not make that statement as the representative of a vanquished group, but rather as the powerful head of a vast Muslim empire. He made it in defence of the weak non-Muslim subjects of the state. The statement has been taught to Muslim school children for many generations. Ahmed Orabi, leader of the 1882 Egyptian Revolution, stood side by side with Khedive at Abdeen Square on 9th September 1881 and said to him: 'We have been born free and shall never, after this day, be enslaved again.' Orabi could not have been aware of the American Declaration of Independence or the Universal Declaration of Human Rights or the *declaration des droit de l'homme et du citoyen*. He was reciting what he had learnt as a young boy at the village school!

The Qur'ān addresses the whole of mankind when it asserts the unity of their origin, saying: 'People, We have created you of a male and a female' (Qur'ān 49:13). The Prophet, in his ʿArafāt 'farewell sermon', said: 'Mankind, your God is one, and your father is one. You are all descendants of Adam and he was created of dust.' He went on to affirm that there would be no preference of an Arab over a non-Arab, or of a red man over a black man 'except by their piety'. Thus, unity of origin confirms equality of all human beings, while the Prophet's words indicate that distinction between people is determined by faith in God and their free actions and behaviour. People can only excel one another by actions they willingly undertake, and are available to them all, for which they are accountable. Equality eliminates discrimination among people on the basis of qualities they inherently possess or incidentally acquire, which remain with them in perpetuity and they are unable to remove or overcome by their own volition. Such qualities must apply to specific groups of human beings and be commonly shared by them, and that is the case with race, ethnic origin, skin colour, and language. Equality means that society looks at all its members purely as individuals, and without preference of one individual over another except on the basis of *relevant* acquired merit, such as education, skill or expertise. Preference may be based on factors that are particular but not permanent, such as the age required for certain jobs or appointments, because although it is not acquired, age is decisive and can be overcome.

I. Equality Among Citizens in Public Service Appointments

1. Having asserted in Article 1 equality of all human beings 'in dignity and rights', the UDHR goes on in Article 2 to condemn 'distinction of any kind, such as race, colour, sex, language, religion, political or other opinion, national or social origin, property, birth or other status.' This gives rise to the following question: To whom is this Article

Participation of non-Muslims in Government

addressed? We read in the Preamble to the Declaration that its implementation and promotion are urged upon 'every individual and every organ of society, who shall strive by teaching and education,...and by progressive measures, national and international, to secure their universal and effective recognition and observance, both among the peoples of Member States themselves and among the peoples of territories under their jurisdiction.' The answer to our question is that it is addressing 'States' with respect to peoples under their jurisdiction.

2. The rights and freedoms covered by the Declaration are all conditional on equality and non-discrimination. These fall under two categories:

a) Rights and freedoms of national groups, such as the right to life, housing, resort to law, freedom of movement, ownership, freedom of opinion and expression, all of which are recognized and equally upheld by conventional and Islamic law, and cause no problem in our discussion.
b) Rights and freedoms relating to public service, referred to in Article 21 of the Declaration, which says: '1. Everyone has the right to take part in the government of his country, directly or through freely chosen representatives; 2. Everyone has the right of equal access to public services in his country; and 3. The will of the people shall be the basis of the authority of government...'

3. There is need for further clarification of this point with respect to human rights. While the Declaration speaks in general terms of absolute equality in all rights and freedoms, the Preamble refers specifically to 'States' and 'the peoples of territories under their jurisdiction.' Article 21 establishes the right to take part in government and public service for 'everyone' in his country. The right here is linked to the state and the political entity.

4. This takes us to the constituent elements of the state that distinguish one nation from another and one human group from another, and which affect the apportionment of the rights guaranteed by the

Declaration. This means that certain provisions of the Declaration could not be implemented absolutely and abstractly, but can only be applied within the context of the existing relationship between the state and its citizens. The state, in other words, is obliged to equate among its citizens regardless of their 'race, colour, sex, language or religion…' This obligation, however, does not apply to all rights and freedoms with respect to non-citizens, and therefore their rights to ownership and to freedom of movement are not considered to be absolute.

5. The right to take part in public administration and public service, on the other hand, is not absolute but depends on the nature of the relationship between the individual and the state. The dispensation of this right is influenced by the overall structure of state authority and the political affiliation upon which the state is founded. If the state is founded upon 'nationalism' and is an outright nationalist state, problems of equality or discrimination would not arise, since citizens would either belong to the relevant nationality, and would therefore be entitled to all human rights, or they would be 'foreign' and would have no entitlement to such rights based on their relationship with the state. The problem always arises in multi-ethnic states, or states that have no ethnic or nationalistic foundations, such as tribal societies or those consisting of several political communities, each adhering to one religion or one religious sect or school.

6. We conclude that human rights declarations prevalent in the world today have all been formulated on lines of modern Western thinking and are the outcome of the historic experience of Western Europe, in particular, where nationalities had emerged and grown as political entities during the eighteenth and nineteenth centuries. Peoples and political entities were defined on the basis of language, common territory and history, resulting in collective social adhesion. When it is said today that countries with the best human rights and equality records are those of Western Europe and North America, it is because the concept of equality with respect to public affairs is based on the nation-state idea in purely nationalist states where the political body consists of one nationality and there is one state for the one nationality,

Participation of non-Muslims in Government

and where there are no minorities or multiple ethnic groups, or where minorities have become more or less assimilated. Those who are not entitled to these rights would be classified as aliens who do not belong to the state nationality and are not recognized as citizens. Such a state, in other words, has no ethnic minorities. This model begins to change as we move eastward towards central and eastern Europe, the Balkans and further on to Asia and Africa, where nationalities, ethnic groups and tribes proliferate, mix and overlap within the same state, and where religions reflect political affiliation, giving minorities prominence in the state structure.

7. Nationalism emerged first in Western Europe during the late eighteenth century, augmented by the American Revolution of 1776 and the French Revolution in 1789, from where the famous human rights declarations originate. These declarations treated individuals as citizens of states based on a common nationality defined by language, territory and history with no regard to religion, colour, race, or social status. Thus, the free national state was born. As this concept spread towards eastern Europe during the nineteenth century, sweeping the Austrian empire, Bulgaria, and the Ottoman empire, certain forms of multi-national, multi-religious and multi-racial states began to emerge in the late nineteenth and early twentieth centuries. The nation-state became multi-national as well as uni-national, embracing nationalist affiliation based on language, territory and history as well as religious affiliation based on faith and culture, as we see among many Asian and Arab peoples. It also incorporated racial identity based on tribe and clan, as we find in desert regions and among peoples of central and southern Africa. This multiplicity and the interaction of various constituent social groups have given rise to the concept of equality.

8. The Western concept of the state underlying modern principles of human rights is based on three main elements: people (nation), territory and authority. The 'people' (nation) is the most fundamental element in defining the relationship between the ruler and the subjects, and is the basis for the legal framework and the allocation of authority. By definition, people of the same nation possess common features that bring about a certain degree of harmony among them, and form the

bond that moulds them into a single entity. The concept of state is, therefore, based specifically on the idea that it is a nation-state, and in Western Europe has emerged as a state without minorities. Principles of human rights have been formulated within an environment with no experience of minorities and along the nationalist concept of the political community, common in Europe.

Minorities are defined as human groups whose members are linked by a common element of religion, language or race, which distinguishes them from the majority in their community. A minority's awareness of its uniqueness gives rise to political demands, either for equality with the majority, for special treatment based on recognition of such uniqueness, for self-rule or for separation as an independent political community. One may conclude that equality as an essential concept for human rights is closely linked to the political association underlying the idea of nationality and the overall concept of the modern state. This concept determines the existence or otherwise of minorities and defines the framework for equality.

9. In order to separate the concept of equality from the nationalistic context which has influenced human rights declarations inherited from the Western political experience, one ought to link equality, and the concept of political association adopted by different groups to express their origins and relationships, with the type of state that has been created in accordance with that political association, whether defined by geographical, linguistic, tribal, traditional, religious or cultural factors. Equality, in the present discussion, is linked to nationality (citizenship) by virtue of the identity adopted by the political association as a criterion for its rise and existence. Egyptians are equal on the basis of the 'Egyptian-ness' they have chosen as their distinguishing factor as people of the same state. Likewise, equality among Arabs or Muslims depends on the definition of 'Arabism' or 'Islam', the respective communities consider as a distinguishing factor. Once the deciding factors are established, there should be no discrimination between members of the same community. Those lacking in these factors would be treated as alien to that community.

We are not dealing here with equality as an absolute ideal, since we have already differentiated between equality of inherent and special rights and freedoms and equality in the public service structure and the subject of Part III of this paper. This is what I mean by linking equality to nationality within the context of a specific political community, whether based on religious doctrine, language, territory, racial factors, or on any combination of them, which is often the case due to the complexity of the social and historic realities that rule out a simplified classification.

10. Our discussion centres on equality in public service affairs, and this implies acting on behalf of others in the administration of their affairs. Public service can be special if the commissioning relates to appointees, and general if it is unrestricted and concerns non-appointees, and it finds its most evident expression and manifestation in the state structure. A state is built around a well-defined political community, which is the most important of the three elements of nation, territory and authority. This indicates the necessarily evident link between appointment to state posts and affiliation to the political community upon which the state is founded, that is to say, the qualification for political association, otherwise known as nationality or citizenship. Equality in public service appointments or in participation in the administration of public affairs is contingent upon the fulfilment of the criteria for membership of the political community, and equality is undermined by any impairment of the public rights granted by nationality as a legal status related to affiliation to the community. Public service is a right by virtue of nationality or citizenship. We can see that this concept links the states to the political community upon which it is founded, and linking the political community to its members bestows upon them attributes that define that community and give rise to it. This, in turn, becomes a condition for appointment to public service, and so on. Modern legal jurisprudence encapsulated this in the concept of 'citizenship', which is a direct link between the individual and the state, and a recognition of the individual's membership of the community upon which the state is founded; the state thereby admits the individual as a member of the nation.

Reservations

Two reservations may be made on this concept.

1. The first one stems from the multiplicity of the criteria according to which individuals and groups are classified, and the way in which these classifications may overlap. Societies consist of several groups of different forms and categories, based on various criteria, including, among others, profession, ideology, geography, and language. The political community arises as a result of the dominance of one or other of these factors, and of it becoming the overriding criterion. Accordingly, when we speak of the political community as an entity based on a certain criterion, we ought not to imagine that it is a simple collection of individuals with a common description. Egyptians are all those inhabiting a defined territory. But this is not the only factor that characterizes them. They also belong to different communities defined by other factors based on region, religion, ideology, profession or vocation, as well as education. Each of these factors, though contained within the overall description of 'Egyptian-ness', overlaps and interacts with it, leading to the conclusion that the general description of a political community is influenced by the secondary affiliation criteria in proportion to their material and moral influence in society. In Egypt, for instance, although the dominant identity factor that defines the political community, and upon which the state is founded, is that of being Egyptian, Islam is the dominant religion among Egyptians which leaves a prominent impression upon the 'Egyptian-ness' factor as the criterion for nationality. The same was true of the Umayyad, Abbasid and Ottoman eras in which Islam was the dominant factor of affiliation to the state and the symbol of nationality. Nevertheless, Islam was being influenced by other cogent affiliation factors, Arab, Persian and Turkish, without upsetting the overall framework upon which the whole political community is founded and by which it is identified.

In this way, the principle of equality in participation in public service administration remains intact, and the overall identity of the community continues to be determined by those characteristics that are dominant in society by virtue of size or influence. As an example, we may take the Egyptian constitution which stipulates 'Egyptian-ness'

Participation of non-Muslims in Government

as the general description of nationality and the factor determining citizenship and equality among those who fulfil the relevant criteria, but it also states, at the same time, that Islam is the official religion of the state and that Shari'ah, or Islamic law, is the prime source for legislation. We have a similar situation in the United States of America with respect to provisions relating to the Anglo-Saxon descent, the English language and to the Protestant church. All this has its effect on the overall composition and disposition of the state and society and on the selection of their leaders, such as the president. It is to be noted that the criteria here are implicit rather than explicit.

2. Secondly, there is no contradiction between equality in participation in public service administration of society and the stipulation of certain qualifications as conditions for appointment to public service positions, such as age, education, or expertise. As already pointed out, these are voluntary conditions and distinctions whose stipulation does not undermine the principle of equality. There are other conditions for public service, which are neither discriminatory nor voluntary, but whose stipulation does not impair equality, since their stipulation for public service is a matter of technical or specialization requirement for the proper execution of the task involved. Of these are linguistic skills in a multi-ethnic multi-linguistic society. These conditions are not a violation of equality or human rights, notwithstanding Article 2 of the UDHR proscribing, among others, discrimination on the basis of language.

The reason these conditions do not violate the principle of equality among citizens is that they represent what might be called qualifications or specializations required for the performance of certain tasks or duties, as long as these can be justified, such as the requirement for teachers at al-Azhar Islamic University to be Muslims. This holds so long as these requirements do not become so prevalent as to target one particular social group with the aim of barring them from jobs available to their fellow-citizens. It must be clear that the specialization required is directly linked to the specified job, without it becoming a discriminatory factor amongst different groups. For, once a condition becomes general it would no longer be aimed at one group and cannot be applied to one group at the expense of other members of the same political community. Furthermore, such conditions should not be attached to public service posts that are basically open to all citizens by virtue of their being qualified members of the political community as defined by its dominant factors that identify the society and its collective character upon which the state is founded.

II. Traditional Islamic Jurisprudence and Minorities

In his book *Al-Aḥkām*, Abū ʿUbaid ibn Sallām points out that, in his agreement with the people of Cyprus, Muʿāwiyah, the fifth *Khalīfah*, granted them the status of *ahl al-dhimmah* among both Muslims and the Romans, a form of neutrality. His successor, ʿAbdul Malik, decided that the people of Cyprus had broken their agreement, and sought counsel from a number of scholars of his time on whether he should go to war against them. Abū ʿUbaid gives a summary of their submissions, and says that the majority advised him not to resort to war against the island. The actual incident itself and the individual opinions are of no interest to us, but I mention it as an illustration of how a *fatwā* or a particular religious ruling is arrived at. I am concerned with the method, or the technical aspects, of arriving at a religious ruling (*fatwā*) or a legal opinion with respect to the various issues and problems that arise.

In this instance, we have a single event on which the opinions of several scholars or jurists were sought, who had separately carried out their research and formulated their own opinions. These views related to the same issue and a specific problem, which they had contemporaneously and simultaneously studied and analyzed. We also know that, despite the difference of views, they had adopted more or less the same approach. They would each state the incident, as they understood it, cite the religious texts that, in their view, applied to it, and finally formulate a judgement or ruling. This is what judges and jurists would, as a matter of course, do today. Each of the jurists selected the religious text that he thought applied specifically to that incident. The variance in their views was not due to a difference in their interpretation of the text but rather in their understanding and analysis of the situation. This was a vindication of the adage that: 'Judgement is dependent on

Participation of non-Muslims in Government

understanding.' Here is a summary of those views as reported by Abū ʿUbaid:

- Al-Layth ibn Saʿd wrote: 'We continue to accuse the people of Cyprus of disloyalty towards the Muslims and of sympathy towards the Romans.' Then he quoted the Qur'ānic verse that says: 'And if you (the Prophet) fear treachery from any of your allies, you may likewise fairly retaliate by breaking off your treaty with them' (Qur'ān 8:58). Pointing out that the mere fear of treachery, even if it did not actually take place, would be sufficient reason to apply the rule, Al-Layth concluded by suggesting a grace period of one year to be granted to the people of Cyprus to choose between joining the Muslims, going over to the Roman camp or remaining under a state of war. The key words in Al-Layth's statement are: 'We continue to accuse the people of Cyprus of disloyalty,' which indicates that he seriously suspected their treachery and betrayal. He immediately associated this suspicion with the Qur'ānic verse, which he had clearly correctly interpreted.

- Sufyān ibn ʿUyainah wrote: 'With the exception of the people of Makkah, we know of no other who had broken a treaty and were spared.' He quoted the verses: 'Will you (the Muslims) not fight against those who had broken their oaths and conspired to banish the Messenger (Muḥammad)...Fight them and God will chastise them at your hands and humiliate them, and grant you victory over them' (Qur'ān 9:13–14). He concluded that the people of Cyprus had no right to any protection from the Muslims because they had unanimously broken their agreement. Sufyān based his opinion on the opinion that the people of Cyprus were unanimous in violating their agreement with the Muslims, and selected the relevant Qur'ānic ruling, concluding that the Muslims were under no obligation to abstain from waging war against them.

- Mālik ibn Anas wrote: 'The peace and security of the people of Cyprus had been guaranteed by the rulers who decided not to disturb them and keep them under Muslim authority. None of the rulers had repealed the peace agreement with them.' He then cited the Qur'ānic injunction: 'Proclaim a woeful punishment to the unbelievers, except to those idolaters who have honoured their treaties with you in every detail and aided none against you. With these keep faith until their treaties have run their term' (Qur'ān 9:3–4). He concluded by advising the ruler not to pre-empt the situation by revoking their agreement or declaring hostility, but to give them time and wait for positive proof of their infidelity or treachery before going to war against them. Mālik's view of the problem was clearly different from the others. He saw no need to break the peace that had been made with the people of Cyprus, and was in force for a considerable period of time, since they did not violate that peace and the Muslims clearly had the upper hand over them. He cited what he saw as the relevant Qur'ānic text and formulated his opinion accordingly.

- Mūsā ibn Ayman wrote: 'None of the previous rulers had revoked or amended the peace agreement with the people of Cyprus of whom a majority did not seem to support the minority view to break the peace.' He also did not see any proof of treachery or any unanimity to break the agreement, which might have been advocated by a minority among them. He upheld their entitlement to peace and protection, provided they maintained their loyalty and faith.

- Ismāʿīl ibn ʿAbbās wrote: 'The people of Cyprus are a vanquished and humiliated people and the Romans are subjugating them and taking their women, and it would be our duty to protect them.' He cited earlier encounters between them and the Muslims, concluding that peace with them should be upheld and they should be protected.

- Yaḥyā ibn Ḥamzah wrote: 'If Cyprus were to be taken over by an enemy, as happened with the people of Sousse, maintaining the *status quo* and accepting it, while its people are paying taxes and the Muslims continue to have access to its products, is recommended.' This is a purely pragmatic way of looking at the problem. He seems to say that the decision should be taken in the light of what would be deemed appropriate at the time, and that would be the right decision from the *Sharīʿah* point of view.

- Abū Isḥāq and Mukhallad ibn Ḥusain recalled the agreement with Cyprus when it was conquered which, they said, imposed certain obligations on both sides. They argued that 'the agreement could not be breached unless their was clear proof of betrayal or infringement on their part.' Accordingly, they recommended that the agreement, with its conditions, should be upheld.

We note from the above that as the understanding or evaluation of the situation changes, the jurists would cite different Qur'ānic texts to support their respective views. This gives us a glimpse of the technical practical process adopted by the jurist or the *Sharīʿah* scholar in applying religious text to real-life situations. At the outset, a link between the two has to be established in order to determine the *Sharīʿah* view of the problem and its potential material and moral consequences.

The process always begins with the articulation of a situation that is faced by the investigator, or one that might arise in the future, in terms of the *Sharīʿah* legal framework. If it were a financial transaction, for instance, it would be important to determine whether it was in the form of grant, payment, loan, settlement of loan, trade, rental payment, theft or fraud. Once the category, or categories, is identified, reference would then be made to rules under that category or categories. The jurist would then systematically sift through the general rules of *Sharīʿah* with a view to matching the situation to the category and identifying the most relevant texts that deal with it. The text is then analyzed and examined very closely in an attempt to formulate a legal ruling that would fit the situation in question. The articulation of the problem in hand is similar to a physician's diagnosis of an illness aiming to define the ailment in medical terms, which would then be followed by selecting the right treatment and the way it would be administered.

I cite this example at length to draw attention to the technical aspects of the mental process that takes place in such situations. I also aim to show that the differences that arise among jurists are not always due to the derivation of the ruling from the relevant text, or to deductions from that text. Most differences arise as a result of a jurist's understanding and articulation of the problem in legal or *Sharīʿah* terms, which would guide him in seeking the appropriate text and its legal or religious implications. The Cyprus problem is a good illustration of this point and an excellent textbook case.

III. Minorities from an Islamic *Fiqh* Perspective

The way Islamic *fiqh* views minorities stems, in my view, from the stance of the minority towards Islam and the Muslim community. This was how the late Professor Abdul-Wahhab Khallaf put it, as summarized by Dr. Abdulhameed Mitwalli:

> Throughout history, the position of non-Muslims in Muslim countries has not been governed by religious considerations alone, as political factors also were taken into account, especially with respect to their loyalty and transparency towards the Muslim state and its people.

As already seen, this was clear in the rulings on the Cyprus example. Islamic history is rich in incidents and examples of dealings with non-Muslims following the sweeping Muslim conquests of the early period and the domination by Muslims of public affairs, which, due to restrictions of space, we are not able to go into here. However, I shall attempt to draw attention to some general pointers that could be of value to us today.

On the purely religious matter of building churches and synagogues, we find that Muslim jurists differentiated between non-Muslim lands taken by force and others entered by agreement. In the former, most jurists, with few exceptions (such as ʿAbd al-Raḥmān ibn al-Qāsim who insisted on obtaining the ruler's permission), were opposed to the idea. In the latter case, the matter would be determined by whether the peace agreement had made any specific provisions for building such places of worship. Some were of the view that if the non-Muslim inhabitants were paying land tax, they would be permitted to build churches, while the Mālikī school allowed it unconditionally as long as no Muslims lived there with them. The point here is that even on a matter of faith and worship, jurists had a variety of views, as a result of political considerations; in this case whether the land was taken by conquest or by agreement. This relationship between matters of worship and political realities has its rationale in the degree of loyalty or perfidy (Arabic: *al-walā' wa al-barā'*) shown by the non-Muslim subjects towards Islam and the Muslim community.

Participation of non-Muslims in Government

Based on historic and jurisprudential evidence, one may conclude that the status of Jews and Christians (Arabic: *Ahl al-Kitāb*) in Muslim society, as protected minorities, had arisen out of the conquest of non-Muslim lands: a historic event that later became a legal and religious issue. As Islam spread in various parts of the world, and Muslim governments were set up implementing Islamic laws, rules and regulations, the natives gradually embraced Islam and adopted it as a religious faith and as a political system.

Those who held unto their original religion continued to be subjects of the Islamic state, but their affiliation to the Muslim community remained incomplete because it was political only. They were treated according to how loyal, or otherwise, they were to the state and the community. It is against this background that the jurists had to perform their role of understanding the issues, codifying the rules of the *Sharīʿah*, reconciling, analyzing, interpreting, and eventually issuing *fatwā*s and opinions. They had to take all aspects of the prevailing situation into account: whether the conquest was by force or by agreement, how well were the minorities assimilated into the Muslim society. This had led to dealing with issues of public and government service in the Muslim state, drawing, all the while, on the experience of the early period of the spread of Islam.

Some changes have occurred in this over the years. Since the late eighteenth century, Western powers have spread their domination all over the world. The Dutch reached the Cape of Good Hope, and the British armadas ruled the sea routes in the Gulf and the Indian Ocean, and reached the borders of Afghanistan in the north, throwing a huge cordon around the eastern and southern parts of the Muslim world. Russia expanded eastward and southward into Asia, taking control of central Asia down to Persia and Afghanistan, slicing as much land as it could from the Persian and Ottoman empires. All through the nineteenth century, one by one the central parts of the world of Islam, including Algeria, Tunisia, Egypt, the Sudan, Morocco and Libya, began to fall, completing Western domination over the Muslim world by the end of the nineteenth century. By the end of the First World War, Istanbul, the capital of the Islamic *Khilāfah*, fell and Syria, Lebanon,

Palestine and Iraq were divided, bringing an end to the political association that had united the Muslims for many centuries. The new situation gave rise to national liberation movements, which emerged to defend Muslim lands and drive away colonialist occupation and foreign political domination. Many non-Muslims, as citizens and members of the political community, joined the fight for freedom and independence.

The question then became no longer one of conquest by force or by agreement, but who, of the non-Muslim minorities, had participated in the liberation of our countries and who had not. This ought to be a major criterion in the regulation of the role citizens might play in public service affairs, using loyalty in our countries to the emerging (predominantly Muslim) political community as a guide in this regard. We ought to view the development of our contemporary history through the struggle for political independence, national unity, resistance to foreign colonization and the desire to free our people of foreign political, economic and cultural dependency.

In view of the changes that have swept our societies today, a major difference between our contemporary situation and that of early Islam is that the Muslims then represented a dominant political and military power but represented smaller numbers in the regions they governed. This had forced them to restrict the administration of public service affairs to Muslims as a means of keeping tight control over the country and of protecting themselves from being totally absorbed into the larger mass of population who had not, until then, embraced Islam or come into contact with it. They were able to do so due to their indisputable political and intellectual superiority in comparison to their opponents in those lands.

Today, the situation is completely reversed. Muslims are the dominant majorities in their countries and they have nothing to fear from the participation of non-Muslims in public service. Politically, militarily and economically, the Muslims are clearly weaker compared to other world powers, and any instability in their countries brought about by unequal treatment of other citizens or by the breakdown of the bonds of nationhood, could pose a real threat and open the way

Participation of non-Muslims in Government

for foreign powers to exploit the situation. Let our scholars and intellectual leaders today learn from ʿUmar ibn al-Khaṭṭāb who cancelled the right of new converts to Islam (Arabic: *al-muʾallafah qulūbuhum*) to receive the *zakāt* money when he felt that Islam was strong enough as not to be in need of appeasing this group of people in society. By considering loyalty and good faith in arriving at rulings to regulate the relationship between Muslims and non-Muslims, we are taking a leaf from the book of our great predecessors without actually adopting their views. There is nothing more crippling to innovation than transforming the approach into a doctrine. All we are advocating is exploration of wider means and resources than the mere idea of loyalty and good faith. We are calling for a widening of the scope of loyalty and good faith for the sake of the stability and progress of contemporary Muslim societies.

5

Non-Muslims in Muslim Society

FAHMI HUWEIDI

THE SUBJECT I have been asked to speak on here is: non-Muslims in Muslim society. I have written a book on this subject which has gone into its fourth edition. I have to confess, however, for the first time in fifteen years, that I owe the credit for writing that book to none other than Dr. Fathi Osman. He may not remember that in 1980 he wrote an article in *Al-Aman* magazine of Beirut on the rights of non-Muslims in Muslim society. While I was preparing this paper, I looked through some of my old papers and came across the original article, written sixteen years ago in Dr. Osman's own elegant handwriting. It had his famous marginal notes and arrows criss-crossing all over every page. I had in fact borrowed the book's title, *Citizens not Subjects*, from a phrase in Dr. Osman's article, a copyright which I now acknowledge; we might discuss his share of the royalties at a more appropriate time.

The other thought that came to my mind while preparing this paper was that if a Muslim who had lived during the Prophet's time, or during the following one hundred years, were to enter this hall now and find us talking about non-Muslims in Muslim society, he would be astonished. For the disputes that had arisen among the Muslims themselves at the time were far more serious than those among Muslims and non-Muslims. These latter were living in peace and security, totally reassured under the covenant offered them by Islam. The dispute with the *Khawārij*, on the other hand, involved Muslims who dissented over the entitlement of the Fourth *Khalīfah* ʿAlī to *khilāfah* or the arbitration procedure between him and Muʿāwiyah, his rival and successor.

Non-Muslims in Muslim Society

Nobody then had the feeling that non-Muslims had a problem, and they were seen as part of the social fabric of Muslim society and active participants, in their various capacities, in building what we now call Islamic civilization. There was no attempt to distinguish them as non-Muslims. Indeed, in certain cases, the privileged status they enjoyed intimidated some Muslims and provoked their jealousy. We have to admit that this vast and rich mosaic of races, ethnic groups, colours and traditions we see all over the Muslim world owes its origins to this important fact of Muslim history, which has been established in the Muslim psyche from a very early date. To this very day, in many Arab countries, you will find Muslims, Jews, Christians, Magians, fire-worshippers and many others, living side by side. This colourful array of social groups has been a constant feature of Islamic life, absorbed into the very consciousness of our people and our thought.

The Crusades and Muslim Decline
One wonders, therefore, at what point in history did non-Muslims become a contentious issue? One may point to three major factors as having contributed to the rise of this problem, which has today become one of the major controversies associated with Islam as a whole. The first factor is to be found in the days of oppression and decline of Muslim civilization. One must say for the record that Muslims as well as non-Muslims were victims of bigotry and oppression during the years of decline of Muslim civilization. The second factor was the Crusades, which Muslim historians have always viewed as European wars against Islam, while Europeans associated them directly with the Cross and the Church. It is important to note that Muslims did not view the Crusades as religious wars, but they were perceived as such by the European invaders who swept eastwards brandishing their crosses and swords. Muslims were suddenly made aware that others were not prepared to tolerate them or co-exist with them, especially as some eastern Christians welcomed the invading Crusaders, leaving a painful and lasting impression in Muslim minds. This led a great scholar and jurist, Ibn al-Qayyim, to devote a whole book to the laws and rules governing the status of non-Muslims in Muslim society, in which he leant very

heavily against them. Intellectuals such as Ibn al-Qayyim must, therefore, have been greatly influenced by the Crusades and the atrocities committed against Muslims and the support the European invaders had received from Christians of the East. The third factor is the external threat to Islam. Ever since the days of Prophet Muḥammad, the West has been working to penetrate Muslim societies, and has used non-Muslims to undermine them, and to sow conflict and division from within. This continued until the nineteenth-century French campaign in Egypt, when Napoleon recruited and armed Coptic militias to assist his army. Similar methods were used in all colonialist incursions into the Arab world under the guise of protecting minorities and through the appointment of consular officials during Ottoman rule, as spies and operatives to infiltrate the Muslim world. Foreign powers have, therefore, used the non-Muslims issue to further their interests, especially during times of hardship when our people, including non-Muslims, were weak and vulnerable.

Today, we still find evidence of attempts to stir-up non-Muslim minority issues. I can mention a certain 'Research Centre' in Cairo (that will remain nameless), which is financed by institutions in the United States. This Centre is totally dedicated to the study and monitoring of non-Muslim minorities in Egypt. It organizes regular seminars to which the most bitter and hostile opponents of Islam are invited, and quarterly meetings devoted to hurling insults and abuse against Islam and Muslims. It has never solved any of the problems it purports to examine, but it never ceases to inflame the atmosphere and cause continual agitation. Some of us in Egypt tried to organize campaigns calling people to deal with their common problems as one people, belonging to one country. But those organizations, heavily subsidized by outside agencies, approach our problems with divisive intent, supporting the supposedly down-trodden minorities who are denied their rights.

A Frame of Reference

In order to understand Islam's attitude towards non-Muslims in Muslim societies, it seems to me that we must define our frame of reference, and whether it should be the Qur'ān and the *Sunnah* or history or the opinions of jurists and scholars of one period or another. What I believe ought to be the correct approach is to refer to the Qur'ān and the *Sunnah*, the only authoritative sources we can all agree upon. We should give due respect to opinions of individual jurists or scholars, which are not binding on us, and take from them what we find useful and constructive. History is a dynamic process and every generation is accountable for their contribution to it. I appreciate Dr. Zaki Badawi's comments that the West, just like Islam, is not homogeneous, which is true but needs some qualification.

There are different approaches to understanding Islam, but there is a unified immutable point of reference represented by the Qur'ān and the *Sunnah*. In the West, however, there is no such conformity, and people talk and debate without any restrictions or restraints. In our case, once we agree on the Qur'ān and the *Sunnah* as the authoritative reference and ultimate arbiter, non-Muslims will have no problem with Islam whatsoever; the contrary would in fact be the case, because Islam acknowledges other religions and addresses everyone on an equal basis, whereas other religions refuse to recognize Islam. Accordingly, the Islamic approach is extremely accommodating and tolerant.

Why do I say this? I say this because the incontrovertible principles which the Qur'ān and the *Sunnah* have laid down for dealing with non-Muslims give rise to a fair and objective framework which, if Muslims and their leaders adhere to and respect, would not allow minority problems to occur. These principles may be summarized in the following way:

1. The Qur'ān recognizes the dignity of man. All men are seen as possessing an inherent dignity, regardless of colour, race, creed or religion. As some people were talking of 'God's chosen people', the Qur'ān came to affirm that man is God's chosen creature. Accordingly, every human being has the inalienable right to dignity which implicitly includes the right to life, freedom, equality, education, work, and all the other rights one may find in any contemporary human rights charter, all of

which we respect, support and must benefit from and incorporate into the right to dignity which jurists consider a fundamental principle of Islamic *Sharīʿah*.

2. The Qur'ān is very clear on this matter, and so was the Prophet Muḥammad. When a funeral procession once passed by, the Prophet called on the company to rise in order to show respect. One of his Companions pointed out that the deceased was a Jew, to which Muḥammad said, 'But he is a human being, is he not?' Our Shaikh, the late Muḥammad al-Ghazālī, used to say that man has a Divine pedigree, because when God created man, He blew into his soul. This entails a whole series of rights to which every man is entitled. Islam does not differentiate between Muslims and non-Muslims with respect to their basic human rights. God, in His infinite wisdom, has created men in different types and forms. He clearly says in the Qur'ān that, had He wished, He could have created mankind as a single community, but did not. This tells us that differences of creed, religion and race are natural and part of God's scheme of creation.

3. The Qur'ān says: 'There is no compulsion in religion' (Qur'ān 2:256). This statement was revealed in connection with Muslims who wanted their children, who had been brought up among Jewish tribes, to convert from Judaism to Islam. Now, since Islam teaches us that 'there is no compulsion in religion,' it would only be logical to conclude that 'there is no coercion in life,' either.

4. Qur'ānic statements clearly point out that difference of religion and faith should be left to God's discretion. As human beings living on the same planet, we are required to work together and cooperate for the good of all mankind, and defer judgement on differences between Muslims, Jews, Christians and Sabaens until the Day of Judgement that is to come. We

may advise people and call them to what we believe to be the right path, but their religious and other beliefs are not an immediate concern of ours. Moreover, the Qur'ān has clear instructions for Muslims to show kindness and benevolence towards non-Muslims, and treat them as they would their own families, as long as they do not show hostility or perpetrate sedition against Muslims. It says: 'God does not forbid you to be kind and equitable to those who have neither made war against you or your religion nor driven you from your homes' (Qur'ān 60:8).

5. The Prophet Muḥammad, God's peace and blessings be upon him, had specifically decreed that non-Muslims should have equal rights and obligations as Muslims, thereby opening the door for normal relations based on parity, equality, and mutual respect.

6. The charter (known as *Ṣaḥīfat al-Madīnah*, or the Madinah Document) drawn up by Prophet Muḥammad on his arrival at Madinah, on the eve of establishing a state there, is quite relevant in this context, as it had granted non-Muslims full citizenship rights, specified their national obligations on an equal footing with their Muslim fellow-citizens, so long as they accepted to co-exist with them.

While these principles, in my view, give a concise view of Islam's atti-tude towards non-Muslims, misunderstandings in this area seem to persist with respect to three important issues: *dhimmah* (protection), *jizyah* (poll tax) and *wilāyah* (public service). Since Mr. Tarek al-Bechri has dealt with the third issue, I shall only deal with the first two.

To the early Muslims, *dhimmah* referred to the protection granted to non-Muslims by God and His Messenger, i.e. by the Qur'ān and the *Sunnah*, rather than by any individual Muslim. This had been an established tradition among the Persians well before the advent of Islam, by which the powerful provided protection for the weak. This would take place between individuals as well as tribes. When Islam came, *dhimmah* was conceived of as a gesture of benevolence towards non-Muslims from God and His Messenger, rather than from any particular individual. It was taken out of the personal and into the public domain, giving it an equivalent status to what we now know as citizenship, a concept that has arisen out of the modern concept of state, which was unknown fourteen centuries ago.

The concept, as we now know it, does not derive from the Qur'ān or the *Sunnah*. Rather, it is one that had been formulated and articulated by Muslim jurists several decades after the Prophet's time. As time went by, the protection envisaged in the system continued to contract until, towards the end of the Ottoman empire, it came closest to what we call citizenship, albeit of an inferior class. Thus the impression has come about that non-Muslims in Muslim society are considered second-class citizens. At one stage, in certain parts of the Muslim world, a narrow strip of the road was designated for non-Muslims to walk along in order to distinguish them from the Muslims. Traces of this can still be seen today in parts of Lebanon. Dr. Fathi Osman has long ago called for this whole episode to be consigned to history and under no circumstances should it be considered representative of Islamic teachings or binding on anyone. It is true that, to begin with, *dhimmah* was not a matter for Muslims to be ashamed of, but in practice it has been widely abused. Indeed, with the establishment of citizenship laws and rights, the system has become redundant.

The more I think about *jizyah*, the more I find it an extremely agreeable idea. Incidentally, the rate of *jizyah* which non-Muslims used to pay to the state was far lower than what Muslims themselves used to pay in the form of *zakāt*. In return, they were granted rights to all essential public services and guaranteed personal security and protection, and were not expected to fight for the state. The term *jizyah* derives from the Persian word *gazit*, meaning war duty or tax. Jurists have written extensively on this subject; some of them spoke about it as a means of denigration of non-Muslims, to put them in their place and preserve Muslim status and prestige. Such scholars must be held accountable for their opinions that clearly undermine respect of human dignity, which we believe to be a fundamental and binding Qur'ānic principle. The Qur'ānic statement that non-Muslims should be made to pay *jizyah* 'with humility and submission' (Qur'ān 9:29) refers to a state of war and is not relevant to issues of citizenship and state loyalties. When Muslims were not able to defend non-Muslims, they would not take *jizyah* from them, and they paid it when citizenship rights were established and all subjects of the state took part in fighting and enlisted in the army. Everyone became obliged to pay war duty and national taxes. Moreover, there was no justification for restoring the *jizyah* system again, since it had become obsolete and, like *dhimmah*, it has become a matter of history.

Similar opinions are often expressed by Muslim thinkers and intellectuals, led by Dr. Fathi Osman to whom we owe a great deal. Others have differed with them, maintaining that non-Muslims should pay *jizyah* and should be treated on a par as 'People of the Book'. There are, however, two points to be made in this regard. The first one is that those who hold these views brand people like us, who differ with them, as heretics, thereby taking the whole argument to a completely different level, much farther than a simple difference of interpretation. Some people are simply not educationally or culturally sophisticated enough to appreciate what we are saying, but what is more serious is that there are certain Arab regimes today that wish for this unhealthy and erroneous understanding to survive and take root, regardless of its world-wide repercussions and effects. The second point is that in view of this gap of understanding among us Muslims over this issue, I believe that we must agree on the need to support our view, which to me is more rational and representative of the true spirit of Islam. Let us reinforce this view and enrich it with further research and elaboration.

I pray to God to give Dr. Fathi Osman the strength and long life to contribute more in this field, and may we continue to gain from his knowledge and wisdom.

6

Minorities in the Muslim World and in the West

MUNIR SHAFIQ

THIS CHAPTER, as indicated by the above title, follows an approach that attempts – as objectively as possible – to determine the various aspects of the current situation, with regard to understanding the prevalent power balances and the nature of existing relations between Muslims and the world around them. The aim is to enable us to analyze the situation with a view to formulating policies and/or specific lines of action. This study calls for the relevant questions and issues to be presented to Muslim policy-makers with utmost accuracy, and objectivity in order to enable them to determine the Islamic position on the contemporary issues facing the Muslim *Ummah* today. This approach contrasts with those approaches that treat our problems today as if they were abstract issues needing only a general abstract answer from the Islamic juristic point of view. It also stands in contrast with the approach that treats today's issues as if our *Ummah* is reliving the era of the *Khilāfah*, or as if this were the Umayyad or Abbasid era.

Western Hegemony

At present, the West (i.e. Western Europe and the US) exercises hegemony over the world including the Muslim world. This hegemony is almost absolute, especially with regard to military superiority in the sea, air and even in outer space, as well as control over strategically important geographical locations. This Western domination extends also to areas of science, technology, industrial production, and world trade and transport facilities. It also extends to areas of the media, education, culture, arts as well as major international institutions. In addition to that, the West enjoys unrivalled influence and control over most of the Third World countries. Countries that ceased to be colonies, but only to become areas of influence in various aspects, are burdened with financial debts to the West, and have relinquished control over their internal economic policies to the World Bank and the IMF. These organizations exercise more control in these countries than the imperial powers used to enjoy in the colonies. It is fair, therefore, to state that the world order that has prevailed in the last two centuries has been – and still is – dictated by the Western great powers. This world order today determines the pattern of international relations and the international economic order with the effect of maintaining the monopoly on the technological know-how, determining the price of raw materials and dictating international trade rules. A similar pattern of Western hegemony persists in other areas such as arts and culture.

Another aspect that has characterized the last two centuries has been the fierce initial resistance put up by the conquered nations against the colonial incursions into their territories and the struggle they later launched to rid themselves of colonialism. Most of those nations actually managed – in the past 50 years – to end direct colonization and set-up their own 'sovereign' independent states. But these states have inherited their laws, their systems, and their modes of operation from the departing colonial powers. They also inherited a backlog of backwardness and underdevelopment, which had accumulated during the colonial period. This made the transformation of political independence into a real one more difficult than the stage of struggle against foreign conquest. These states have suddenly found themselves operating within the aforementioned world order whereby the West holds overwhelming control over world resources. They also found themselves – on the political level – caught up in the Cold War struggle between East and West.

Even a cursory look at the situation of most Third World countries today would reveal that, for them – with the exception of less than ten countries – the stage of independence has now been superseded by a relationship of dependence on the West, which now has far exceeded that of direct colonization. It is evident that the West now maintains far more control in the international arena than it had during the colonial era. This Western hegemony is being pursued and enhanced by new economic developments towards globalization, the expansion and liberalization of trade and the advances in transport, communications and media. This Western hegemony is amplified by the failure of most development programmes in the Third World where external debts have risen, and economic conditions have reached crisis levels due to high unemployment, rocketing prices of consumer goods and the cost of living, and continuous resort to borrowing to service debts or to keep incumbent regimes in power. Added to all this is the widening gap between the people and their respective governments. These are primary factors that explain the extent to which Third World countries have reached in subservience and dependence on the West.

The Situation in the Muslim World

If we now focus our attention on the Muslim world, we find that this adverse situation is even more evident and persistent in Muslim countries – particularly in Arab countries – where extensive territorial disintegration, and overwhelming Western influence has given rise to unnatural situations. We also find that the Muslims have resisted colonization vehemently before and after their territories were overrun by conquerors. They have also shown strong resolve in accomplishing the liberation process after their states became independent. Today they continue to show strong resistance to what has been termed 'The New World Order' or the 'New Middle Eastern Order'. One should also note that the colonial powers pursued in Muslim countries – unlike in other countries of Asia, Africa or Latin America – a policy of encouraging fragmentation (territorial, ethnic and political). The worst practice of this policy has been in dismembering the Arab region and planting the Zionist entity in Palestine, in addition to the impact of East-West polarization of the Muslim *Ummah*.

The fragmentation of the Muslim and Arab countries had several serious consequences, made more profound (and institutionalized)

Minorities in the Muslim World and in the West

through the independent states which later emerged. These consequences were instrumental in defeating the attempts at liberation in the Muslim world, regardless of the ideological or political form these liberation efforts had taken, given the huge existing imbalance with regard to military strength and political influence between the West on the one side, and the rest of the world on the other side (let alone the Muslim world). Revivalism was also hindered by the imbalance in scientific and technical capabilities, financial and industrial capacity, and the imbalance in control over the international economy and media. Moreover, the Muslim world is torn apart and divided between spheres of influence and suffers from the presence of the Zionist entity, which was transplanted at its heart.

In addition, one should also take note of the blatant scaremongering pratised by Orientalists and certain groups of academics and politicians, who wish to constantly provoke and alarm the West against the supposed danger of revivalism in the Muslim world, and the threat posed by such revival to 'Western civilization'. This has greatly enhanced the West's keenness to keep the Muslim world torn apart and weak, even in comparison to other regions in the Third World. The increased influence of Zionism in the United States acts to maintain and intensify Western concerns towards the (supposed) danger from the Muslim world.

Consequences of the Imbalance

In the light of this characterization of the situation, one can reach the following conclusions:

- Regardless of any emphasis or evaluation of the extent, depth, and importance of the various forms of resistance which the Muslim people have shown in their struggle for revival and liberation, and regardless of the extent and importance of the Islamic revival trends and activities, one can only be struck by the huge imbalance in power between Western hegemony on one side, and the Muslim world on the other, even if the latter were to be unified. The imbalance becomes much more striking when one considers the extent to which the Muslim world is fragmented and the extent to which rivalry and conflicts are endemic among its member states. Such conflicts are often over resources, territory or loyalty.

The imbalance is widened further if we also consider the many cases of despotism, internal struggle, draining of resources, underdevelopment and violence and counter-violence which prevail in Muslim countries. This is exacerbated by the fact that many incumbent regimes derive their strength from foreign powers and rely on them in varying degrees.

- Therefore our first consideration must be that Islam and Muslims today are in a position that requires of them to defend their strategic international domain, and they are not in a position to mount any positive or offensive action.

- The West is on the offensive strategically and on all fronts.

- On the tactical level the West is also generally on the attack and the Muslims are generally on the defensive, except for very few situations that swiftly get contained before being themselves the object of new counterattacks.

We can therefore confirm that the Muslim countries are generally in a very weak position *vis-à-vis* the might of the West and its hegemony, which means that the Islamic revival or any form of revival, in general starts from a position of weakness and from exposed territory. It is therefore not possible to manage the conflict wisely and correctly if due consideration is not given to the current circumstances and to the imbalance of power in the various fields, and if the strength and weakness of the opponents and within the Muslim *Ummah* were not clearly identified at both the strategic and tactical levels.

Minorities in the Muslim World and in the West

The Question of Minorities

If we now look in light of the above considerations at the issues of minorities in the Muslim world, and Muslim minorities in other countries of the world, especially in the West, we find that the question of the relation between these minorities and the host majority is one posed by the West. And although such an issue has always been present and has its historical roots, it is clear that this question is posed today within a framework that serves purposes other than its traditional one, and is aimed at introducing the dynamic for a new equilibrium. Reference to the historical roots should be made by one way or another to help in drafting policies for tackling current issues, but the problem today should not be understood as if it were the same problem as in the past.

Today, the most prominent theories that are purported in the Muslim world in general – and Arab world in particular – treat the matter as if we were dealing with a mosaic of communities or minorities with various different national, tribal, geographical, or ethnic associations. According to these theories there is no such thing as the Islamic identity, or the Arab identity, or the Arab-Islamic identity – or even a national or territorial identity. *All that exists is a vague belonging to a geographical location, the people of which share no common identity, existing only as a mosaic of numerous identities and associations.*

This theory is the background for the Israeli strategy in setting up a Middle Eastern order, which gives the Hebrew state – itself one alien entity serving the interests of one minority in the region – a dominant position and absolute legitimacy. The peddlers of this image of the Muslim world seek to encourage and support all the narrow (and divisive) tendencies in every Arab or Muslim country, while the hegemony that the West enjoys on the international level guarantees that such tendencies are protected, supported, and given prominence. The West does this by initially giving protection for such tendencies until they develop and reach the stage of becoming separatist movements. At this stage some historical grievances are revived, and current injustices or alleged discrimination befalling a certain minority are exaggerated and exploited, while references are made to the Western outlook of another minority enjoying a superior scientific and cultural edge, and so on.

In short the West has taken the initiative on the issue of minorities and is manipulating it as part of its offensive strategy in subjugating any particular country, and in tightening its grip on the Muslim *Ummah* as a whole in a way that strangles any revival attempt. This offensive, targets the close ties between the Muslim majorities and their historical partners in the homeland and civilization who share with them many vital interests.

Bad Diagnosis, Wrong Prescriptions

Today, there are many voices that have arisen among the Muslims, seeking to repulse this attack. But, sadly, many of them do not start from the correct analysis of the current international situation and the extent of the conspiracy against the Muslim *Ummah*. Nor do they try to comprehend the extent to which the *Ummah* suffers from weakness and subjugation. These voices do not recognize that we are, at most, on the defensive. And instead of understanding the limits of our capabilities and our need for a wise management of the conflict, they rather respond in a way that increases provocation against Islam in the West and stirs up enmity and hatred towards Muslims. *They thus feed the campaign of the enemy, and help in breaking up the inner structures of Muslim societies.* They do all this in the belief that they are exercizing the duties ordained by the Islamic *Sharīʿah*. However, Islamic *Sharīʿah* urges that due consideration should be given to the prevalent state of affairs, and that lines of action should only be pursued within the range of existing capabilities and with utmost care, wisdom, and foresight. The Islamic *Sharīʿah* goes even to the extent of outlawing 'duty of forbidding evil' if such action could lead to an even worse evil. It may also forbid duty of 'enjoining what is good' if it may conflict with another good or lead to the spread of another evil.

This approach contrasts with the tendency to formulate the Islamic position on various vital issues without proper regard to circumstances or consequences. Such tendencies constitute an approach that cannot be justified by good intention especially when it can lead to negative

Minorities in the Muslim World and in the West

results, which affect not only its proponents, but also the Islamic *Ummah* as a whole. Thus we find that those people who, in addressing the issue of non-Muslim minorities in the Muslim world, merely end up accomplishing the aims of the enemy. They do this through offering policies which inflame the internal struggle, revive old wounds and promote hatred, thus giving satisfaction to those who stirred up the issue in the first place, who are responsible for bringing the situation of the country or the Muslim *Ummah* to this stage of deterioration. This means that the Muslim *Ummah* would be weakened and torn apart further, while its enemies become stronger and more capable of maintaining their hegemony. This course of action thus represents a position that contradicts the basics of a proper understanding of Islam and proper management of the struggle. It reflects a bad reading of the provisions of the Islamic *Sharīʿah*.

The current conditions require, as far as the issue of minorities in Muslim countries is concerned, the drafting of policies that aim at strengthening the ties and consolidating the shared bonds based on the common interest of the state and the nation. This may include the formulation of new 'treaties', agreed by the leaders and opinion moulders of the parties concerned. It may also call for the initiation of programmes that reformulate the question of justice, equality and reconciliation in the context of today's equations. This is one of the fundamental demands that need to be satisfied by the Muslim revivalist movements, since facing the external threat requires consolidation of the internal front and giving sufficient assurances to the constituent communities of Islamic territories, thus enabling the minorities to achieve full and positive participation in running their countries, and for defending them against external domination. Perhaps one of the ways of defeating external conspiracies is for the Islamic movements to adopt the strategy of building broad alliances with all factions and forces that seek a national consensus to forestall external schemes. Such broad alliances should include forces such as the nationalists and representatives of various minorities. The success of such strategies requires a firm stand against all forms of injustice and discrimination to which the minorities may be exposed. This, after all, is a religious duty. Success in fulfilling it will neutralize any potential for outside interference seeking to sow discord between the minorities and the majorities, or exploit any form of injustice, discrimination, or cultural oppression. Such potential must be eliminated through clear and firm positions emanating from the alternatives that are based on the Islamic principles of justice, equality, and unity. If the leaders, thinkers, and scholars of the majority adopt such a position, they can go a long way towards achieving unity and reconciliation in their societies.

Our religion and our civilization can only be presented to the world through the way the Islamic, Arabist or nationalist movements treat the question of the relation between the majority and the minorities in our countries. Our treatment of such issues is the *working model* that the others can see. We do not need to talk to the world about the principles of Islam as much as we need to make the world see these principles put into practice. The world needs to see how Islam can enhance our lives, and through us, our countries and the world at large. Those who lead the way in provoking the world against Islam, do not fuel their prejudices from books or from history, but mainly from actual practices and attitudes that taint the image of Islam with regard to this issue. It is true that much of their propaganda against Islam is based on lies and misconceptions. Such propaganda is baseless and can be countered and defeated easily. However a small part of the propaganda against Islam is based on realities. It is this kind of propaganda which constitutes the most effective weapon which we can neutralize only if enormous effort is exerted and if Muslims manage to present very bright alternative '*working models*' of Islam.

Perhaps one living example of the 'right position' that we should adopt with respect to the issue of 'minorities' is expressed in a communiqué on the subject by the Muslim Brotherhood (dated October 1995). This communiqué represented the crowning of many writings by Shaikhs Rashid al-Ghannoushi, Yusuf Qaradawi, Abdul Karim Zaidan, Muḥammad al-Ghazālī, Hasan Turabi, Fahmi Huweidi, Adel Husein and others. The following is an extract of this communiqué:

Minorities in the Muslim World and in the West

Our position towards our Christian brethren in Egypt and in the Arab world is clear, and has been stated and known for a very long time. They are entitled to the same rights and duties as ourselves, and they are our partners in the long national struggle. They are entitled to all the rights of citizenship, be they material or symbolic, civil or political. Kindness and cooperation with them on good causes is an Islamic duty, which no Muslim should undermine or take lightly. And whoever takes a different position on this, with words or deeds, we declare that we renounce any association with him, or his words and deeds.

Muslim Minorities in the West

There is a set of characteristics that distinguish the Muslim minorities in the West from similar minorities in other countries. Perhaps the most important difference is the Muslim minorities in most of the Western countries, especially Western Europe and North America, materialized as a result of migrations, while Muslim minorities in other countries have their roots deep in the histories of their region and constitute a part of the indigenous culture and education. We can include in this category the Muslim minorities in Asia and some East European countries, because they are of the indigenous population who became Muslim or inhabited the land for hundreds of years. There is therefore a difference between the minorities that came into existence mainly after World War II, and others that share a long history and cultural heritage with their co-national majorities, as in India and China.

While our main concern here is the position of Muslim minorities in the West, we wish to also draw attention to the importance of the issue of Muslim minorities in Asian countries, in Russia, in Africa, or Latin America (this issue in Latin America needs a different perspective than that of Western countries, in spite of the fact that Latin America shares broad cultural characteristics with the West). The issue in these countries is no less important than that of the West, perhaps more important from a strategic point of view.

It is also important to note that any treatment of this issue in Asia and Russia must pinpoint some serious burdens. For example, before India gained independence and before the secession of Pakistan, it was possible to treat the issue positively, through the building of common ties that aim to preserve the unity of India, promote fraternal coexistence and strengthen common associations. Such inclinations had strong support among the Hindu and Muslim communities at the time. But the British scheme, which was based on driving a wedge between Muslims and Hindus, had culminated in the break-up of India, and has found Muslim and Hindu leaders who adopted it and pursued it to the end. This resulted in the very serious decision to separate Pakistan from India, the birth of the problem of Kashmir and the dramatic rise in enmity and hatred between the Muslims and the Hindus, as manifested in Kashmir and in Indo-Pakistan relations. These policies are now repeated in many Asian countries, where Muslim secessionist movements are active, pushing the situation in these areas into dead ends, and threatening serious consequences for Muslims and the Islamic revival.

Here we have to note that the grievances from the Muslim point of view arise mainly from two factors: one is the injustices that Muslim minorities are having to suffer, including denial of rights in the fields of education, health care, development and political participation, etc.; the other factor is related to the general mood of provocation, which affects both the attitudes of the governments and the majorities on one side, and the Muslim minorities which start demanding separation on the other. The West aims to foster hatred which serves its design in some cases, as shown by the example of the Western struggle against China and Russia.

To deal with the situation one has to take into account the current international conditions and the weight of Muslims in the international balance of forces. The West is therefore the centre of international struggle against Islam and Muslims. This means that the conflict between Muslims and non-Muslims in Asian, African, and Latin American countries should not occupy centre stage. If it were to be elevated to that level, the Islamic work in the country concerned will reach crisis situation, and the West, which has capabilities to manipulate both sides of the struggle, will benefit most. In this way, the Muslims may find themselves involved in an endless conflict, as was the case in India, China, Russia and other countries in Asia.

One of the faults in some Muslim conceptual frameworks for

Minorities in the Muslim World and in the West

dealing with minority issues comes from looking at the problem only from the ideological point of view, which makes collision with the majority inevitable and leaves no room for conciliation and cooperation. This in spite of the fact that Islam recognizes and accommodates other faiths, and does not perceive ideological differences as grounds for conflict and enmity, but rather an opportunity for civilized dialogue based on the Qur'ānic injunction that : 'There should be no compulsion in religion.' This flaw in the conceptual framework leads to a rejection of any positive association between the Muslim minority and the majority, and causes some to downplay common factors, such as having the same mother tongue, ethnic origin or partnership in the country's history or culture. It also leads to neglecting areas of common interest, which include facing the exploitation of the external Western forces. They also omit to deal with ideological differences on the basis of dialogue, which is the only solution to avert enmity and conflict.

The right position from the *Sharīʿah* point of view is for Muslims to affirm that they are keen to preserve their territorial integrity, to uphold justice, equality, and common interest and to resolve all differences through dialogue. This position is also more appropriate to the realities of the international state of affairs, and it leaves the Muslims in a stronger position while weakening and exposing the forces of division and dissent.

As to the injustices and provocations to which the Muslim minorities are often exposed, and which sometimes reach intolerable thresholds, it is important to struggle against these, not on the basis of seeking separation, but on the basis of seeking to remove injustices and secure full rights of citizenship, equality and freedom of worship for Muslims, and to end all forms of oppression and terrorism against them. And even when these injustices push Muslim minorities in some countries to the extent of declaring rebellion or adopting armed resistance, they should still aim at preserving the territorial integrity of the countries they live in, while struggling to alleviate the injustices and claim back their rights.

Here we have to note two important points:
1. It is not clear that secession to form tiny states, in the present

international circumstances, will serve the general cause of Muslim revival. Newly independent small states soon find themselves caught up in regional struggles for power and fall at the mercy of the World Bank and the IMF. This in addition to pressure from many quarters can cost these states their independence; some of them may become 'states for rent' as is the case with Eritrea today.

2. The principle of separation, which divides both state and its people on religious, ethnic, linguistic or other grounds, is usually unacceptable at both official or popular levels in almost all countries. All states and people reject calls for separation for any minority. We see some countries, especially large states, encouraging separatism against their opponents, while suppressing such tendencies at home. Such dual standards often bring about international tension and cause chaos, instability and harm to relations between different peoples.

Therefore it is important that Muslim states, Muslim scholars and Islamic movements should adopt a position against the secessionist policies whether the proponents of separatism were other Muslim minorities, whether the fire of separation is fanned in a Muslim or non-Muslim country. Muslims should know that, in both cases, they would be losers. That is whether separation occurs in their countries or whether a Muslim minority seeks to break away from a non-Muslim country. Therefore separation is a slogan that Muslims should never accept or adopt, if they really comprehend the circumstances and balances in power in the international situation today. There may be one or two exceptional cases, where Muslims may find themselves forced into accepting separation, but this has to remain exceptional and this path should never be accepted willingly and may be pressed only as a necessity and accepting the lesser evil.

There are, of course, those who do not wish to take into account the current international conjunctures, and would like to imagine that the 'Khilāfah State' is still ruling over the world, or that this imaginary state is a major power competing in the contest for world leadership. Such people can appeal to the religious laws of 'compulsory' emigration from the 'Land of *Kufr*' (unbelief) to the 'Land of Islam', or to religious opinions that call on Muslim minorities to seek separation to 'join the

Minorities in the Muslim World and in the West

Khilāfah state'. On this understanding, they may well advocate separation. Similarly, there are others who do not take into consideration the extent of Western and Zionist domination in various international spheres, and do not want to manage the conflict on the basis of countering such domination. Such people can proceed to act as if they were alone in the world, or as if they and their local opponents were alone in the battlefield. For them, what is needed is only to beat this opponent to clear the way for themselves to become an international power or superpower in a few years. All this thinking is at odds with the natural laws relating to the power balances and dynamics of human and state behaviour. All this can only worsen the situation for Muslims, and hamper the development of programmes and slogans that are compatible with the best possible strategies of managing the conflict, in the light of international realities.

It is important to note here that the struggle against international forces of domination requires a search for, and identification of, areas of cooperation and solidarity on the broadest possible front within any single country. The same applies to relations among Arab countries and in the broader Muslim world, as well as amongst all oppressed communities. Only thus can official and popular forces be lined up to resist the onslaught of the dominant international powers, and force them to some concessions. Even with such a broad front, this task may prove to be too difficult and the outcome may not be guaranteed in view of current international balance. However one can only imagine the alternative when our policies contribute to widening the international cracks in the Muslim countries between Muslim majorities and the minorities, or widening the gap between Muslim minorities and other 'oppressed' majorities around the world, including majorities who represent large countries such as Russia, China, and India, but are themselves subject to conspiracies of the dominant Western international powers.

In short, any policy that is not based on a deep understanding of the realities of the international situation, and a careful calculation of the consequences of a particular course of action, is not a credible reading of Islamic *Sharīʿah*, and may lead to overburdening the Muslims with tasks beyond their capabilities. This can lead to even worse conditions.

A Strategy for Cooperation

In summary, one can argue that a careful analysis of the situation of Muslim minorities in Western countries necessitates looking at the following facts:

The Muslim minorities in the countries of Western Europe appeared when migrants were brought to Europe after World War II, or migrated on their own seeking a better life or education. Some of them were people who served in the armies of colonial powers, while others were people who fled persecution in their own countries. In contrast to the case of immigrants in the US, Canada, New Zealand and Australia, most of these migrants found it difficult to obtain citizenship in the host countries, and their integration into societies of those countries did not progress very smoothly. This was either because of the policies of European countries, or because the immigrants were deemed different from the host communities with regard to religion, culture or colour.

Their presence started to become a problem when demand for their labour greatly declined, and as unemployment reached crisis levels in the capitalist economies. The situation worsened after migrations started from Eastern Europe and Russia after the end of the Cold War. This has resulted in a crisis for both the minorities and the host countries. Their repatriation was out of the question, while at the same time the host countries were not pursuing positive policies to integrate them. Recent international economic developments, particularly the advent of globalization, made these minorities more exposed to threat of impoverishment and social rejection, and this crisis was made even worse because conditions in the Third World have deteriorated, sparking fresh waves of migration to countries in the north. This is one cause for the rising tide of racism against migrants, which has led in some instances to the use of violence against them to force them to return to their countries.

We note from the above that the crisis has some objective dimensions, and that it is not based solely on ideology or cultural and religious differences. What we have is an economic and social problem in the Western countries and an international crisis that is crushing Third World countries and sparking migrations to the north through all possible avenues. This requires that the Muslims should help to devise solutions to address these two crises and cooperate with concerned governments and with the active political and social forces to find suitable solutions for these two crises. At the minimum, efforts should be made to stop these crises becoming more acute, and prevent the worsening of their associate symptoms, like the progressive sinking into the underground world, which includes organized crime and drug trafficking.

If the Western governments and the institutions concerned in the West were to exclude minorities in general, and the Muslim minorities in particular, from dialogue and from participating in the solution to the problem facing these countries, then such exclusions could lead to solutions which are based on indiscriminate crackdown and oppression. This would increase racism against the immigrant minorities, and can only deepen the crisis rather than ease it.

On the other hand, inclusive policies and open constructive dialogue represent the best way towards finding a solution, which can also advance the ability of the concerned economies to compete. It can also lead to stopping further migration and can possibly encourage migration in the other direction, especially if plans for real development in the Third World countries were to be part of the solution.

From this perspective, Muslim minorities can adopt, through their representatives, the principle of dialogue and openness in tackling the real problems that are facing their adopted countries. This should be based on mutual acceptance of them being part of that country and their conviction that it is their Islamic duty to contribute positively in solving common problems. Muslims have to stick to this position even if they were to be faced with a snub or unjust assault from the other party. They have to show that their position is clear and positive and that it can withstand any provocation or rebuke without falling apart as a reaction.

We note here that the problem also has another dimension related to the ideological and cultural differences, especially with regard to the spread of secular values in Western societies and the way they are affecting families, personal conduct, and one's relation with his/her body and relations with other people. Here the crises transcend the ideological and cultural differences and sometimes blur them. That is, the crises should be viewed from the perspective of the new developments sweeping through the Western societies. These developments are causing deep divisions within the majority, where the new trends are threatening all the traditional values of the Western civilization, especially those related to the family.

Western civilization and the Western societies are today facing radical changes in their values and lifestyles, and these changes pose great challenges to the minorities, especially Muslim minorities, and touch their values deeply. However, this can present an opportunity because the concerns of Muslims and non-Muslims overlap here. In confronting these challenges the Muslim minorities will find themselves on the same front with all the live forces of the Western societies.

7

On the Dilemma of the Islamic Movement: A Political Party or a Reformist Organization?

RASHID AL-GHANNOUSHI

THE ISLAMIC MOVEMENT is embodied in, and denotes, the totality of collective and individual efforts undertaken by tens of thousands of believing men and women who are engaged in propagating the Islamic message throughout the world. Their cherished aim is to guide humanity to Almighty God, enlighten hearts with the light of divine guidance and increase the harmony between their individual and collective conduct. They seek, in addition, to reinforce this guidance in such a way that nurtures their effectiveness in every aspect of life, with the ultimate objective of securing God's pleasure.

The fulfilment of this objective can be achieved only through continuous individual and collective struggle against visible and invisible obstacles which stand in the way of renewal and reformation of all aspects of Muslim life: thought and practice, politics and society, literature and the arts, with the aim of bringing these in line with the values and message of Islam. This, actually, is the requirement of the monotheistic creed, *tawḥīd*, which rejects polytheism in all its various forms and demands the universal realization of *tawḥīd*, whether at the philosophical level, as belief in the unity of the creation and Creator, or in the realm of morality and legislation, as an acceptance of the supremacy of revelation over every other source of reference that attempts to define truth and falsehood, good and evil. Any authority seeking to compete against this supremacy is seen as nothing but an act of rebellion against God and the attribution of partners to Him.

The realization of *tawḥīd* on the metaphysical, theoretical level, as well as the political one, is the core of the Islamic mission. It has, indeed, been the focus of the reform missions undertaken by all the prophets who endeavoured to erect the lofty edifice that was finally completed by the Arab Prophet, may God's blessings be upon them all. With the passage of time, this edifice, like all others, was exposed to forces of destruction. As the direct role of the prophets came to an end, the task of leadership was transferred to the *Ummah* (community) of the final prophet, which was led by its scholars (being, as the prophetic tradition goes, the heirs to the prophets).

The role of the vast majority of prophets was, however, confined to doctrinal, intellectual and educational reform, as this task exhausted all their efforts, leaving little scope for the passage to the next stage of restructuring the economic, social and political life of the people on religious foundations. This problem was compounded by the prevalence of materialist philosophies and the authoritarian customs associated with these, in addition to the influence of the despotic forms of rule that protected these and obstructed the reform aspirations of the prophets. The despotic rulers did not hesitate to incite the masses against the prophets, and regularly threatened to detain the prophets, murder them or force them into exile. '(And remember) when the unbelievers plotted against you, to keep you in bonds, or slay you, or drive you out of your home' (Qur'ān 8:30). 'And the unbelievers said to their messengers: "Be sure we shall drive you out of our land or you shall return to our religion"' (Qur'ān 14:13).

Only a small number of the prophets succeeded in going beyond doctrinal and educational reform to achieve significant political and social reform. Some, like Moses, led their people in movements of liberation, but their mission faltered, partly due to serious deficiencies in the people's faith and moral commitment, which caused them to yearn for some aspects of their former life of servitude, and even hearken back to some polytheistic traditions. 'O Moses! fashion for us a god like unto the gods they have' (Qur'ān 7:138). Moses therefore abandoned them and died in grief, leaving them in the wilderness. As for David and Solomon, even though they enjoyed some success in merging doctrinal reform and political work, establishing a state on a limited area of land, the Children of Israel themselves recoiled from assuming the responsibility of protecting this state. As a result Solomon had no choice but to relinquish his horses and his army. He pleaded to God to replace them with an army of supernatural creatures (Qur'ān 38:33, 35–9). This, in retrospect, appears as a stark expression of his failure to complete the mission of doctrinal and political reform simultaneously. It was, moreover, a signal of the collapse of the state and society together and a return to reliance on non-human agencies.

The Arab Prophet, Muḥammad God's peace and blessings be upon him, was in many ways unique among his fellow-messengers in having attained success both in doctrinal and political reform. He managed to forge from the ranks of the divided and backward Arabs a unified, organized, civilized community that was prepared to take the Islamic project from the level of theory to the level of practice. The community was transformed from conditions of weakness into the nucleus of a state that, though small in size, was strong in its structure, aims and capacities. Within a short period, the Prophet's community was able to overthrow and replace the entire system on the Arabian Peninsula. It engineered sweeping changes not only in the beliefs of the people but also in the prevailing social and political structures. Thus, a unified state founded on the doctrine of *tawḥīd* was established which, by the time its founder died, extended beyond Arabia into the territories of the Persian and Roman empires. His successors adopted the same methodology of combining the missions of doctrinal and political reform, creating a state that was subjected to serve the society and entrench the foundations of faith and justice. 'Those who, if We establish them in the land, establish regular prayer and give regular charity, enjoin the right and resist wrong' (Qur'ān 22:41).

The Umayyad *Coup*: Separation of Religion from Politics
It did not take long for this unique and unifying generation which established the model Islamic society in Madinah to be overwhelmed

by winds of change emanating from the revival monarchical and tribalistic tendencies. The rapid expansion of the state incorporated disparate communities, many still beholden to their recent tribal and monarchical heritage. A qualitative transformation was, therefore, effected in the direction of public opinion, enabling the supporters of the old order to exploit the new conditions and engineer a radical transformation in the character of the state and its relations with religion. As a consequence, the first and most dangerous political and intellectual schism took place in the history of Islam, converting in the process the Muslim community from being a unified body into one of disparate parties. The state was also diverted from being in the service of religion and society, in the process alternating between this original objective and putting both religion and society in its service. It often imposed its authority by force and abdicated from the service of religion and the society together.

In the face of this situation, the Muslim élite became polarized into two broad tendencies. On one side, there were those political groups and activists who adopted a stance of political and military opposition toward the state, rejecting the arbitrary Umayyad transformation of the state from a consultative caliphate into a despotic monarchy. This aggressive political opposition continued to engage in a bitter and bloody conflict with the state, constantly engaging in new forms of resistance. It refused to give loyalty to the state, which it believed to have betrayed the model founded by the Prophet God's peace and blessings be upon him and his Rightly-Guided Caliphs. However, it is to be noted that, when some of these very parties were given the opportunity to take over the state, they failed to offer a better model. On the contrary, they only managed, in spite of the many priceless sacrifices exacted, and in deference to the backward conditions, to reproduce the same models of individual rule that were prevalent at the time. Indeed, the legacy of autocratic rule and the repressive measures deployed against these parties led to the emergence of alternative theoretical models which were furthest removed from the ideal of consultation and government of the people, and to offer solutions that were even more autocratic than the Umayyad model. Even the

On the Dilemma of the Islamic Movement

Khawārij, who were known for their extreme rejection of the hereditary system, did not themselves differ from their adversaries; for when they established their state, they also did so on the basis of hereditary and family ties. The Shīʿah, for their part, totally abandoned the principle of *shūrā* in favour of the concept of divine appointment.

The other tendency among the élite, reflecting that of the vast majority of the community, adopted an entirely different approach after considering the destructive consequences of the bloody conflict between the authorities and the opposition. They abandoned the struggle for power and remained content to respect the general Islamic laws, paving the way for the scholars to carry out the tasks of social and educational reform. Thus it was the men of learning (*ʿulamāʾ*) who were called upon to provide social services through the utilization of charitable funds to build mosques and to organize education, in recognition of the fact that the rulers had neglected these duties. They were expected, moreover, to assume the responsibility of caring for the needy, opposing the spread of social ills, defending thereby public interests and making representations to the rulers on behalf of the oppressed. The fact that the scholars provided advice and guidance to the rulers did, in the final analysis, give a sense of legitimacy to the latter's authority in the eyes of the people. This, therefore, was how the majority of Sunnī scholars preoccupied themselves, constituting as it were, the largest and most powerful source of influence on the administrations that followed the Rightly-Guided Caliphs. Although the scholars gave these authorities a semblance of legitimacy, they knew in their hearts that these systems were all based on power and the imposition of force.

The Modern Era

The Islamic *Ummah* thus remained, over the centuries since the collapse of the early Caliphate, governed by this balance or historical compromise based on a division of labour between the scholars and rulers. For whereas the rulers focused their attention solely on governmental affairs, the scholars devoted their time entirely to matters of social reform. Neither of the two approaches prevented the emergence of armed opposition here and there. This happened when educational and reform groups were transformed into parties seeking to seize power from the incumbent authorities. These movements quickly shifted from a stage of revolutionary education and evolved into that of organized and clandestine action, which frequently exploded in attempts to seize the reins of power in the state. When these undertakings failed, as was often the case, they were explained away by the scholars with the official rationalization of *fitnah* (dissension, sedition). If, on the contrary, these operations succeeded in capturing power, they gained immediate allegiance and legitimacy; such was the level of pragmatism that invariably prevailed. This continued until the civilizational cycle, which started from unity and strength in Arabia, ended in division and weakness in Istanbul, thus enabling its enemies to finish it off. The unity established by Islam was thus destroyed, leaving the field to national entities fashioned by the victors in line with their interests.

The Muslim community thus entered a stage of complete fragmentation, leading to the collapse of the formula based on the historical compromise between scholars and rulers. In the new states, where brute force and loyalty to foreigners became the basis of power, the *'ulamā'* no longer represented a pillar of legitimacy side by side with political power. Religion and its institutions became mere tools in the hands of rulers, to be used in case of need, and often were seen as mere adjuncts of the security apparatus of the state. The ordeal of the *'ulamā'* was more severe under repressive states that were secular in form and content (as is the case in Turkey) or Islamic in form but secular in content (as most Muslim countries are). Some of the *'ulamā'* chose to collaborate with the rulers, either to achieve perceived public or private ends. In this, they were following the established tradition, whether aware or not of the radical transformation which took place in the nature of the state. Others chose political opposition, through the formation of societies or political parties. These start by appealing to the people, spreading a message of radical religious consciousness, and end up as opposition groups, using either peaceful methods or resorting to violence on the understanding that the new states have moved outside the confines of Islamic legitimacy. The writings of Sayyid Abul A'lā Mawdūdī, Sayyid Quṭb and Ḥasan al-Bannā lend

On the Dilemma of the Islamic Movement

themselves to interpretation that could legitimize the use of force to right the wrong established by the secular state.

However, the resort to force against the existing regimes cannot be based solely on their forfeiting Islamic legitimacy, but must also presuppose the ability and capacity to effect change. Islam obliges the Muslim, therefore, to struggle against oppression. It broadens before him the choices, using reason and discretion, to choose the more appropriate and least costly methods of change. These choices must be decided in line with the prophetic advice: 'Whoever from among you sees an abomination, should change it with his hand (physical force), if he is unable to do so, he should do it with his tongue (words) and still if he is unable, he should hate it in his heart and this is the lowest level of faith.'

Today, most Islamic parties have rejected the use of force to achieve political ends, and instead, initiated a search for opportunities that would enable them to effect changes through peaceful means. They are, indeed, well aware that it is possible to realize their objectives through the creation of legally recognized political parties and agencies or by joining existing ones. The combined effort of both the first group (official Islam) and the second (opposition Islam) has given a considerable impetus to the call of reformist Islam, leading to the penetration of reformist ideas into all strata of society, and thereby representing the widest cultural and political currents in the Islamic world. On a practical level, the Islamic trend demands political change with the objective of setting up Islamic democratic and consultative institutions instead of the existing dictatorial and secularist ones. Likewise, it demands social, economic and cultural change and the establishment of all social activities on an Islamic basis. By so doing, the Islamic trend seeks to ensure that the state apparatus serves both religion and society, while guaranteeing the independence and unity of its people and contributing to world peace built on just premises. In effect, this emerging tide aims to protect the image of Islam and its minorities throughout the world in their struggle against renewed Western and Zionist aggression.

The Problem Today

There is no consensus among Muslims today on the most appropriate methodologies of change. And the issue is not confined to differences about the degree of legitimacy or the propriety of using force as a means of change, nor to determining the legitimacy of existing Islamic states. For at a time when the idea of an Islamic party has become so established that there is hardly an Islamic country in which one or more Islamic party is not found, this idea is still the target of severe criticism in some quarters. We are not concerned here, as we discuss the dilemma of the Islamic movement between the state and the society, to dwell on the contemporary views that reject the idea of an Islamic party altogether, let alone accepting a multi-party system. This notion they argue, is essentially alien and does not accord with the unitary concept of *tawḥīd* that proclaims the primacy of the *Ummah* and not the party as the focus of political work and loyalty. It is significant to note that this criticism is shared by the ultra-traditionalist (*salafī*) militant groups which reject the concept of multi-party politics and also those states founded on the ideas of modern Islamism such as the Islamic Republic of Iran. The same can also be said of certain scholars who enjoy special relationships with their rulers. What concerns us here in this paper are the ideas which Imām Ḥasan al-Bannā (founder of the Muslim Brotherhood in Egypt in 1928) sought to implant, and which are echoed by many of his disciples, as well as many Islamic scholars who are supportive of existing regimes, defending the legitimacy of these regimes by their words as strongly as the regimes defend themselves with their arms. The gist of this thought, as it was articulated by the martyred Imām, is that the Islamic movement, of which the Muslim Brotherhood is a prototype, is larger than any political party. Certainly, it is a body that stands above all political parties. According to one of its thinkers, Sayyid Dusuqi Hasan, the Islamic movement must be a reformist movement which establishes its work upon social interaction and the awakening of man to construct, do good and display the Qur'ānic values embedded in his being. This individual must also transform these values into potent systems in life.

In the light of this view, the movement emerges as a global reformist

On the Dilemma of the Islamic Movement

one, focusing the vision of mankind toward the Divine. It guides people to the Qur'ān so that they may extract its valuable treasures in every domain of life, enabling them to build their lives around systems. The movement is thus not an executive political movement. It is the duty of the Islamic movement to send into society cadres who possess an array of leadership abilities. It should not imprison them within its ranks.

According to this outlook, the Islamic movement has the closest possible resemblance to a civilizational school, which produces generations of reformists who will then seep into every nook and cranny of the society and assume the burden of assisting the Islamic re-awakening. The political party becomes, under these circumstances, an integral organ of society, in the same way the judiciary, military or economic institutions are functional components of this society. This perception of the Islamic movement was advocated by our late friend, Muḥammad Abdul Halim Abū Shuqqah, proprietor of Dār al-Qalam and author of the *Encyclopaedia of the Liberation of Woman in the Prophetic Era*. He believed that the Islamic movement must be a conglomerate of parallel and complementary, but distinct and independent, organizations, each undertaking to inspire sectors of the society whether it be in the areas of trade unionism, culture, politics or economics. According to Abū Shuqqah, therefore, the political party is to merely constitute an expression of the reformist effort in a special area: the political arena. With respect to the leadership of the Islamic movement, it is necessary that it should embody a spiritual, intellectual, advisory and educational nature, directing every sphere through its intellectual and spiritual influence, for it must remain above competing with any party for position or office. In other words, the leadership of the Islamic movement must not be distracted from its primary mission of calling to God and advising both rulers and ruled, without isolating itself and taking the side of any particular party. It should not permit itself to become preoccupied with the immediate rather than long-term objectives or sectional rather than all-embracing issues (from a lecture delivered by Abū Shuqqah in Tunisia in the Summer of 1985).

This idea was articulated with exquisite clarity by one of the most outstanding contemporary Islamic scholars, Shaykh Saʿid Ramadan al-Buti in his controversial book, *Jihād in Islam*. There, he unleashed a scathing attack upon the Islamic political groups which, he argues, had become distracted from reformist Islam and its main task of calling to God the stray sheep from every walk of life, and turned into partisan groups the activities of which serve their specific interests only, and have no relationship with the mission of calling people to God. As a consequence, their focus becomes the support of one party, the primary concern of which is the assumption of power, thus distancing themselves from the tasks of reforming hearts, convincing minds and inspiring souls. Quite to the contrary, their main preoccupation is to convince people of the need to propel them into the seats of power and leadership. These activists have, therefore, been transformed into a party competing as any other for prestige and material gain. This, for all practical purposes, is how the Islamists have earned for themselves enemies and rivals from the other parties and groups. Accordingly, it is very difficult to perceive how or by what means will these people be motivated to accept the call of such Islamists who compete against them for the hearts and minds of the masses in order to gain power.

Shaykh al-Buti, it must be noted, was himself a member of the ruling Nationalist Progressive Front in Syria. He was on one occasion approached to form and lead an Islamic faction within the Front. He pointedly refused, saying that would be giving the impression that Islam had approved of a division of influence and power between it and the other members of the Front, its share thus representing a fifth or sixth or whatever. The relationship between Islam and the other members of the Front had become a competitive political relationship. This, he argued, represented a reduction of the influence and scope of Islam, an attack upon it and, indeed, an attempt to crush it. He went on to say:

> In reality, it is Islam that should be the common denominator that would unite the members of the Front. And so if Islam connects them as the hand connects all its five fingers, who is he that will be satisfied to retract and assign for the unifying hand neighbouring fingers. Who is

he that will be pleased, therefore, to ascribe a competing force to this common factor or convert it into an adversary. In the present context, I am the furthest away from competing against them for the division of immediate booty, and who is close to their sensitivities of faith and their Islamic nature. I am thus able to address in them this shared element without there being between me and them any dividing gap or broken bridge. But what good awaits my appeal to them when I find myself sitting among them as an equal, struggling against them as an adversary who aims to secure profit at the expense of others. Surely there will be no time for *daʿwah* or explaining the truth of Islam in the smog of this competition.[1]

An Old Ambition Revived

Throughout the ages, the concept of the righteous and learned caliph has remained alive in the Muslim imagination, abating only to be rekindled again. From time to time, it would flare up to revive Islam's vitality, and rebel against plots to marginalize it and confine it to a sanctuary or a mosque, or to make it into the tool of an ignorant secular ruler. This represented the enduring attraction of the Prophetic and Righteous Caliphate model, in which Qur'ān and power coincided, while mosque and government seat were one and the same. The mosque was indeed the centre of life in all its aspects. It continued to trigger a series of revolutions against the attempts to marginalize it or convert it into an institution subservient to deviant or ignorant rulers seeking to impose their will on it, appointing its *imāms* and attempting to transform it into an instrument that served their interest and justified their policies.

The Islamic experience concerning the relationship between the ruler and scholar became stabilized in a division of labour in which the state became the sphere of the ruler's authority, and society the sphere of the scholar. This general pattern was not, however, without exceptions as some non-Sunnī Islamic groups generally formed rejectionist opposition movements that did not hesitate to resort to force in their attempts to wrest power from existing rulers. Similarly, there

---

[1] Shaykh Ramadan al-Buti, *Al-Jihād fī al-Islām*, pp.75–7.

were among the majority Sunnīs those who advocated both peaceful and violent means of change. Even on the level of theory, some Sunnī scholars strove to place the scholar in the position of the Supreme Guide in relation to, and on behalf of whom, actual rulers exercized executive authority. This type of reasoning was reflected in the thought of the prominent Sunnī Imām, al-Juwaynī, as well as that of Imām al-Mahdī ibn Tumart, the founder of the largest Islamic state in North Africa (the *Muwaḥḥidūn* state). In our era, it was Imām Ayatollah Khomeini who succeeded in reviving this idea of al-Juwaynī's, establishing it in the context of a modern Shīʿah state headed by a leading scholar, assisted by an executive arm subordinate to him.

The question remains, however, given the fact that Islam is a unitary faith which does not distinguish between religious and worldly matters, does this entail that the state established under its auspices must be an all-embracing, totalitarian state? Likewise, should the parties that function in Muslim societies and aspire to reform it be themselves also inclusive and all-embracing? Or are we to assume that the comprehensiveness of Islam does not necessarily entail that the state, party or parties should be all-inclusive? After all, we have recognized that prophethood has been ended, and the responsibility of the implementation and expounding of the message had been transferred to the *Ummah* as a whole. This in turn has prevented the rise of a 'church' emerging to claim exclusive authority in the name of God, and also barred the emergence of an absolute rule in which despots claimed to be God's representatives on earth as did occur in Europe during the Middle Ages. Instead, the vicegerency on behalf of God was vested in the whole *Ummah*, and no individual was deemed infallible.

This perception has shifted the central interest, responsibility and focus of the historic Islamic movement to rotate around the *Ummah* rather than the state. Hence, the mission which has been given special priority over others was that of dedicating time to reforming society and educating it until it fully assumes the duties entrusted by Islam, including the supervision of rulers. Islam has indeed made it incumbent on the *Ummah* to establish a state in order to establish justice among men in accordance with the commands of God and in defence of them. Yet, despite the primacy of this mission, it still cannot have the same urgency as social reform and the proper establishment of social institutions. Social institutions must be strong enough so as to be capable of holding political leaders accountable and removing them from office when necessary. This may lead us to conclude that, when conflict arises between the two missions of reforming society and that of political reform, the former must prevail and have priority. Even when it appears that the rulers are obstructing the scholars' efforts to implement social reform, the matter could not be resolved by devoting all the time to opposing the rulers and inviting the people to rebel against them. This certainly will not achieve anything except the weakening of both state and society. For success, quite to the contrary, lies in patience, enjoining it, giving good advice and seizing opportunities to contact the people and standing by them. Surely the mission of Muḥammad God's peace and blessings be upon him as an appointed messenger and reformer was paramount and much more important than his position as a ruler. 'And keep you soul content with those who call on their Lord morning and evening, seeking His Face' (Qur'ān 18:28).

Conclusion

There is always an ever-present danger of the Islamic movement sliding into the status of a mere political party, distinguishing itself with the Islamic label and standing as an adversary and competitor to other parties. Likewise, the suspicion of monopolizing the authority of Islam by a political group which condemns its opponents as unbelievers is also a possibility. In the same vein, one must also not ignore here the likelihood of the preoccupation with state reform and neglect of the primary mission of the prophets, which is essentially one to reform souls. The main focus of this mission has to permit hearts to reach out to God and be conscious of the Hereafter, to strengthen bonds of love, togetherness and brotherhood between people and to support and strengthen the institutions of civil society. All this makes it necessary for Islamic parties to be aware of these dangers, and would entail the following:

1. That these groups should present the people with their reformist agenda and programmes rather than the empty slogans of electioneering campaigns.
2. That they avoid giving any indication that they want to monopolize the authority of Islam, or brandish a threat of condemning rivals as unbelievers.
3. That they steer well clear of adopting the totalitarian methodologies of communist parties, permitting the Islamic party to dominate every social activity such as trade union activities, cultural affairs, mosques and economic institutions. On the contrary, it would be much better to curtail party involvement in all these activities, and concentrate only on political party activities, leaving the civil society to organize itself. The Islamic movement would be better off releasing some of its highly trained cadres and professional élite into civil society, and permit them to concentrate independently on social reform. These cadres, unencumbered by party affiliation, would thus be able to concentrate on what is undoubtedly the noblest of all missions and the loftiest of all undertakings: to propagate the message of reform to all parties without prejudice or partisan tendencies. 'And who is better in speech than one who calls men to God, works righteousness, and says, I am of those who bow in Islam' (Qur'ān 41:33).

8

The Burden of the Muslim Intellectual: Fathi Osman's Jihād for Human Rights

ABDELWAHAB EL-AFFENDI

WHEN I JOINED *Arabia, the Islamic World Review* in London in the Autumn of 1982, it looked like the most exciting place on earth to be. The Islamic Revolution in Iran was fresh in all memories, and the second oil shock, the good side of it, was transforming the Gulf, and with it the whole Muslim world. Politically and economically, the Muslim world was asserting itself. *Arabia* was, in a sense, a celebration of this fact. It also reflected the vision of some liberal Muslim intel-lectuals who were concerned that the Muslim world's self-assertion should not translate into hostility to the West. *Arabia* was seen as the Muslim world's 'ambassador to the West'. It represented an enterprise in bridge-building and dialogue, keen that the Muslim world, in its hour of emergence on the modern world scene, must seek understanding and cooperation, not confrontation.

At the heart of this endeavour was the self-effaced, fatherly figure of Dr. Fathi Osman, the Editor-in-Chief. In a paradoxical way, his towering presence asserted itself precisely in the self-limit he put on his own authority. He allowed the editors a wide margin of freedom, rarely imposing his will, and thus permitting a thriving (even bewildering) diversity of standpoints to find expression in the magazine. But there was one instance in which he would assert his authority with uncharacteristic vehemence: when someone else tried to interfere with the freedom of his editors and contributors. There were several occasions when Dr. Fathi clashed with the publishers over the right of editors and staff to write what they believed to be the truth.

The Genesis of a Vision

Fathi Osman came to *Arabia* via a long detour, which took him from his native Egypt to Algeria, to Saudi Arabia, to the United States, and finally back to Saudi Arabia where he teamed up with like-minded intellectuals and financiers to establish the publishing enterprise which gave rise to *Arabia*. Born in al-Minya in Egypt in 1928, Fathi arrived in Cairo in 1944 at a very young age for his university education to find a boiling cauldron of cultural and political effervescence. He was less than twenty years old when he was admitted to the Arts Faculty of Cairo University to read History. Like all good Egyptian patriots, he had been an ardent supporter of the Wafd Party. But the post-war era in Cairo was not a time of settled allegiances. The Wafd's image as the bearer of the banner of nationalism had been tarnished when the British forces of occupation used their tanks in a rare overt and crude show of force in 1942 to impose a Wafdist government on the palace which, for once, was more in tune with the anti-British sentiments of the wider Egyptian public. The post-war era, with its promises of independence and the end to the British occupation of over seventy years, also witnessed the emergence of rival patriotic movements. Foremost amongst these were a variety of left-wing groups and, most prominent of all, the Muslim Brotherhood led by Ḥasan al-Bannā.

When Fathi arrived in Cairo, the Muslim Brotherhood had been fighting a fierce battle with the Wafd for supremacy on the campus at Cairo University. His sympathies were naturally with the Wafd, but he was alerted to the existence of the Brotherhood by these clashes, and soon began to be drawn into its orbit. He took to attending the meetings addressed by the movement's charismatic leader, Ḥasan al-Bannā. But those were times of turmoil, and the Brotherhood became involved in a whirlwind of struggles. In 1947, the movement joined the war in Palestine, thus increasing its popularity and raising its profile, but also coming into conflict with the powers that be. Its leader al-Bannā, was assassinated in 1949, following the ban on the movement the year before after one member assassinated the prime minister of the day, Mahmoud al-Nuqrashi. In 1949, following the movement's dissolution, Fathi, then a young school teacher was transferred

The Burden of the Muslim Intellectual

summarily to the remote village of Kom Ambo near Aswan, in a step clearly intended as a punitive measure. This forced him to resign from the Ministry of Education and seek employment at al-Azhar.

Al-Bannā was succeeded in the leadership of the Brotherhood by a judge, Hasan al-Hodaybi, who lacked al-Bannā's charisma and was somewhat rigid in his views. But he was also a cool-headed man, who immediately came into conflict with the more arduous members, especially those who formed the backbone of the 'Special Order', the movement's secret military wing. The movement supported the military *coup* of July 1952, but later clashed with its leaders because of al-Hodaybi's uncompromising stance on constitutional propriety. This led to the movement's implication in an attempted assassination of the new military strongman, Colonel Gamal Abdel Nasir (Nasser) in October 1954, the disbanding of the movement and the arrest and execution of its key leaders. Hasan al-Hodaybi and six others were sentenced to death, but he was later spared and his sentence was commuted to life imprisonment. He was to spend nearly 20 years in jail.

Although never a formal member, the young Fathi stuck with the movement through these lean years. He was in particular very close to al-Hodaybi, and also maintained a close liaison with Sayyid Qutb, who later came to prominence as one of the movement's foremost ideologues. Having graduated from university in 1948, Fathi found a job as a schoolteacher of history in Cairo. Due to political persecution, he had to leave this job and seek work in the private sector. Worse was to come. In 1954, he was one of tens of thousands of people arrested and detained in connection with the crackdown on the Muslim Brotherhood. When he was released from prison two years later, he had been formally sacked from his job in state schools, and was forced again to seek work in some private schools. But he made a virtue out of these adverse circumstances and started to study for another university degree in Law at Alexandria University, while also starting work on an MA degree in History at Cairo University. He obtained both degrees in the same year: 1960. His thesis for the MA was, significantly, on the history of Islamic-Byzantine relations, an early indication of his keen interest in Muslim-Western relations.

That year also witnessed the publication of Fathi's first major book, *Al-Fikr al-Islāmī wa'l-Taṭawwur* (Islamic Thought and Change). Before that he had published a book in 1955 entitled *Aḍwā' ʿalā al-Ta'rīkh al-Islāmī*, which was an introduction to Islamic history and historiography. His later ideas were anticipated in two works: *Al-Dīn li'l-Wāqiʿ* (Religion for Reality) and *Afkār Taqaddumiyyah min Turāth al-Islām* (Progressive Ideas from Muslim Heritage), in 1957 and 1958 respectively. But his line of thinking reached its maturity in *Al-Fikr al-Islāmī wa'l-Taṭawwur*, which was seen by many modern Islamists as a seminal work, being the first instance where a committed Islamist came out forcefully in favour of a liberal interpretation of Islamic tradition. In this book, Fathi was decisively in favour of a liberal interpretation of Islamic heritage in the areas of democracy, human rights, the rights of women and the status of non-Muslims. However, while the work was welcomed by many, Fathi was disappointed in the response it received from most liberals, who ignored it completely. Few writers to whom the book was presented even bothered to review it. It is most probable that this response was occasioned by the fact that many liberals had thought then that, with the prison gates firmly locked behind the bulk of the leaders of the Islamist trend, and with the rest on the run, there was no need to bother about what Islam said about this or that aspect of life. There was a new religion in town: scientific socialism. For that year witnessed the start of the decisive shift in the Egyptian regime towards socialist ideas, and the bulk of intellectuals started to look in that direction.

The year 1960 was good to Fathi in another respect, for he was finally given his job back. And no sooner has this happened, than he had a rare opportunity to put his reformist ideas into practice. In 1961, he was appointed to the Department of Islamic Culture at al-Azhar University, which was run at the time by the famous scholar Muhammad al-Bahi. Al-Bahi immediately took a liking to his new aide and when al-Bahi became rector of al-Azhar, he elevated Fathi to the job of Director of Planning. Osman followed al-Bahi on when the latter was appointed Minister of Awqaf in 1962, and for the next few years, the two men cooperated closely in implementing the most

The Burden of the Muslim Intellectual

ambitious reforms al-Azhar was to see. Thereafter followed one of the most exciting periods in the history of Islamic reform in Egypt, and Fathi became intimately involved with this effort, himself moving to al-Azhar in 1965 as deputy controller of libraries and research.

The reforms included a complete overhaul of the syllabus and teaching methods, as well as the addition of new faculties such as Medicine and Engineering. Osman regarded those reforms as vital not only for al-Azhar's survival and progress, but also for modernization in the Muslim world. However, he judges them as less than successful, because they were instituted from above and did not have strong support within the institution, with the result that as soon as the influence of the charismatic al-Bahi receded, things started to fall apart. It is probably this impression that prompted Fathi to leave al-Azhar in 1969 and move to Algeria, where he was at first employed as an advisor on Islamic affairs and education at the Ministry of Religious Affairs in Algiers and then as a lecturer on Islamic History and Political Thought at Oran University. In 1972, he left Oran for Saudi Arabia where he became Assistant Professor at Riyadh University, teaching courses on 'Cultural Issues in Contemporary Islam'.

In 1973 Osman moved to Princeton University in the United States, where he started working on his Ph.D and also taught courses on Modern Islamic Reform and Modern Arabic History and Literature. In 1975 he became Assistant Professor at Temple University, teaching a course on 'Issues in Contemporary Islam'. He obtained his Ph.D from Princeton in 1976. His thesis was 'Conquered Land and Land Taxation (*fay'* and *kharāj*): Origin and Development in Medieval Islam.' In Princeton and Temple he came in contact with Orientalists such as Bernard Lewis, as well as Muslim intellectuals such as the late Ismail Raji al-Faruqi, with some of whom he formed a life-long association.

From the US he went back to Saudi Arabia, where he became Professor at Imam Muhammad ibn Saud University and Director of the university's Research Centre. It was in Riyadh in 1978 that he published his book *Ḥuqūq al-Insān bayna Sharīʿat al-Islām wa'l-Fikr al-Gharbī* (Human Rights between Islamic *Sharīʿah* and Western Thought). It was another attempt by Fathi to advance his central idea on the compatibility of Islamic values and modern liberal ideals. The setting may not have been ideal, and in fact I heard someone who was completely unaware of the author or the background of the work, express scepticism at a conference in the United States about the work, asking how was it possible for someone who was a professor at Riyadh University to write convincingly about human rights. This is an easily made misunderstanding. And it was probably because of these constraints that Fathi Osman's works took a long time to become widely known in the Arab world, even in his home country. However, already a small but vibrant trend has grownup around his ideas, and at one time this trend tried to go under the name of the 'Islamic Left'. But it was never a homogeneous trend, nor was Osman the only or predominant influence upon it.

It was with *Arabia*, however, that Fathi Osman became best known to the wider world.

The *Arabia* Experience

Arabia, the Islamic World Review was launched in October 1981 as a London-based monthly magazine. The keynote speaker at the launching ceremony was Shaikh Ahmad Zaki Yamani, the then Saudi Minister of Petroleum and Mineral Resources, who called the magazine an 'ambassador of the Muslim world in the capital of the West – London.' He saw its main task as improving Muslim-Western understanding, which he believed was essential for a just world order. The main obstacles to cooperation between Muslims and the West, he argued, were the designs of communists and Zionists who benefited from sowing bitterness between the two camps. But there is also the historical animosity created by the legacy of the Crusades and colonialism. The Crusades bequeathed to the West an anti-Muslim mentality, while colonialism and its extension in the Zionist occupation of Palestine created bitterness against the West among the Muslims.

But Yamani believed that what united the Muslims and the West was much more than what divided them. The strategic position of the Muslim world and its vast resources are indispensable for the West, while Muslims need the West and its technology. There is, moreover,

The Burden of the Muslim Intellectual

a common outlook that unites Muslims and Christians, especially in opposition to Communism. Muslims respect Christianity and regard it as a precursor to their own religion. If the injustices perpetrated against the Muslims are corrected, then there will be no limit to cooperation between the two camps. *Arabia*'s mission, according to Yamani, was thus to combat the age-old misunderstandings about Islam in the West by revealing Islam's true image. It should also transmit to its Western audience the sincere desire of Muslims for cooperation, and explain how best it could be achieved.

The line adopted by Yamani was reiterated again in later interventions by the Shaikh. It was based on recommending Islam to the West by appealing to the common values and perceptions, arguing that Islam was 'a religion of peace which was nearer to Christianity than any other religion.'[1] He also tried to show that Islam agreed with Western values on such issues as human rights and democracy. In addition, Islam was portrayed as treading a middle road between capitalism and Communism, supporting what was best in both. It agreed with capitalism in supporting individual political rights, but unlike capitalism it did not neglect the economic rights emphasized by Communism. Western civilization also has a common root with Islam, highlighted by Islam's significant contributions to modern sciences. The current Islamic revival is set to reform the Islamic religion and lead to even greater convergence between the two civilizations. Both groups should thus work to remove misunderstandings and suspicions.

The vision enunciated by Yamani was the one that prevailed within the Saudi establishment during the reign of the late King Faisal.[2] Yamani was the leading intellectual exponent of the establishment's agenda; he drew on some of the ideas of the Austrian-born Muslim writer, Muhammad Asad, who had a long-standing association with the

---

[1] Shaikh Yamani, 'On Avoiding Misunderstandings about Islam', *Arabia*, December 1981, pp.40–1.

[2] For more insights into this period and the Yamani-Faisal relations see the account in Jeffrey Robinson, *Yamani, the Inside Story*, Simon & Schuster, London, 1988. Robinson apparently based his book on information provided by Yamani, and of which I have independent corroboration.

House of Saud. Yamani and King Faisal's son, Prince Muhammad al-Faisal al-Saud were *Arabia*'s principal backers. But it was also a vision shared by Fathi Osman himself and a growing band of Muslim intellectuals. Another proponent of this viewpoint was Temple University's Ismail Raji al-Faruqi, who expressed his ideas in an article entitled 'How the US and Islam can work together' (*Arabia*, June 1982). Faruqi's thesis was that the tension between Islam and the US was tragic and unnecessary, given the common interests and perceptions uniting the two. The Muslims regarded the US traditionally as a haven from persecution and poverty, and saw it as a defender of freedoms. But the post-war role of the US as a 'neo-colonialist' power that wanted to fill the 'vacuum' left behind by the departing European colonial powers caused anger and disillusionment among Muslims. The US support for oppressive puppet regimes in the name of the war against Communism caused resentment among the Muslim masses and lost an opportunity in which Muslims and the US could have cooperated for their mutual benefit and against the common Communist enemy. The growth of the new revolutionary Islamic movements offers a golden opportunity for cooperation. However, the shortsighted might not grasp this opportunity.

The intelligent, on the other hand, will realize that Islam is the religion closest to Christianity; the Islamic culture has been a primary foundation for Western culture; that the Muslim revolutionary youth of today are the nearest embodiments of the traditional American revolutionary ideal.

The publishers of *Arabia*, the Islamic Press Agency (IPA) professed adherence to this line in their charter. IPA affirmed the role of the modern mass media as 'the most formidable weapon of political action in modern times.' The charter also lamented the stark backwardness of the Muslim *Ummah* in this vital domain and the total dependence of Muslims on the West for their media output. Western media persistently distorted the image of Islam, thus deepening the gulf between the Muslims and the rest of the world, especially the West. The dependence of Muslim media on their Western counterparts enhanced the influence of the latter and further demoralized the Muslims and

The Burden of the Muslim Intellectual

undermined Muslim societies. Zionism contributed further by inciting hatred for the Muslims in the West, and provoking hatred for the West among the Muslim masses, and thus deepening the divisions between the two cultures and driving Muslims to espouse Communism. IPA was launched to break out of this cycle by breaking the monopoly exercized by Western media organizations and present world events from a viewpoint that was sensitive to the Muslim perspective. IPA sought to put the Muslim world firmly on the world map and help bring the *Ummah* up to the challenge of modernization. As well as facing the external challenges the *Ummah* also needs to come to terms with itself and affect internal reforms. The contribution of IPA to the promotion of free debate, research and communications will greatly ease the growth pains of the *Ummah* and help guide it to the right path.

Arabia's first issue (September 1981) printed a message from the publishers entitled 'For Islam and the West', reaffirming the view that the magazine was for all Muslims, regardless of their diverse ethnic, regional or doctrinal background. The magazine, it was stressed, was 'not published to undertake "missionary" work in the West, nor will it provide the Muslims with apologetics or wishful thinking. Only truth will help the Muslims.' The message also affirmed its role of promoting mutual understanding between Islam and the West through informing Muslims about the West and its cultural achievements and also informing the West about Islam.

> The barriers between the Muslims and the West built during the Crusades and the colonial era should be broken down by today's Muslims and Westerners...*Arabia* is keen to undertake the difficult task of bridging the gaps and opening up channels for a fruitful dialogue between Muslims and the West. *The Islamic World Review*, published by Muslims in London, is managed and edited through solid cooperation between Muslim and Western journalists. It represents, in its daily practice, this much needed 'dialogue', and it looks forward with enthusiasm to embodying that dialogue in every word on its pages.

The approach adopted by the organization was further elaborated by the Editor-in-Chief, Fathi Osman himself, in a magazine interview.

He explained that the Islamic media must address itself to all Muslims regardless of their schools of thought as well as to non-Muslims. The Muslims needed a forum on which to exchange views and a medium for dialogue with other inhabitants of the Globe. The need for Islamic media is primarily a need for inter-Muslim dialogue. Muslims need to share their experiences as they try to make sense of Islam in the modern world and engage in experiments designed to give a modern-day expression to Islam. It is vital that all those engaged in these activities and movements should communicate with each other, so that all will be aware of what the others do or think. Dialogue between different schools and approaches could then take place. The media could thus transcend the borders between countries and schools and help bring Muslims together. The media should also be a forum for an assessment and evaluation of the results and approaches of Muslim activism, allowing Muslims to focus on successes and failures and an explanation of both. However, Muslims must not speak just to themselves, but to others, and they should explain to them their beliefs and demonstrate that the ideas they propose are beneficial to the whole of humanity. They should enter into a serious dialogue with the rest of the world on the issues that concern all men on earth, such as the problems of famine, nuclear proliferation and the environment. In other words, Muslims should concern themselves with global rather than parochial issues, and attempt to speak to the world in a common language which Muslims and non-Muslims share.[3]

The Vision and the Reality

From the beginning, the vision and ideals thus put forward faced serious problems when confronted with the reality. The apparent connection the magazine had with Saudi Arabia, and its very name, fed scepticism and the suspicion that the magazine was no more than a PR exercise for the oil-rich monarchy. At the same time, Muslims were not as united as the magazine had supposed about which message they wanted to present to the outside world. And it was here that Fathi's insistence on

---

[3] *Al-Umma*, Rabiʿ al-Awwal, 1406 AH (December 1985).

The Burden of the Muslim Intellectual

giving space to the largest possible number of diverse voices brought him into conflict with others who did not share his open-mindedness.

Consistent with its liberal inclinations, *Arabia* campaigned vigorously on human rights issues, and was adamantly opposed to all forms of dictatorship. Such radical and dictatorial secular regimes as those of Syria, Iraq, South Yemen and Libya faced overt and persistent criticism. Secular autocracies with slightly better human rights records (Egypt, Morocco, Jordan, Tunisia) received a more lenient treatment. The response to Islamically inclined autocracies was mixed. Iran was supported consistently but received criticisms, Pakistan received more criticisms than support and Sudan received criticism first and critical support later. But the magazine maintained a liberal and pluralist policy even on its editorial pages. Thus one could find articles expressing diverging points of view on some subjects in successive issues, and sometimes in the same issue.

The most dramatic example of this approach was the publication of a six-page report on Pakistan by Javed Ansari in June 1983. The article was severely critical of General Zia-ul-Haq's regime, prompting a full-page notice by the publishers the following month, disavowing the views expressed in the article in the name of the publishers and the Editor-in-Chief. But the publishers affirmed their commitment to free expression of opinions. And although they took issue with many points expressed by Ansari, they maintained that all writers on the magazine were free to express their views and publish them. Those opposed to these views will be given the opportunity to reply. And indeed Ansari continued to express his critical views in the magazine. But the continuation of 'Zia bashing' elicited from publisher Muhammad Salahuddin the unprecedented public criticism in his not-so-regular column 'Alternative Thoughts' in May 1985 where he wrote: 'I fail, as a journalist who is familiar with Pakistan's political scene, to understand the logic behind, and disagree with, most of the articles published in *Arabia* on Pakistan.' And he proceeded to offer point-by-point refutation of some of the pieces the magazine published. Later, Salahuddin tried to compensate for this perceived bias by a lengthy interview he personally conducted with president Zia, but he did not get the prominence he desired for the interview without a fight, since the Editor-in-Chief was opposed in principle to what might appear to be too close an association with autocratic regimes.

Another controversy erupted in early 1985, and this time Javed Ansari was on the opposite fence from his Editor-in-Chief Fathi Osman. The latter was enraged by the US stance on Sudan in the Spring of 1985, when a short visit by the then Vice-President George Bush in March resulted two days later in mass arrests of Islamists in Sudan and an apparent volte-face by the Nimeiri regime on its Islamization policies. Osman joined the radicals in lashing at the US. Quoting pro-US papers which reported that the crackdown on Islamists and the backtracking on Islamization were conditions for the resumption of US aid, Dr. Osman expressed the shock and dismay of liberals at the way the US was prepared to recommend extreme measures and support dictatorship and repression in order to extinguish Islamic activism. 'The US seems to prefer cooperation with dictators who can easily carry out American "advice" without constitutional or institutional hindrance,' he wrote. While the US tries hard to understand and accommodate Communism and accept the existence of Communist states in the Muslim world, it adamantly refuses to deal with political Islam:

> While Islam proved to be a dominant factor in the politics of Muslim countries, the West in general and the US in particular, insist on ignoring Islam as a political power...they cannot tolerate Islamic political activities either from the rulers or from the ruled...
>
> The US may claim that it is not against political Islam as such but against extremism and violence, but is there room in its policies for moderation and dialogue? Several Islamic movements – of whom the Sudanese movement and its leader, Dr. Turabi, represent a model – have tried to exclude all violent measures, rely only on political activities and open dialogue with the West to assure that the time for crusades from any side is over. But they are labelled, with all others who may use force, as fundamentalists! (*Arabia*, April 1985).

Fathi Osman's anguished *cris de coeur* was music to the ears of radicals like Dr. Javed Ansari, the former General and Economic Editor, who

The Burden of the Muslim Intellectual

was quick to fire an I-told-you-so letter from his Viennese exile. Ansari, the chief proponent of the radical view, had resigned in the Autumn of 1984 in protest against the way the establishment was run. He was a vocal and consistent critic of the liberal line espoused by the Editor-in-Chief Dr. Fathi Osman with tacit support from the publishers, even though he had been a beneficiary of Osman's liberalism, as the case of Pakistan revealed. Ansari found vindication for his stance in Dr. Osman's apparent disillusionment with the West. Osman's recognition of the futility of advances to the US, wrote Ansari, 'ought to be the beginning of a debate about the nature of Western civilization and the appropriate attitude of Muslims towards it.

'Muslim modernists in the tradition of Muhammad ʿAbduh – including Fathi Osman himself – have been attempting to engage the West in a protracted dialogue about issues which are of supposedly common interest. In [his article] Fathi Osman admits that this has remained a fruitless exercise.

'The reason for this failure is that Fathi Osman and his friends have been addressing the wrong people. They have attempted to develop an understanding with Western intellectuals, political leaders and opinion makers (particularly within the media) and religious scholars. But these people have the greatest interest in maintaining the West's present political and economic hegemony. They are also deeply contaminated by the major vices flourishing in the West.'

Ansari's counter-prescription was for the Muslims to exploit the inherent contradictions of Western society, which in theory advocates liberty, equality and prosperity in a society in which 'man is god', but in practice 'consists of turning men into self-centred, egotistical beasts willing to accept the dominant priviligentsia as long as the priviligentsia guarantees material well-being and prosperity.' Muslims should not waste their time in attempting to win over the élite wallowing in their vices and luxurious lifestyles, but address themselves to the 'millions of oppressed and dispossessed ordinary people who are increasingly bewildered and frustrated by the contradictions of social theory and social practice.' He concludes: 'Whereas there is a vital need for a dialogue with the West, we must address ourselves to the broad masses, not to the deaf, dumb and blind within these societies.' (*Arabia*, June 1985).

Fathi Osman replied in the same issue, castigating Ansari for importing 'Marxist concepts' into the dialogue, relying too much as he did on the role of contradictions in material interests. These ideas were not acceptable from the Islamic perspective, as Muslims had been instructed to carry their message to all people, regardless of race or class. They are required to do so peacefully, avoiding confrontation as much as possible. This precludes the advocacy of revolutionary methods such as those prescribed by Ansari. In addition one should not assume that Western societies are static. The appeal to the philosophical background of present Western societies misses the point by imposing on them the straitjacket of history. The truth is that many Western intellectuals question some of the basic philosophical assumptions of their civilization, and many are amenable to dialogue over these assumptions. The values of tolerance, justice and respect for human rights are not a mere camouflage. They are a practical aspect of Western societies that many Islamists can vouch for, especially those who have found refuge in the West from tyranny in their own countries.

The two controversies go to the core of what *Arabia*, and Islamic liberalism in general, was all about. The magazine had been launched in the optimistic view that the liberal values prevalent in the West and the modernizing influence of Islamic revivalism were going to push the West and the Muslim world closer together, a convergence that was going to be beneficial to both. But the problem with this vision, which Yamani outlined in his inaugural address at *Arabia*'s launch, was not only that it did not accord closely with reality, but that it was flawed from the beginning, and in more than one sense, mainly because it was not reciprocated by the supposed Western interlocutors. The passionate belief in an automatic convergence of vision and interests between Islam and the West appeared problematic and unfounded even in the pre-Gorbachev years. It was clear for many even then that the East-West contradictions on which this vision was based were not as irreducible as they appeared then. The ultimate absurdity of this vision was put into sharp focus by Henry Kissinger's ridicule of the

The Burden of the Muslim Intellectual

late Saudi King Faisal's reiteration of some of its ideological justifications in front of the Secretary of State during a visit by the latter to the Kingdom in the early 1970s.[4] If anything, this encounter must have impelled Kissinger to redouble his efforts to achieve détente with the Soviet Union.

In addition to the manifest self-contradiction of this vision, there was from the beginning an ambiguity over whether *Arabia* was addressing the West or the Muslims. Yamani's intervention in the second issue entitled 'The roots of Saudi society' embodied this ambiguity. Overtly, it was addressed to the West, explaining how Islam was central to the Saudi self-perception and the Kingdom's role in the world. The article urged the West to understand Islam, to correct its misperceptions of the Muslims by adopting a more objective and sympathetic attitude and to review its stance on Palestine to win the hearts of the Muslims. It emphasized the common bonds that united Islam and Christianity and the common interests that united the West and the Muslims. Behind these overt arguments lay another, deeper meaning. In this other sense the statement by Yamani was an intervention in an internal Saudi debate, at a time when the historical commitment to Islam and the traditional friendship with the US and the West were both being questioned by radical secularists inside and outside the kingdom and, more seriously, by new Islamic radicalism championed by the Islamic revolution in Iran, which was gaining in popularity, and by the Kingdom's own Sunnī hard-liners. Yamani was thus speaking to several audiences on several issues. But the central pillar of his argument was an appeal to the West to rescue his brand of 'moderate' pro-Western Islam by showing some sympathy and understanding, arguing that it will be in the interest of the West to do so, since the alternative could be the rise of anti-Western radicalism or even Communism.

This view was reiterated again and again by leading Muslim intellectuals who contributed to the magazine. And at first the publication appeared on target towards achieving its goal of engaging the West in

---

4 Henry Kissinger, *The Years of Upheaval*, Weidenfeld Nicolson and Michael Joseph, London, 1982, p.661.

some kind of real dialogue. Its contributors were heavyweight intellectuals, usually liberal, living in the West and often occupying leading positions in academic institutions or other important organs. Some leading non-Muslim intellectuals were also enlisted. Professors Edward Said and Richard P. Mitchell addressed the meeting organized to celebrate *Arabia*'s launch and thereafter figured repeatedly on the pages of the magazine, mainly through interviews. Others, like Peter Mansfield, a former British ambassador in the Middle East and leading Arabist, actually joined the magazine's staff. Many others contributed in various ways.

But this stance did not go unchallenged. Even in one very early issue where Yamani was busy expounding and arguing this viewpoint (December 1981), some dissenting voices started to be heard. Thus we find in that month Javed Ansari challenging this perception of things. In an article entitled 'Forward from Liberalism' he rejects the position of economists who wanted to support a synthesis of either socialist or capitalist ideas with Islam.

The struggle between Islam and the dominant Western civilization is part of the continuing conflict between religion and materialism. The central problem of Islamic economics must be the creation of a policy framework which increases the social power and political viability of a group committed to a rejection of materialist values.[5]

Ansari goes on to challenge a cherished idea of Yamani's: the advocacy of a synthesis of Islamic and Western economic values. Instead, he argues that an Islamic economy cannot be created by marginal changes in existing systems '[n]or can it through the creation of public and private sector institutions to enhance the bargaining power of Muslims in international commodity and factor markets.'

Challenges also came from other quarters. Even from its early issues, the magazine found its letter pages cluttered with attacks on its liberal line, deemed too pro-Western by readers. This was a side effect of its marketing strategy that targeted primarily Muslim readers. At that time, Muslim readers were mainly the Islamically-inclined students and

---

[5] *Arabia*, December 1981, p.82.

The Burden of the Muslim Intellectual

activists in the West, or Muslim activists in the Muslim world. This sector was then in no mood for pro-Western compromise. At a time when the US and leading Western countries were engaged in a head-on fight with the forces of Islamic revival from Indonesia to Morocco, not to forget Iran, advocates of cooperation with the West were miserably lonely. US support for Israel and its disastrous Lebanon campaign, and its alliance with too many corrupt autocratic regimes all over the Muslim world, caused anger and resentment among many Muslims.

The magazine found itself forced to adopt a defensive posture, repeatedly justifying and explaining its stance. It also found the gap increasingly widening between its editorial pages, which advocated cooperation with the West, and its reporting, which graphically described how Western policies were laying to waste practically the whole of the Muslim world, and how leading Western powers were waging war on the Islamic revival. However, Fathi Osman maintained his optimism both as regards to the viability of liberalism and the utility of cooperation with the West. He appeared to be put off by the West only when the West was not truly itself: when it was not Western and liberal enough. This is the abiding crisis for all Muslim liberals. How can one have a rapport with the West when it appears to be doing less than justice, not to say flagrantly violating, its own value system when it comes to dealing with the Muslim world?

To complicate things more, another line of attack was launched by disillusioned liberals who were upset because the magazine did not live up to its initial liberal promise. This line was represented by, among others, Dr. Hashem Sharif (from California) who wrote in November 1985 attacking *Arabia* for supporting Islamic regimes in Iran, Sudan and elsewhere in clear contradiction to the Editor's commitment to the liberal ethos and human rights:

> Has 'Islam' become a ready-made mantle to cloak crimes against the dignity of human beings, against their freedom to think, to speak, to live? It is poignant that, while hailing the application of 'Shariʿah' in Saudi Arabia, Iran, Pakistan or the Sudan, you have preferred to enjoy the protection of 'kaffir' [infidel] laws in England in your publishing endeavour.

In his reply, Fathi Osman wrote: 'It may be significant that while some of our readers find us too "liberal" and even "odd" in deviating from the ideas prevalent among committed Muslims, including those who are associated with current Islamic movements in several countries, others find us in need of more reformation (*iṣlāḥ*) and renovation (*tajdīd*).' Dr. Osman implied that this dual attack could be taken as a sign that the magazine was indeed treading the right path. But it would have been more realistic to conclude that the magazine, it appeared, was liked by no one. This was more so since the liberal attacks also reflected another problem. As the magazine's finances worsened, the quality of its editorial content declined, ushering in a spiral that could only lead downhill. Material constraints, no less than ideological ones, thus prevented the magazine from giving a true and full expression to its potential.

Under pressure from its readers, publishers and some of the staff, the magazine witnessed a shift towards more radicalism. But in spite of this progressive radicalization, it maintained its lively and pluralistic approach to the end. Its increased radicalism coincided with more determined input from its critics, especially in the Forum section, which accommodated a wide variety of viewpoints. It was clear, though, that the magazine suffered from a lack of focus. But its predominant shortcomings were technical. It was simply not well equipped enough in terms of personnel and material resources, and could not afford to be. But the dilemmas it faced with regard to its conflicting ideological orientations severely taxed its already meagre resources and made its task that much harder. The ideological handicap was thus enhanced and compounded by the technical and financial straitjacket.

The practice of open disputes over editorial policy was itself criticized by many who saw in it a sign of disarray in the publication, where the publishers appear to be unable to control their magazine. But for Fathi Osman, who staunchly supported the right of staff to express divergent views and protected them from the wrath of the publishers, this was the ultimate expression of the democratic ethos he so vehemently espoused. And the editorial freedom enjoyed by the staff was indeed admirable, compensating significantly for the problems they faced elsewhere.

The Burden of the Muslim Intellectual

After *Arabia*

Eventually, *Arabia* was forced to close down in 1987, due to a series of financial and managerial crises compounded by adverse political circumstances affecting its main markets and sources of finance. Fathi Osman then moved to the US, where he continued to engage in teach-ing and research in several institutions, including the University of Southern California, the Islamic Center of Southern California, the Center for Muslim-Christian Understanding at George Washington University, Washington, DC and the Islamic University of Malaysia. Since then he has published quite a few books, including *The Children of Adam* (1996); *Jihad: A Legitimate Struggle for Human Rights* (1991); *Muslim Women in the Family and Society* (n.d.); *Fi'l-Tajribah al-Siyā-siyyah li'l-Ḥarakah al-Islāmiyyah al-Muʿāṣirah* (On the Political Experience of the Contemporary Islamic Movement, n.d.).

The list of Fathi Osman's publications is long and varied, running into hundreds if we include his papers and articles, and is still growing. But the thrust of his thought centres on the idea of human rights. He has argued consistently for democracy, freedom and respect of individual rights from an Islamic perspective, and spoke against all forms of authoritarianism and abuse of power. The novelty of Osman's approach resides in the fact that while most earlier Islamic writers who touched on the issue of human rights did so from the perspective of apologetics, labouring to demonstrate that Islam had espoused human rights and justice long before the West, his perspective and motive were different. His concern was not to demonstrate how the Islamic perspective was great, but to really *make* it so. He discusses human rights and justice with a view to how they could be promoted and protected. 'I believe,' he writes, 'that human rights and human dignity must be the cornerstone of the call for Islam among the contemporary masses.' Human rights must also be the basis of any modern Islamic state, he adds (*Fi'l-Tajribah*, p.16). In another contribution (see his paper in this volume) he reiterates his firm belief that Muslims should not have a problem with the concept of human rights in principle, and downplays the divergence between the Islamic perspective and that of the universal perception of human rights. The problem appears to be rather, in implementation, he argues. It is the liberal Muslim's dilemma once more. Will the (supposed) forces of liberalism in the Muslim world and in the West, put their money where their mouths are and support genuine, universal human rights? 'Can the developed countries which lecture [others] on human rights resist the temptation of exploitation and its fast gains to extend a hand for real development of those who need it, a hand which will have the long-term rewards of the whole world? Can they go beyond their short-term and short-sighted strategic and economic policies of supporting undemocratic regimes, to say the least?' The questions are themselves heavily loaded with scepticism, but Osman makes it clear that the world has no hope if the whole of humanity cannot join hands to promote equal rights for all.

Osman urges the Muslims not to be discouraged by the apparent double-dealing of the major powers, calling on them to take a lead in promoting human rights. The Muslims must reach out positively to others, and 'talk the common language of the world,' even if this meant a rethinking of traditional Muslim terms and concepts. They must put themselves at the heart of the emerging universal global community, and not isolate themselves within their own traditions.

While Fathi has always regarded himself as belonging to the broad Islamic trend, he has maintained a healthy distance between himself and specific Islamic groups. In his writings, he adopts the perspective of the Islamic groups even when he was criticizing their stance. He is very cautious, in spite of his innovative ideas, and is careful to support every major statement he makes by an appropriate quote from the Qur'ān. In some of his writings, there is more than one quote in every paragraph. Fathi's familiarity with the Qur'ān and tradition is legendary. Even in a casual conversation he could marshal quotes and citations from every conceivable traditional discipline. However, while Fathi recognizes the contribution of the major Islamic groups, including the Muslim Brotherhood to which he once adhered, he has become increasingly convinced of late that these movements might have outlived their usefulness and could have possibly become a hindrance to the Islamic revival rather than its locomotive. He believes that they should be replaced by broad coalitions espousing democratization and human rights so that the intellectual side of the Islamic revival may flourish in a healthy atmosphere.

This brings us to the core of his perception of his own role, that of the committed intellectual who wants to act as a moral beacon for the community. Unlike political parties that may be forced by the necessities of political expediency to compromise, the committed intellectual brooks no compromise. While Fathi, in line with his own disposition, is quite tolerant of various stances, Islamic and otherwise, there are some areas where he is not prepared to compromise, especially in the realm of human rights and respect for them. In fact he argues in his short essay on *jihād* that the only instance where struggle is legitimate is when one is faced with oppression and loss of human rights. That is where he believes all men must make their stand.

Conclusion

It may be too early to assess the impact of Fathi Osman's contribution to renaissance of Islamic thought, but there is no denying that he has been seen by a whole generation of Muslim activists as a beacon of commitment and enlightenment in times of difficulty and turmoil. It is of the nature of such contributions to take time before their full impact could be known. When Fathi Osman began to blaze this trail in the fifties, he was a lone voice. At that time, the political field was dominated by the schism between liberals on one side, and Islamists on the other. Liberal Islamists sounded like a contradiction in terms. As things developed, the 'liberals' became the new despots or their sycophants, while the Islamists were consigned to prisons and exile. The natural outcome of this state of affairs would have been to turn Islamists into liberals and supporters of human rights. However, what happened was quite the reverse. The Islamist trends became dominated by angry and intolerant groups. However, a slow development was taking place elsewhere, with a broadening current of liberal Islamists, at times embracing whole movements, as is the case in Tunisia and Malaysia. This was partly due to the influence of voices like those of Fathi Osman, and it also shows that he had anticipated a trend that is going to dominate Islamic thinking in the future. For it is the condition of survival for Islamism.

9

Summary of the Open Debate

Report by JOHN L. ESPOSITO

THE SECOND DAY *of the conference witnessed a lively debate over the key issues touched on by the speakers, as well as expressing many of the concerns of the participants. We give below a summary of the discussion, which was chaired by Professor John Esposito of Georgetown University. The panellists were: Abdolkarim Soroush (Iran), Tarek al-Bechri (Egypt), Dr. Fathi Osman, Professor Louis Cantori (University of Maryland), Professor Tamara Sonn, Mr Abdel-Halim Hoffman (Germany) and Professor François Burgat (France).*

John Esposito
As I look out and see so many friends – I would like to say old friends, but I am getting to an age where I don't like using the word 'old' – I thought how much this is a testimony to the importance of this event. If nothing else, I am sure, for many of us, when we first received the invitation, we thought: another conference, but then we realized who the organizers were, and more importantly, who this conference was to honour. It seems to me that the theme of the conference is most appropriate, Islam and Modernity. For, as was said yesterday by Fathi Osman, ABIM and Ennahda represent, from my point of view, organizations or movements *par excellence* who have grappled with the question of the relationship of Islam to Modernity. The founders of the organizations, and the current leaders embody this approach, and we have seen that already in some of the presentations that have occurred, for example Shaikh Rashid's presentation yesterday.

Open Debate

But I can think of no scholar today who epitomizes in his life and work what this conference is about than Fathi Osman. He embodies what to me it means to be a true scholar, a true intellectual. I like to say an intellectual activist, that is someone who speaks to reality, someone who may study and know the past, but relates it to today and attempts to have an impact on today. If we look at his career – and others have referred to it so I am going to be brief – think about what he managed to embody in such a short period of time. To be a scholar who has taught all over the world, in the Muslim world and the West; and to have that kind of impact, to be someone whose writings are known all over the world; to be someone who until recently, I would say, would seem to be in every conference all over the world. I said to someone, I first got to know Fathi Osman, not so much from his writings, but from the fact that I would be in a hotel lobby almost any place in the Muslim world, and I would see Fathi sitting across the way. And that is how I would know that there was a conference in that city or that country. He is so prominent and so much in demand that whether you are talking about West Africa or Southeast Asia, or any place in the United States, there he is. To have been the editor of *Arabia*, and to bring together the remarkable team, and listening yesterday to one of his former 'reporters' talking about the way in which he ran that magazine in an open way, so that you had tension between the editor and the publishers, and the publishers and the writers, but that kind of freedom is allowed, I think that is a testimony to who he is. That, in other words, he embodies what he writes or what he says.

I can say that we were delighted in the experience that we had with Fathi at Georgetown because, in addition to bringing his scholarship, he embodied what I see as a special characteristic, and it is a very curious one. He is a genuinely nice person, and for academics, that is not always there. He says what he thinks, but it never really gets personal. You almost get suspicious. How can someone be so frank and straightforward and be so nice? There must be something that is happening here, at least for those who have been around academia enough. The audiences that he has addressed, therefore, have been multiple. His interpretation – and in fact interpretations I would say – of Islam are remarkable. Throughout his life, he has been addressing the issues that fall under the umbrella of 'Islam and Modernity'. He has not been afraid to speak out, and at times very courageously. But, more importantly, he has not been afraid to change his mind. That is the other thing that becomes difficult when you really establish a body of work. There are two things that I have noticed. One is, you establish a way of seeing the world and people respond to it, but the real test is whether or not you can later on say, getting into self-criticism, I made some mistakes and I need to correct them. The other test is to realize when you are at a conference and you begin to notice that the only person you really like listening to is yourself, that maybe there is a bit of a problem there too. But Fathi would not be that kind of person. He would not have that problem. People like myself tend to. So I think it is important that we are here and that we have honoured him. But I think that this round table is perhaps the best way to honour him, because our charge this morning is to really engage many of the issues that were raised yesterday, and to do so in an honest and open discussion and even debate, among ourselves, and also with the audience.

It seems to me that the challenge is to really address some of the key issues raised yesterday and push them. Yesterday we heard ourselves discussing, re-examining ideas of the nature of the state, legitimacy, non-Muslims, pluralism, women, many of these are very hot issues. Our challenge though, it seems to me, is to be very honest in pushing them. Yesterday, we were not. From my point of view, we had some very good speakers, we had some honest discussions, but a lot of people were pretty polite. There is no way everybody in this audience agreed with everything that was said yesterday – whether we were talking about the nature of the state, or whether we were talking about *ḥijāb* – at least not in my experience in listening to these topics discussed.

So what I suggest today is that we take on some of these issues and really try to push them, in terms of not only ideas, but also how we have seen them played out. Has the Islamic movement hit a blind alley with regard to some of these ideas? Are there areas for self-criticism? If so, what are these? I think all of these issues are up for grabs. To lead off, I will open it up to any one of my colleagues who wishes to begin.

Open Debate

Saad Jabbar
I have a few points and I will be brief. First, it is very unfortunate that this conference is being held under the title Islam and Modernity, and there was no woman speaker. But as the organizers have involved so many women at the door, and a female chairperson, I might say this time that we may forgive the organizers. The second point is that yesterday, I think, we heard very good papers, and for the first time, even though I attend many conferences and round tables, I heard people – or at least those counted in the Islamic movement – speak with some frankness. However, I think that the Islamic movement and thinkers have not yet addressed issues of politics and Islam, especially *vis-à-vis* Islam and party politics, although Rashid al-Ghannoushi touched on that yesterday. But I think that in this age, especially with the new technology, with the communication explosion, the Islamists should think again. They have to provide very good information, and not to stick to the ancient 'yellow' books, because there are many people who talk in abstractions. I think that Dr. Fathi Osman, from what I heard about him yesterday and today, really tried to address these issues. For the Islamists to be part of this world locally, regionally, and interna- tionally, they have to address the issue of how to do things. What are we going to do about democracy? Are we going to say it is '*kufr*' like many people do? Are we going to say there are general principles, there are fundamental principles, but when it comes to the instruments, to the procedures, we are free to innovate. I think Dr. Zaki Badawi touched on this.

Louis Cantori
I would like to address the question of the concept of modernity, from a critical point of view in terms of the position a number of people took yesterday in their presentations. I think they essentially adopted the liberal perspective of modernity. So to begin with saying that, today, modernity belongs to us all. There was perhaps a time when it was Western, but now it is globalized, it is a global phenomenon. But we, as people sitting in this room, as believers – I don't want to be misunderstood, I am a Christian, I am not a Muslim – but as believers,

we want to adopt a religious point of view. We have to see the world from a religious perspective. But as intellectuals, we also have to distance ourselves from the subject of religion in order to look at the subject of religion from a more critical perspective as well, to examine it and to evaluate it. And this is what I am concerned about: that we need to be careful when we approach the subject of modernity not to uncritically accept the Enlightenment principles that accompany the concepts, the ideology and the philosophy that accompanies them. This ideology is one of individualism, of secularism, of a weak state, of the fragmentation of power, of confrontation and conflict as a model, and so on and so forth. I am critical of that model. But I think the most important thing is that we need to be aware that it is a model. So even if you are adopting that point of view, it is important to understand more self-consciously that is what we are doing. Because then we can better express ourselves in a meaningful way about one's religion when we deal with this topic.

I wanted to contrast points of view about the subject of modernity. I would suggest the following, that is, unless you are very specific and very simple, modernity seems to have as part of its baggage an emphasis on individualism, to begin with, and secondly some formula for secularism. I would suggest that what we need is a different perspective that I would call 'conservative' (*muḥāfiẓ*). This perspective is one that exists in fact in the Western world philosophically, identified with [the British philosopher] Edmund Burke and Hegel, the German philosopher, and Hegel's concept of 'corporatism' (or *takāfulīyah* in Arabic). This perspective is one I find a persuasive alternative for the following reason: if the modernity of the West is one of individualism, the reality of the Islamic world is the family, or in other words, it is the unit of analysis, the institution that takes precedence over everything else. The individual is subordinated to the family within Islam, according to the teachings of religion and in the sense of practice.

Secondly, it goes without saying that, within Islam, one is not going to accept secularism. It is just contradictory to the mission and to the reality of the religion. Therefore, what I would argue for is necessarily a different current, a different way of looking at things. Once one

Open Debate

adopts these different assumptions, one then becomes critical of the ideology and the philosophy surrounding the Enlightenment. One begins, for example, to look at the concept of democratization which is obviously a dominant concept, properly so in the Middle East and the Islamic world today, and ask: is this democracy one of one man, one vote, or is it the democracy of the *shūrā*, or as some people call it 'shuracracy'. In other words, is it the democracy of consultation, and representation through consultation? Is it the democracy of the political class, which is another reality of the Middle East and of the Islamic society? Or is it a democracy, for example, where there is a more top-down, rather than bottom-up [structures]? The Enlightenment perspective on all of this is always to go 'bottom-up', because they want to deny the state, they want to deny the concentration of power, and so on and so forth, whereas the reality of the Islamic world is exactly the opposite. So when you begin to adopt these conservative concepts, it leads you in logical terms to quite different interpretations. It does not mean that the Islamic state needs to be less democratic, but I would suggest that it needs a different democratic formula, because the question of mass participation is also there. But the reality of the Middle East today is that we seek mass participation, so-called presidential elections and so on. These are not elections of course. By definition, these are samplings of opinion in order to legitimize the government in power. I think the challenge to Islam is to think about the subject of democracy the way I am suggesting from a critical point of view, and to improve on the practice, but I think it is very important to understand the theory and the reality of top-down. It is just simply different, and I think it is very important that it looks this way.

I would conclude this kind of suggestion on my part by addressing a subject that I am thinking a great deal about at the present time, and that's the question of economic productivity. A number of economists, including a very outstanding one of the World Bank, has been doing some writings and lectures under the title 'Why not the Middle East?' In 1965, the per capita income of Syria and Japan was the same as Thailand and Malaysia, and today the per capita income of those countries is less than it was in 1965 in the Middle East, and it is ten times greater in Asia, among the so-called dragons, or little dragons, or little tigers. I think there is a reason for that, and I am basing this partly on some research that I am doing on privatization in Morocco. But I think the reason is that Islam needs to think about this issue critically. And the critical issue is: is there within the Islamic theory of economics a sense of the public, a sense of public responsibility? And I think one other thing that has been happening along with this Enlightenment theme that I have been talking about: the discovery that Adam Smith is not rele-vant to the Middle East, and is not relevant to Asians. The Asians now are increasingly talking about the 'Asian Way', one that is based on solidarity and the homogeneity of society. It is the disciplining of so-ciety for the purposes of achieving national objectives. But the way I understand the subject presently is that, as far as Islamic economics is concerned, the issue of Islamic economics is not *ribā* (interest). That is an archaic concern. It is understandably an important theological issue. The real issue ought to be productivity, however. How can we increase per capita growth in the Middle East? I am suggesting that we need to pay attention to theorizing in terms of Islamic economic theory in such a way as to establish a public identity and a public res-ponsibility. Germany happens to be an example of the kind of country I am talking about, and certainly Malaysia, which is a very interesting Islamic example. And, by the way, the Malaysians happen to be quite self-conscious and very aware of what I am saying, because I have heard and spoken with a few Muslim Malaysian leaders. They have adopted the Confucian system in Malaysia. So I would suggest that is a very interesting point of reference for people, for the Muslims to be looking at. They say we value our Chinese minority because we have learnt how to conduct our economic affairs on the model of the Chi-nese and the Asian model. What happens in the Middle East by con-trast is a neglect of this very capital. Islam has too quickly embraced what is called in French *capitalisme sauvage*. They want to show how Islamic economics is the same as that of the West. What I am suggest-ing is that in fact it is inappropriate; it is as socially irresponsible as Western capitalism is itself – or at least the American version of it. And what is needed is social responsibility, and that comes from these conservative principles I am talking about, but it is in practice in Germany for various historical reasons, and in Asia.

What happens in the Middle East instead is a practice that affirms the priority of politics and regime survival, so that economics becomes subordinated to the particular individuals or the particular groups in power. We therefore pay little or no attention to, for example, industrial planning. It just does not happen, and if it does happen, it is because the IMF or the World Bank says if you do not engage in this planning, you will not get a reduction in your debt. Egypt or Morocco will then go along dutifully with what the IMF or the World Bank wants. It is usual, but they do it rhetorically, and they hardly ever do it sincerely, and that is because the name of the game, as usual, is politics and not economic advancement or productivity. These are some thoughts that I wanted to share with you. I think I will conclude by suggesting we ask ourselves the intellectual question: whose modernity, whose paradigm? What set of assumptions are we bringing to bear when we think about modernity as intellectuals? What I tried to share with you are some critical perspectives that suggest that a great deal of thought needs to be given to the alternative to the liberal set of principles that accompany the concept of modernity. Thank you.

Tamara Sonn
I will have to split Professor Cantori's comments into two subjects: one is the question of modernity, the other is economics. I will not deal with economics, but I feel compelled to address the question of the terminology we have been using. We have to prevent ourselves from being cast into the past. The very title of the conference is 'Islam and Modernity'. Modernity does not have a positive image in Western academia at present, as I am sure you are aware, although I don't think the presentations yesterday made it clear that this group is aware of the negative image of modernity in Western academia. Modernity in general is not considered a set of ideologies primarily. There are ideologies associated with modernity, but modernity as it is being discussed in Western academia now, deals primarily with methods of interpretation, and that is what I would like to focus on in my comment.

Rethinking Islam and Modernity

Pre-modernity, as we learn in Western universities, that is European-American universities nowadays, was a period during which primary authority was granted to the Church; certainty was derived from Church teachings. Modernity was a revolution against pre-modernity, whereby the primary authority of the Church was separated from political and intellectual life. It wasn't abandoned altogether. The certainty and the authority accorded to the Church, were relegated to the personal level, so that religion became a personal thing. One did not have to abandon the certainty of moral teachings, but one kept them to oneself. Modernity was a period during which primary authority in the public sphere was granted to science, to reason. Post-modernity came along, in reaction to that period, questioning the certainty according to reason in the period of modernity. In modernity, under certain circumstances, philosophers taught us that human beings could not be absolutely certain that the processes of their reasoning would end up with absolute certainty. Unfortunately for most of the world, among those certainties that Western intellectuals came up with was that Christians were better than non-Christians, that white people were better than non-white people, that white people have a burden or a mission to civilize the non-Christian and non-white world which was the Southern hemisphere for the most part. It was in reaction to those kinds of atrocities permitted in the name of rational certainty that post-modern thinkers arose.

I want to focus on the question of interpretation. Post-modern thinkers, (Derrida in particular, and Foucault, to name two) wanted to question the processes by which those certainties were achieved, looking at the text of modernity. The texts of modernity, the ones that carried basically Orientalism among other things, were considered to be authoritative and they were the basis of political decisions that were atrocious in the view of modern thinkers. Colonialism was based on the certainties according to human reason in modern thinking, or modern misthinking. So post-modern thinkers want to question the processes by which these decisions were made, they want to question the texts upon which these political decisions were made. Questioning the text, questioning the authority of human reason, is the hallmark of post-modernity. So I think that is what we have to be aware of.

There are, of course, ideologies concerned with, or connected with, modernity as well as post-modernity. Professor Elmessiri yesterday pointed out some of the ideologies associated with both. I think he focused more on ideologies associated with post-modernity, but those I think have to be looked at separately. Those are by-products. The actual process of questioning texts, which is the hallmark of post-modernity, is something that I think contemporary Islamic thinkers have in common, which has in fact paved the way for in the modern world. It is in this context that I think that the bifurcation of the world into West and non-West collapses. In fact, among the analyzes we heard yesterday, let me point to some of them: 'Look at the text with suspicion', Professor Osman mentioned; Shaikh al-Ghannoushi, talking about the reform of thinking; Fahmi Huweidi talking about differences of opinion being not only allowed, but expected in Islam; Zaki Badawi talking about a sociology of *fiqh*. These are the kinds of things that Islam has incorporated from the very beginning of its institutionalization, and these are revived in the contemporary world. These are the hallmark of contemporary Islam, and they have far more in common with post-modern thinking than with modernist thinking. I don't know if this is a very interesting point, but I think it is very important to be clear on our terminology, because when certain Western academics look at a title like 'Islam and Modernity', they may believe that they will be looking at authoritarian structures. Their immediate response to modernity is: Oh, dictatorship of the mind.

Contemporary Islam is not concerned with dictatorship of the mind. In fact it is concerned with dismantling political dictatorships through rethinking the texts or interpretations upon which those dictatorships are based. Questions of secularism, individualism, separation of church and state, these are secondary issues, as I think Fathi Osman was very clear yesterday in pointing out. Individualism is something that comes with industrialization and the breakdown of the standard family. These questions can be dealt with within Islam, they are well incorporated in Islamic principles. So we need not concern ourselves primarily with those, but concern ourselves instead with methods of interpretation. Questioning the text is post-modern in Euro-modern academia. Questioning the text is contemporary in Islamic thought, but it has been part of *ijtihādī* thinking from the beginning of institutionalization of Islam.

John Esposito

I just want to add one or two observations. One is that all this was interesting. The second observation is that one of the things that I have been amazed at over the years is how Muslims, like many of my Jewish and Christian friends, slip into equating Islam with their interpretation of Islam, so that rather than saying you have Islam, then you have multiple interpretations or multiple discourses, usually each individual somehow manages to say in effect, 'I am right,' which means: 'You are wrong.' An example of that is what we sometimes see today, when some of those who talk about Islamization also advocate what I call an alternative policy of 'kufrization': if you disagree with me, you are guilty of *kufr* (infidelity), whether you are a Muslim or a non-Muslim. That then falls on a very authoritarian kind of concept that always gets in the way. Many of those Muslims who say it will always, when talking to a Western audience, want to say: 'Islam has *Ikhtilāf* (diversity)'. It has always recognized difference. But usually it is 'my' difference that is the authoritative one.

Ibrahim Moosa

I have three comments. One concerns freedom, or the lack of it, in the Muslim world generally. I know I am going to be incoherent in these points, but I will say things that hopefully the panellists would pick up for discussion. One finds, as shown by the case of Nasr Hamid Abū Zayd [Egyptian thinker], persecution for a whole variety of reasons. In Iran, I think, one of the panellists has been subjected to intellectual scrutiny. In other parts in South East Asia, intellectuals feel very uncomfortable in universities that are supposed to bring about the new type of intellectual renaissance. I think that there must be a strategy on the part of a forum such as this one, to continuously and relentlessly

Open Debate

make this space available for Muslim intellectuals to think, and I believe it is not people like myself – loud mouths – that are going to make an impact. It is people who have a track record, who are weighty individuals, and who should continue speaking about this in every forum. Sometimes one keeps quiet in the interest of politeness or decorum, but I believe, as someone said, evil flourishes when good people do nothing. That continues in the vein of what Tamara Sonn has said, dictatorship of the mind, and the whole question of re-thinking and critical thinking in Islamic thought. There is a lot of dictatorship of the mind because, I think, intellectual critiques are not taking place.

Movements like Ennahda or ABIM might want to start the re-thinking. But the mainstream Islamist thinking, including the modern Islamist paradigm, is not engaged in real re-thinking. One of my concerns about this whole thing is: are there ways of confronting, on a whole variety of fronts, new taboos? For example if you look at debates in the last part of the nineteenth century and the twentieth century, modernity was something that was attacked by everybody. Children going to English schools, or women going to school for the first time in Egypt, were attacked. We are now beginning to create a new language of taboos. Now modernity, post-modernity, all these are but names of periods and eras that had some particular consequences intellectually and materially. I am just concerned that we start to condemn post-modernism as the road towards nihilism, because people said equally bad things about modernity when it came out. And I think we are engaging in giving terminology and names that disable intellectual conversation.

This leads me to the question of *Ikhtilāf* that someone has just raised. To what extent can people say: we can have differences, but there must be boundaries. One of my students asked me what are the boundaries of re-thinking? I said there were none. It is the context that will determine the boundaries, but philosophically and intellectually, there are no boundaries. But I have to put my foot down now: that is my boundary. I have to address the question of women in the mosque, or organ transplantation, that is my contextual boundary. The limitations of my knowledge, the limitations to my consequences, that is my boundary. But there is no theoretical boundary. Many people want to put the boundary at ʿaqīdah, dogma, or the boundaries drawn out by Ibn Kathīr, or any other type of interpretation, or that the text can only be interpreted in those forms which have been outlined by classical authorities. Even the explanations presented by the classical exegists are open to negotiation, to re-interpretation, and to creating new interpretations again. Obviously on the same point, I heard the question being asked if we must separate between Islam and Muslims. I believe that is a type of an 'opt-out presentation'. We must take responsibility for what we do, because I think as long as we maintain this distinction: Islam is good, but Muslims are bad, it leads to a type of dualism that leads to moral inactivity. For example, is it conceivable to have Islam without Muslims? No one can go to that type of Hegelian understanding that Islam is conceivable without Muslims in a utopian way. We can only talk about Islam in the world that exists. Islam is inconceivable without Muslims, and Muslims are inconceivable without Islam.

All this leads to the question of strategies of reform, what form they should take. Often when you engage in critical issues, you would get advice that you should not push it too far; the time is not yet right. Well, I ask the question: when is the time going to be right? I hope that some of you will address this question. Then we come to the issue of the type of Islam that we are engaged in and re-thinking. We have to know that when we go out of these halls, there are people who are going to say that this is CIA Islam, this is American Islam, these are traitors and so on and so forth. Obviously, it is only when we start making a lot of noise that people will ascribe some type of seriousness to this type of thinking. We have to really address the marketplace of ideas. I have a lot of faith in the people here and a great deal of respect for their work, and I believe that they can make an impact, and not allow the space for other interpretations to completely dominate the marketplace of ideas.

The second point I am making touches on the question of translation of concepts. I often hear people talking about shūrā, equating it with democracy; ʿaqd, the type of social contract of early Islam, equating it with the social contract of Rousseau and others; creating a type of analogy between the rights and obligations in pre-modern Islamic understanding of rights and obligations to rights as entitlements, because in modern human rights, you have rights *qua* human. Just because you are a human being, you have certain rights. That is the philosophical underpinning of the Universal Declaration of Human Rights. It might not turn out like that in legal terms, but the philosophical underpinnings, and that is the crux of the debate, hinge on you having rights *qua* human in the modern human rights debate. The Islamic declaration of human rights and other Muslim interpretations talk about rights and obligations. My question is when we engage in those intellectual questions, the type of quantum leap that they make from pre-modern, or from 1400 years ago, or what happened in the first 500–600 years of Islam, to use that as an analogy and make a kind of intellectual jump, I think it creates a number of gaps. It creates a problem in the type of terminology and language of that debate. I believe that it can help to say that there was an elementary notion of that value, but that we need to re-make that notion right now. But many times you see young Muslims out there who want to have confidence that Islam has the answers, that 'Islam is the solution' and so on. It becomes a type of psychological armament, psychological armour, but when he or she is faced with the hard questions, that person is destroyed. That means that the intellectual must go beyond this type of superficial analogy that they create between early concepts and contemporary concepts.

John Esposito
Ideas do not have an impact unless they enter the marketplace and unless they are aggressively put out into the marketplace. Otherwise, it seems to be an occasion for old friends to get together, to look at each other and to agree and everybody has a nice meal and goes away feeling good about themselves.

Bashir Nafi͑
Well, yesterday there was a very important point of agreement between Shaikh Rashid and Dr. Fathi Osman. As these two prominent

Muslim scholars agreed, it can be considered a point of consensus and a point of certainty, though I am going to listen to Tamara Sonn and try to become post-modernist today. Between the state and society in the Islamic experience, we would have to understand the role of other institutions. Of course, there was a kind of transformation between the Madinah state and the Umayyad and Abbasid states. But there is no need to discuss the model of the Madinah state and the departure from the model in the following centuries. What happened is that the ʿulamāʾ of Islam were not only guardians of Sharīʿah, were not only guardians of revelation and the text, but there was a much larger role that the ʿulamāʾ played. The ʿulamāʾ were at the same time guardians of the societal basis. The ʿulamāʾ were in charge of education, of the market, of artisanal associations. The ʿulamāʾ also succeeded in depriving the state of the right of legislation, which is the most powerful instrument in the modern state, in the modern civilized state. That model, the Islamic model, is not, as many people might think, a reflection of a condition of underdeveloped societies which do not have a competent system of communication. For, several centuries before the emergence of Islam, legislation, the right of legislation was in the hands of the Roman state, and was in the hands of the Greek state. The Islamic experience was unique, in that the society led by the ʿulamāʾ kept pushing the state into the corner, be it a caliph, a corrupt caliph, a dictatorship, or whatever, good or bad, it was always confined to a small part of the Muslim life.

Louis Cantori has been saying that the state in the Middle East and the Muslim world had always been powerful. The state was powerful, but also confined, because society controlled most of its field of action. The problem here is that we are looking at the Islamic experience from the perspective of our times, because implicit in the contemporary Islamic historians is the idea of Islamization of the traditional state, Islamizing the Iranian state, etc. by (as Fahmi Huweidi said yesterday) injecting Islamic values. I do not know if anything can be Islamized by injection: Islamizing the Egyptian state, for example, by injecting Islamic Sharīʿah, as some people say, is not going to work. You cannot Islamize a thunderstorm. You cannot Islamize an octopus. I mean that the state as a social organization is the nearest thing in human history to a natural phenomenon, and the only way to Islamize a state is actually to limit the power of the state, to confine the state to the corner.

Rafik Bouchlaka

The dominant perception within Western academic circles, or even within the Arab and Muslim milieu, is to contrast Islam and Modernity, Islam and the West. Often this contrast is also seen as conflictual. A more sober reflection would occasion a new way of looking at this relation. Islam's relation to modernity is not necessarily one of conflict and opposition, but could be one of complementarity and interaction. The condition for this is to view modernity as a project that is open to many possibilities, and not a standard model waiting to be applied universally. One must also look at Islam as an open project, and not a closed and final vision of things.

It is true that there is sensitivity towards, even open rejection of, some aspects of modernity by Muslims. However, this is because Muslims did not confront modernity as a cultural project, but in conjunction with the military might of the ascendant Europe of the eighteenth and nineteenth centuries. As Muslims, we did not see the brighter face of the French Revolution and its liberating values, but only its dark face presented by Napoleon as his guns shelled Cairo. However, this should not hide from us the interaction between Islam and 'modernity' which took place during the last two centuries. (I use 'modernity' between inverted commas to emphasize its multiple possibilities and to deny all claims of centrality put forward on its behalf.) In addition, we should not neglect the other dimension of modernity, the ongoing Islamic revival movement, which seeks to renew Islam and reformulate its language and symbols. This movement is not isolated from the challenges and big questions put forward by modernity. The phenomena of extremism and rigidity, which the world media emphasize and exaggerate, must not blind us to the revivalist and modernizing face of modern Islam. To sum up, Islam is moving towards embarking on its own venture of modernization, on its terms and not necessarily replicating either the Western approach or rate.

Rethinking Islam and Modernity

The other question touches on the matter of the relation between modernity and secularization. Since Max Weber, Western academia seems to have established a necessary relation between modernization and secularization. Weber affirmed that the triumph of modernity and the necessary conditions attending it, namely rationalization at the level of the economy and of social values generally, necessarily leads to a retreat of religious values in favour of more secular ones. But is there a necessary connection between modernity and secularism? The parallel advancement of industrialization and secularization in Western societies does not appear to have been replicated in the Muslim experience. On the contrary, religious values appear more dominant and effective today in Muslim lands than they were three or four decades ago. It is likely, therefore, that we are going to witness a new form of modernization in the Muslim world, one that would not necessarily be secular. We may then be forced to revise the dominant assumptions regarding the interrelatedness of modernization and secularization.

Finally I have a question, directed mainly to Judge al-Bechri and Shaikh al-Ghannoushi. Modern Islamic thought, in its early phase, sought to comprehend and absorb some of the main Western theses, with a conscious attempt to integrate these concepts within its own world-view. Thus Western democracy was 'translated' as *shūrā*, parliament as 'council of *Ahl al-ḥall wa'l-ʿaqd*', etc. Pioneers of Islamic reformism since the last century became prisoners to this logic of compromise, which was dictated by the perceived superiority of the Western model. But should we not consider Islamic thought at present as having progressed beyond absorption of imported concepts to a critical reappraisal of both tradition and acquired ideas?

Fathi Osman

I think very important questions have been raised. All the points recall to me the difference between Allama Muhammad Iqbal and Sayyid Abu'l-Kalam Azad in the modern Indian experience. While Iqbal emphasized change and stressed the need for *ijtihād* to face the change, Azad said: no, we need consolidation or re-consolidation of our

Open Debate

heritage in a new line, or a new light. There is no need for *ijtihād*, we just need to present our heritage in a new light. I believe, as Bashir has raised the point, and before him Ibrahim Moosa and now Rafik, this re-consolidation did not achieve much. I am not talking about how useful it has been in another time to build some confidence. It was appropriate at another time, but it cannot work forever. We need to face the new developments, intellectual and technical developments. And this leads me to another important point: the distinction between Islam and Muslims that Ibrahim Moosa referred to. Definitely we are talking now, not about the whole of our heritage in the development of civilization, or history, that is something else. In our time, our heritage is a point of weakness. Sticking to this heritage, and ignoring the time factor is one of our problems. So, talking about Muslims, one of their problems was sticking to their heritage without considering the time factor. That which was progressive in one time can be a way of keeping people backward in another time. I believe this is very important, and this leads me to another point: Western thinking and articulation. It is not just a difference in terminology or semantics: you choose democracy, we choose *shūrā*; you choose parliament, we talk about *Ahl al-ḥall wa'l-ᶜaqd*. The different mechanisms may rely on different ways of thinking: on what the role of the masses was, and what the situation of the people was. So it is not just a difference in semantics, and we should respect the product of the Western mind in articulation, whether philosophical or legal. We must accept this positive and constructive step in the human civilization, in the human development of civilization, and build on it as the early Muslims did with regard to the Greek logic, Persian literature, Indian mathematics or anything like that. Unless we face this and accept this as a constructive step, neither ignoring it, nor finding what is parallel to it, but making use of these articulations, no progress can be achieved. We are also very slow in coping with the rapid pace of development.

With regard to economics, and this is my final point, I believe that we were hasty to talk about what is called Islamic economics. It has been very suitable to talk about the Islamic philosophy of economics, the Islamic principles, the Islamic ethics in running business, and we would do justice to Islam and to ourselves if we limit our subject to this, and let the so-called Islamic economics develop with time after making these things well-established. If I have a viewpoint on how business should be run, what the ethics of business are, this should pave the way for having a full Islamic economics. The economics in the West developed according to a certain pattern that took a long time to evolve. Industrialization had its impact on this. We ignore all this, and we go to a medieval heritage, to medieval economics to which our jurisprudence refers, without trying to borrow the infrastructure and the superstructure of Marx: build on the facts of the society. We try to build on that, and we think this is good and positive for Islam, to speak about Islamic economics. We may have a viewpoint, we may have some ethics, some philosophy, some principles, and until this can produce something, it would take time, and we should admit this. How can we run our businesses now? There is no choice, in my humble opinion, other than adapting or adopting or accommodating, any word you would like to use, the most recent experience until we have a real alternative, not an alternative of rhetoric.

Abdel-Halim Hoffman
I would like to share a few points with you. One is going back to the translation of concepts that Ibrahim Moosa mentioned. After one thousand and one terrible discussions about Islam has no democracy on one side, and democracy has no value and no ethics, which I hear from lots of brothers on the other side, I find myself in a position where I say: well, I have no problems having grown up in modernity and embracing Islam. There is nothing that keeps me from engaging in the German democratic parties and working in politics. The immediate response was: yes, but you read things into the holy book which are not there, and that of course then creates a problem. Of course I read it with the eyes and the knowledge of a man of the twentieth century, not somebody fourteen hundred years ago. But how do I explain this? I would like to share one term with you, which I came across recently and which I think is extremely helpful. It is the term 'structural analogy' because it is just fruitless to discuss whether democracy is *shūrā*

or *shūrā* is democracy. I mean you come into endless disputes. But if you use this term (structural analogy) you come to the point that each line of thought comes, develops theories and structures that are analogous, but they are not the same thing. I think, with this term, you can just make yourself understand and cross-over between the two systems without equating them.

The second point I would like to make is rather more a question to the other side of the panel. We have been talking about Islamization of knowledge, something, as someone said yesterday, I am not very fond of. And of course now we come to Islamization of the legal systems, and just some weeks ago, I came across something and I would like to turn this into a question. Yesterday, we heard that there is law that is legislated by the political authority, but also law applied in the court, not legislated. And this author I read said that in Egypt and in the Gulf states, you have a legal system which has parts from the French law and parts from the British law, and trying to Islamize this you lose something very important, you lose the law applied in the court which is always a law of the time, a law of the judges. It is flexible, and this author argues that if you take this body that is derived from French and British law, and try to Islamize it, you lose a lot of the flexibility which is basically inherent in the Islamic system. Would you agree with this, and how then could we avoid this because I cannot really imagine an Islamic law that is as rigid as the law that we experience in the West.

Tarek al-Bechri
A few quick points. The main common factor between the modern Western and Islamic experience is the time frame, which does not necessarily entail similar conditions. The question is: to what extent did modern Islamic thought respond, or did not respond, to the challenges and problems posed by the realities of this region inhabited by Muslims? This is the criterion of modernity. In brief, we could discern three disinct periods in the political and intellectual developments in the Muslim world from the late eighteenth century. In each phase, a major problem arose which arrested development generally, and that of Islamic thought

Rethinking Islam and Modernity

in particular. In the first phase, the main obstacle facing Islam, even before contact with Europe, had been the ossification and rigidity of thought. This was caused by the dominant social conditions and the prevalence of superstition, particularly that of the Sufi variety. In the face of this challenge, many movements arose calling for a return to pristine sources of Islam. The aim was to combat the rigidity of traditions by appeal to the basic texts. The external threat to Islam, which came first from Russia and only later from Western Europe, gave impetus to these reforms. But it also gave rise to movements of political and military reform, which were not concerned with intellectual renewal. On the contrary, the leaders of these reforms fought against the intellectual reform and revival movements, initiating a schism between the two strands of reform that affects our societies until this day.

By the late nineteenth century, foreign occupation became a reality, and the need was perceived for an even more radical reform. A conservative reaction arose against Western intellectual influences mediated by the occupation. Thus while renewal became urgent, conservatism also had a useful function in resisting externally imposed changes to the structures of society. Another contradiction thus arose between this conservative streak and the broader movement for renewal and change. This situation persisted until after World War I, when the close link between Islam and nationalism in countries like Egypt was broken, and we had what could be termed 'secular nationalism'. This latter trend wanted to end occupation and to reconstruct the country on the Western model. Conflict broke out between these two strands of nationalism, and it continues until today. The problematic of Islam and modernity thus hinges around these three problems and how to resolve them. I think we already have an outline of what the solution could look like, and it is going to come from within the Islamic trend. Brother Rafik posed a question in this regard which Shaikh al-Ghannoushi could answer better than I could. But I would like to make just one comment. Islamic thought comprehends better the nature of Western accomplishments, and is less enamoured with the superficial aspects of Western thought. I believe that we need Western thought in the area of organization, where Western civilization has shown a remarkable genius in this regard, in organizing the state, firms or societies. We need to make use of this unprecedented achievement. The problem is how to take this idea and adapt it to our values and frame of reference. Several attempts have been made to tackle this matter, and this meeting is a step in this direction.

Michèle Messaoudi
My first comment refers very briefly back to Tamara Sonn. I think many of us have understood modernity as a characteristic of the modern world as it is today, as opposed to the ideology of modernism which you may have not recognized in your explanation about what is normally understood in philosophical circles in the West by modernism and post-modernism. My question is in connection with Islam and culture, and before I ask specific members of the panel to answer, I just want to explain briefly why I am asking this question. In the course of my work, I come across the younger generations of Muslims. Unfortunately, I have to consider myself middle-aged more or less, so I am talking to my younger brothers and sisters here who, in my opinion and in my experience, are fairly confused when it comes to culture. In concrete terms they do not know how to be Muslims living in for example, Germany, or England, or France or elsewhere in what is normally known as the non-Muslim world. One of the many reasons for this is that the word culture has a very negative connotation for them. They are still living in reaction to the cultural baggage that the previous generations brought with them to Western countries, or the cultural baggage in the form of Westernization that the previous generations have experienced in colonized Muslim countries. So the younger generations are under the utopian impression that one can be a Muslim without belonging to any particular culture, or above all cultures, and although this is quite possible or may be desirable at the intellectual level, of course it brings some problems when it comes to the practicality of living in a particular locality. So I would like to put this question to my German brother, Dr. Osman, and to Dr. Soroush.

Rethinking Islam and Modernity

Abdolkarim Soroush

I am not going to answer the question directly, but I would like to make some comments on the subject of Islam and modernity that might include an answer to the sister's question. Concerning the idea of Islam and modernity, I think modernity should be divided into two parts: the roots and the fruits. I think most of our endeavours as Muslims to solve the problem of Islam and modernity usually go to the fruits rather than roots. We are usually concerned with *Fiqh*, the legal system of Islam. The philosophy is much more important. The fruits of modernity, again I would like to emphasize, political institutions, economic institutions, multi-party system, having a consultative assembly, things like that, all these are fruits of modernity. Having in that regard products like computers, planes and so on and so forth, all these are fruits of modernization. These are less important compared to the roots of modernization.

As to the roots of modernity, I am in agreement with two of the speakers here that the roots of modernity consist of the philosophical understanding that came to be known in the West in the Enlightenment values, which later spread out all over the world, including Islamic societies. The idea of individualism, the idea of scepticism should be emphasized here. These two are very important, and when we talk about Islam and modernity, we have to come to terms with these important philosophical issues. Whether in Islamic societies we can accommodate the idea of individualism, whether we can accommodate the idea of scepticism, etc. Can we reconcile certainty with scepticism? You see, we can recognize different phases in the history of mankind, and as far as I can understand and articulate, in the classical period, or in the medieval period, we had an age of the dictatorship of religion, the dictatorship of religious institution. Then in the phase of the Enlightenment, we had the age of the dictatorship of reason. That was the age of modernity, properly speaking dictatorship of reason. Now in the post-modern era, there is no dictatorship whatsoever; there is no god, according to the post-modern philosophers. Reason has become much more humble. Religion has become much more humble, and now it is time for these two to reconcile, to be recombined, to come to terms

Open Debate

with each other. That is the post-modern era, and that is the occasion, the opportunity to try to reconcile again a humbler reason and a humbler religion.

Whilst we had the dictatorship of religion there was no chance of reconciling religion and reason. When we had the age of dictatorship of reason, there was no chance of reconciling reason with religion, because dictators usually do not concede to others. Now we have a humbler reason and a humbler religion and that leads us to be less certain and the unprecedented occasion for recombining and reconciling these two seemingly incompatible products of human and revelation altogether. This is one observation on the idea of Islam and modernity and the relationship between the two. The classical civilization was the civilization of certainty. The modern civilization is one of scepticism, not only towards the text, but towards everything. This is the civilization of fallibism, the realization that human beings are fallible. They cannot attain certainty. We are certain that we cannot attain certainty. This is the absolute certainty that we have attained so far. This is the main realization of the modern era. Now, as philosophers, as theoretical thinkers, we have to think about whether this idea of uncertainty can be reconciled with the dogmatism we have had before in the domain of religion. People usually think that religion has a close friendship with dogmatism. This is a question that has to be resolved in order to reach a kind of reconciliation desirable, to a much-delayed reconciliation between religion and modernity. I am not saying that these ideas of modernity are not criticizable. We have to criticize them. Perhaps we have to redefine them. But these are roots of modernity, and we have to be mindful of these roots. Otherwise, going to *fuqahā'*, asking them about *ḥalāl* and *ḥarām*, asking them to legalize *ribā*, asking them to Islamize economics: all these are superficial acts on the parts of the thinkers, and that does not solve the problem.

You see in all modern so-called Islamic societies, you have a parliament, you have the press, you sometimes have multi-party systems and so on and so forth. But the spirit of these institutions is not there. It is absent, because the philosophy is not behind them. It is only body, with no soul in it, no spirit. So in order to make these alive, we have to inject the spirit, in order to make them work. That is the way to go about modernity and to reconcile Islam and modernity. *Fiqh* then comes in when there is a dispute. In this particular aspect, I am a follower of Imām al-Ghazālī, the fifth/eleventh century philosopher. He declared quite openly that *fiqh* is a worldly aspect. It has nothing to do with *saʿādah* – happiness in the next life. It is for this world alone, and *fuqahāʾ*, the jurists or assistants of sultān are there because living in this world, living in society, we need law, and *fuqahāʾ* are the lawyers or jurists of this world. We need *fiqh* since we are human beings, since we enter into disputes with each other, since we are unjust. He says quite clearly that if humans were just, they would have no need for *fiqh*. *Fiqh* is not a real essential part of religion. It is only because we, as human beings, as unjust human beings, living in this world, that we need *fiqh* or law. He said quite explicitly that if we were just, then the *fuqahāʾ* would be jobless. Thinking in terms of *fiqh*, of jurisprudence, thinking in terms of *fiqh* to Islamize economics, to deal with *ribā*, to deal with politics, and so on and so forth, all this is wasting time. We have to go to the roots. We have to find the roots of modernity, that is scepticism falliblism, individualism; they do not include secularism. Secularism is a contingent effect of modernity in the West. It should not be a part and parcel of modernism, and it is not the case that if we adopt modernity, we are necessarily led to secularism. That is a different issue that can be discussed. So there are roots for modernity, and I follow again Laroui who says that the modern time has a multi-source core for knowledge, while in the classical era, we have only one source, the source of religion. For religious people nowadays, there are different pluralistic sources for gaining knowledge, and this is what made them think pluralistically and non-dogmatically to try to reconcile these different sources, and that is what has made religion and reason much humbler, and that is what has made the task much less difficult.

Abdel-Halim Hoffman
Briefly, I will just try to give a definition of what culture really means. Certainly if my German culture meant roasting pork and drinking

beer, I would have a problem. However, with the youngsters and people from the second and third generations, there is a problem, which is basically a problem within their families and a problem of generations. When I give lectures and discuss culture in mosques, I try to stress that European – not only German but European culture has so many elements from the Arab Islamic world, and also from the Turkish world. And my plea to the Germans is to try and admit this. Don't just think that our roots are Germanic, but try to admit that our cultural roots are also Islamic-Arabic roots. This is on one side. On the other side, I say to my brothers from Turkey and elsewhere: try to discover those roots, because you will discover that even though there was Vienna and the Crusades, we have, through exchange literature and merchandize, been one world. So what I try to do is to just go back to the roots, define culture in an open way, the European system on one side, and the other side of the Mediterranean on the other, not as two antagonistic cultures but as being linked through arts, history, etc. And in this way we can build a bridge for these third generation brothers and sisters into German, European culture. Now if you take it to the theoretical level, I am very much against the term multi-culturalism, because the opposite is monoculturalism, and as I said right now, no country in Europe is monocultural. We have one hundred thousand different influences from the East, from the South, etc. So this concept just does not make any sense to me, because my culture is multi-cultural, so I see no need to use this term because it is just a political term that does not lead anywhere.

Fathi Osman
The confusion about culture among the youngsters, I think, is related to how the anthropologists and sociologists define culture and include religion in culture, while religion is supposed to be divine and culture according to sociologist theorization and to anthropological approach is human. So how can we adjust this? We are Muslims, that means sticking to the divine source. Without going through whether we consider religion a part of culture in a sense that culture can have divine sources or not, I want to say that culture is a human product, and that

there is nothing wrong with a Muslim having a culture based on the diversity of human beings. Diversity is very important. You can be a Muslim and be American, not in the sense of having the American citizenship, but you can have the American culture in food, in cuisine, in dress, etc. I believe that Muslims in China are different from the Muslims in Saudi Arabia, and both are Muslims. The mosques, the patterns and the architecture in an area, can all be different from those of another area. So it must be handled as the lady has pointed out. There is nothing wrong with having a culture. You should have a culture, and the criterion is that it should not be against Islam or anything against the essence of Islam. But I cannot expect anybody to practise his religion in a vacuum, or in abstraction. No, you can have a religion, and the implementation or the embodiment of these principles may be in a certain culture. You cannot split yourself from this culture, otherwise you will have some problems with regard to your identity. A universal Muslim may be a good thing, but it is still a very utopian idea. You cannot cut the relations between yourself and society.

Abdelwahab El-Affendi
I just want to express my dissatisfaction with two terms and the way they have been used. The first term, modernity, has been improperly used, I think. For most Muslim thinkers and activists, from Sayyid Jamāl al-Dīn al-Afghānī to Dr. Fathi Osman, the word modernity was not about individualism, or even about modern living. It was about participation, about being fully human, because Afghānī was worried that the modern world – and I am not saying modernity – the world he was living in at that time, was divided in such a way that there was a part which we now call modern, and the other part which was not modern. And this division of systems was leading to the other non-modern system to become less than human or sub-human. He even used the term that small states were going to rule people like sheep, and in some of the writings of Fathi Osman, he is still worried about the modern state being too powerful. So the issue we are looking at, as Muslims, is how human beings, either Muslims or non-Muslims, are

suffering up to this time from this deprivation, from this less than human condition. It is indicative that we are honouring Fathi Osman not in Egypt but in London, because many of us will probably not be let in there. In the Muslim world we are not in the modern era or the post-modern era. We have states that are too strong to make the people fully human. This is the first point. The second point regards secularism, and it ties in with this problem. I do not think, and I am going to put a revolutionary idea, that Islam and secularism are two separate things. I think the way secularism developed in the West is by stopping certain institutions having dictatorial powers over people. There is no rule under the secular systems for the Church not to act and try to be effective. If there is today a bishop who gets elected for parliament or becomes prime minister, he can if he can get support from the people. Now the states we have in the Muslim world are not secular states. Turkey which is seen as the example for a secular state, is a country where the state can intervene in what people do in their mosques, in what names they use for their children, etc. So I think when we look at these concepts, we have to review the way we have been looking at them, which might need some change.

S. El-Ammoudi
I have two issues here. One is the issue of self-criticism, accountability and responsibility. I think our philosophers have to help us with self-criticism of Islamic movements, and the way they handled the Gulf crisis, mainly the second Gulf crisis. I say that because we are in a different time, whether it is for the Middle East or, as one of the speakers mentioned yesterday, it echoes on us Muslims living in the West. The second issue is how can our intellectual theory help the Islamic movements to be loyal oppositions which will be respected by their own constituency first, by their friends second, whether in the West or at home, and by their opponents within their own communities.

Tarek al-Bechri
I would like to make a point regarding secularism and its incompatibility with Islam. The function and role of secularism in the West

and it is in this context that it is referred to, does not contradict the role and function of Islam. But in our Muslim world, the concept acquired a different meaning due to the social context. Secularism, as understood in Islamic and non-Islamic thought, refers to the displacement of a frame of reference and the installation of another. Another minor point regarding the economy: in my understanding, Islam is not an economic theory, but a frame of reference, instituting values and general principles. Islam cannot provide me with an alternative to the law of supply and demand, but it can influence the model of the 'economic person' as defined by utility theories that hold material utility as a supreme value. Islamic values thus affect the core of social reality, leading to the rise of a different kind of individual who could not be accounted for by the utility theory, in my view.

Abdolkarim Soroush

I have an observation on the question of Islam and secularization. I have to be very careful about what the brother mentioned. There might be some thinkers and activists in the Islamic world who understand secularism or secularization in the sense of separation of church and state, or state and religion. This might be the idea of some of the Islamic thinkers. But they have to be mindful and to be very careful. Secularism has two different meanings: secular mind and secular institutions. We might have secular institutions in a religious society, or at least that is what some Muslim thinkers believe. This, for some people, might seem compatible with the religious outlook. But the secular mind is a different thing. A secular mind cannot be reconciled with Islamic thinking, with religious thinking, because the secular mind in the West preceded the secularization of institutions. Westerners have a secular mind due to the secular philosophers and the secular philosophy, and that was also inherited from Greek philosophy. Then the secularization of institutions began. Here again, we face the roots and fruits. The roots of secularization are the secular mentality. The secularization of institutions, of society, of politics is the fruit of that. Some of the Islamists actually think that they can secularize the institution of state, the government. This might seem to some people feasible and quite easy to do. But we have to be reminded that the secular mind cannot be reconciled with Islamic or religious thinking, because for the secular mind, the idea of God, or spirituality, is totally absent, and that cannot be accepted within a religious context. But secularization as a fruit might seem superficially reconcilable with religion. So my message is to be mindful of the difference between the secular mentality and the secular institutions, and that even if we can accommodate secularization in the second sense in the religious context, the secular mind cannot be reconciled as far as I can understand.

Rashid al-Ghannoushi
It would appear from the general direction of debate that we have placed Islam and modernity on two opposite sides, with a few overlapping areas, such as those pointed out by Hoffman, which occasionally blur the distinction. But we need to remember that we live in a world that is advancing fast, in spite of the persistence of old conflicts (Islam–West, First World–Third World, etc.) towards a wider human unity. Technological advances have created the conditions for positive progress towards Islamic concepts. Islamic discourse, especially in the Qur'ān, departs from this premise of fundamental human unity, addressing all mankind. The Qur'ānic address was usually 'O Mankind,' and not, as in Socrates or Aristotle, 'O Athenians.' We have therefore many obstacles to overcome, as Islamists and Westerners, before the barriers that divide this world into Islam on one side and modernity on the other, or Islam and the West, can be overcome. I think that the value of this meeting is to help the shift from a confrontational situation to one where people believe in the one destiny of man.

Here we find many obstacles, both in Islamic and Western thought. And we cannot deal with the matter just in one camp, because we all face a crisis, each of his own. The Islamic movement departs from the conviction that the West is not a model to emulate, but an experiment to be comprehended, critically evaluated. The point of departure is not one of rejection, but of assimilation. Islam did not deny the validity of earlier revelations, but announced that it had come to complement them. The idea of complementarity between cultures and civilizations is thus a fundamental concept in Islam. This meeting presupposes this point of departure: we are all in one boat, and have to worry about how to save it.

Of the obstacles faced by Islamic thought, one can be summed up in the question: what is our frame of reference? We always say it is the text: Qur'ān and the *Sunnah*. In reality, however, history has always been the dominant influence. In our struggles, we hurl traditions at each other: this one quoting Ibn Taymiyyah, the other al-Ghazālī, some are Shīʿah, others are Sunnī. History thus prevails above the text, in spite of all claims. The idea of 'return to the texts', which was propounded by the modern Islamic movement is thus a truly revolutionary one. But its revolutionary potential has yet to be fully realized, and this can only happen if we liberate ourselves from the burden of history: not an easy task.

Ibrahim Moosa has argued that people seem to exonerate Islam and blame Muslims. But Islam cannot be blamed. Islam is suitable for all times and places, meaning that it could be interpreted from numerous points of view, all of which being valid. The question remains then: how can we read Islam, and how can we apply it to a given reality? If there is a dictatorship, as some have alleged, whether a dictatorship of the *fuqahā'* (jurists) or that of religious institutions, then it is a dictatorship of history. Much of the blood being spilt at the moment, as is the case in Algeria or Afghanistan, is a crime of history. History is still murdering us. The West has liberated itself from its history to a great extent, even if not completely.

There is the issue of dogmatism, considering Islam as the point on which I stand, while all those beyond it are non-believers. But Islam is a space and not a point. You can move within this space, it is not a prison, contrary to the dominant perception among Muslims. Tarek al-Bechri pointed to numerous revivalist movements since the eighteenth century. But most of these movements, all of them, rather, have been aborted. The most prominent culprit continues to be the political authorities. Our problem is how to tame power that has turned wild. The West has succeeded in taming its rulers and in giving some power

Open Debate

to the people. But we continue to be ruled over by tyrants. Each time we express pleasure in the fall of one tyrant, a new and worse tyrant arises. Is this a problem peculiar to us? Is it the fact that our rulers are too powerful while our peoples are too weak?

I believe that this is a problem of culture. The authoritarian spirit is dominant among us, and it starts from the family and the school. But one aspect of the problem of governance in our land comes from outside, from the West. While the democratic movement in Eastern Europe witnessed a phenomenal expansion with significant Western help, in our part of the world, democratization faces not only internal obstacles, but is hindered by massive and direct Western support for dictatorship. Our question to our Western interlocutors is this: how can we transform Western support for dictatorship into Western support for democracy? For if we were to believe that humanity can only have one destiny, this could not be consistent with full democratization in one part of the world and unmitigated dictatorship in another. And why does the West support dictatorship in our lands?

Here, we touch on an important negative element in modernity. In (Western) modernity, and due to certain historical contingencies, the idea crystallized that man can do away with God. Man can organize his life without reference to God. The idea that reason is self-reliant and autonomous from any moral directives is one of the main evils which modernity has disseminated all over the world. This does not detract from other achievements of modernity: the banishment of superstition and the enabling of people to control their own affairs. There is also the organizational genius pointed out by al-Bechri. We were unable to institutionalize our idea of *shūrā*, so we need this organizational input. But the idea of doing away with God is unacceptable. It threatens to destroy the West itself. It destroyed the family and left the individual as an island unto himself, and it made of the economy and the national interest gods unto themselves, without heed to the concerns of humanity or global interests.

In summary, therefore, it can be said that the problems of the world cannot be looked at properly except from the perspective of humanity's one destiny. The group that has gathered here, we think, believes in this one destiny. We believe that modernity is not all bad, and the West is not all bad. We also do not believe that every aspect of the Islamic tradition is good. We need more meetings like this so that rational elements in both camps should reflect on the fate of these two great civilizations from a perspective of cooperation and not one of conflict.

Ahmed Fahmi

When I came to this forum, I thought it was going to discuss practical matters. I thought perhaps the question should be: if you have an Islamic state, for example, what are you going to do about freedom of expression? You cannot just keep on saying 'Islam is the solution'. You have to explain how you are going to do it. Are you going to allow communist people to speak? Are you going to allow people who are against religion, against God, to speak? And if you are going to allow them, up to what limit? So we move from theoretical discussion of modernity and its definition to practical discussions to see whether Islam would be really consistent in providing the civil society that exists and would be capable of protecting it or not. Otherwise, it would remain at the end a merely intellectual discourse that will not affect the Islamic movements at all. And here I bring a question to Dr. Fathi Osman. Suppose that the answers are there, or this can be answered by Shaikh Rashid, how can this filter down to the roots of Muslim organizations and the new generations of Muslims, so that we do not end up in a situation like Ḥizb al-Taḥrīr, saying that democracy is *kufr*, if you go to elections, then you are like a *kāfir*.

Fathi Osman

Well I think that practicality and the practical side are very important, and this can also be connected with the question of Dr. El-Ammoudi about how we can make a loyal opposition and turn Islamic movements into a democratic loyal opposition. I think we have had, unfortunately, a split between the ideas and intellectual pursuits on one side, and the activism on the other, that had been in place since the beginning of the twentieth century. We still have the Islamic movements going

Open Debate

along in some way with this split for historical circumstances. We need, as any action, any movement, like the French Revolution, the American Revolution, the Russian Revolution, this strong relationship and interaction between intellectuality and activism. To attain this, we need some adjustment and reconciliation between intellectuality and the movement, and this is a difficult thing to achieve, but it is not impossible. As for loyal opposition, I believe the way to a loyal opposition is democracy. You cannot be a loyal opposition unless there is a democracy that admits that opposition has a legitimate place. So here we have a problem of democracy.

The other thing that we have within the Islamic movements is an obsession with taking over, that an Islamic state means that you have to take over: that you are a representative of the whole Muslim people in the country, and that it is only some rulers who are preventing the people from ruling in the name of Islam, which is not always really the true situation. You are a political group: some people agree with you, some may be against you, but they are legitimate Muslims like you. So, number one: democracy must be accepted by all the people, by the rulers and the ruled. Number two: the obsession with taking over must be abandoned. You can be an Islamic movement without having an Islamic state until the people are convinced of the idea of an Islamic state, and are convinced of its practicality: that you have a better alternative to give them for reform, not just rhetoric, not just 'Islam is the solution'. Another point is the West and its relation to, as Shaikh Rashid said, the Islamic loyal opposition. The regimes are not helping the Islamic loyal movements to have this role. Tunisia is a very significant example of this, because in the case of Algeria, there is some confusion, but in Tunisia, they have never used force, they have never supported violence, but always the idea in the West is to support who is in charge, whom you can deal with – and accordingly they supported Saddam Hussein at a certain time because he was in charge, and because he was against Iran. Western powers are always looking at Islam as anti-Western, against the Western interest, anti-democracy, anti-modernity, anti-everything. So these three factors: democracy, obsession with taking over, the role of the West in this pragmatic attitude, helping the person who can be easily in charge and whom you can easily deal with and do business with. The first Western comment on former Soviet leader Mikhail Gorbachev came from former British Prime Minister Margaret Thatcher when she saw him for the first time, when she said: 'This is a person that we can do business with.'

Ahmed Jaballah

It seems to me that the main question regarding Islam and modernity revolves around the stance of Islamic movements, and political movements generally, on the main currents of Western thought. It also hinges on how the Muslim community could achieve a comprehensive civilizational renaissance. Here we have two extremes. At one end, there are those who argue that a renaissance can only be achieved through absolute and unconditional openness to all trends coming from the West, accepting the ideas of democracy, human rights, etc. without reservations. At the other, there are those who say that the hopes of the *Ummah* in renaissance can only be achieved if we stick exclusively to our heritage and close ourselves off from any outside influences, restricting ourselves to reviving our own traditions. I think both positions are wrong, and we have to strike a balance in between.

On the issue of how to organize political authority in Islam, we have to admit that Islam did not outline any specific rules to organize the state, leaving that to existing traditions and to discretion. The only overarching principles laid down were the submission to Islamic values as the ultimate reference, while giving the final say in running public affairs to the *Ummah* as a whole. The *Ummah* has been given full authority to choose its rulers and hold them accountable. Islam has also laid down principles that enable the community to regulate its affairs in a manner which protects individual and communal rights and freedoms. Thus while justice and right were made the basis of legislation in Islam, the matter is quite the reverse in Western political thought. In Western legal thought, the philosophical basis of legislation is power and interest. Therefore we find the stance of these societies vary considerably on both internal and external issues. For example, the (Western-dominated) international system as it stands today is perceived as unfair from the perspective of Islamic movements, as well as from that of Muslim and Third World peoples. In our belief, the basis of this manifest unfairness can be found in the philosophical presuppositions which take account only of power relations and interest, and not, as in Islam, of justice and right.

François Burgat
First, Shaikh Rashid made me the least Islamic and the most modernist of the panellists (according to his comment on the arrangement of the panel). My silence was the result not of my laziness, but of my sincere respect for many of my fellow-panellists, from whom I have learnt a lot in not so many years. Our mission in this type of situation is to a great extent impossible, since we must accommodate the requirements of academic debate with the political and identitarian requirements of each of our communities. And this makes it a challenge, but I think we are doing quite well and this is why I was willing to listen more than I was willing to speak. If I was to emphasize only one point, I would stress what Michèle Messaoudi said this morning about the importance of us Muslims and non-Muslims being able to segregate between the substance of our difference and the fact that each of us requires a specific symbolic system to make certain values legitimate in our guts and brains, and this I took from Tarek al-Bechri. If we go further in this direction, most probably we shall not meet all of our identitarian requirements, because the concepts are no longer concepts, they are flags. I am ʿilmānī (secular), you are ʿilmānī so I cannot be ʿilmānī; you are a democrat, so I have to be against democracy. If we go slowly and carefully inside the concept, of course our identities will have to admit the fact that we are cousins, Muslims and non-Muslims. And supposedly for some of us it will be difficult to acknowledge, but for us most probably, we will take the time to realize that. Let us say, to take an example, if the camera of the French television whose representatives were here yesterday, and are today filming the meeting of the FIS so that they frighten the entire European landscape, if they had taken time to film Dr. Osman or Dr. Tarek al-Bechri or Shaikh Rashid al-Ghannoushi, and if they had time to listen to what was said, we

would have come to the conclusion that many of what non-Muslims see as universal can be expressed within the terminology, within the categories of Islamic culture. They would have listened to Abdelwahab El-Affendi recognize that some of what the Muslims do not accept, because they consider it as a too close heritage of the West, can also be connected to a great extent to Islamic culture. But it did not happen. So this is a problem of communication. The cameras of the French TV are filming the meeting where the 'nasty' young people waving flags are frightening my mother who will be asking me what were you doing in London. And for my colleagues there I am not in this meeting, I am in the other one. I would like to give the ending word to a Sudanese colleague when I was a speaker at the conference in Paris. He made a very sophisticated intervention, and we have run out of time to give you the content of the intervention, but I want to propose to you the conclusion. He said: 'I came to the conclusion that, at least in the field of politics, the true meaning of modernity is the ability to participate.'

John Esposito
Let me just end with a couple of observations. We do not have time and I did not intend to make this point that I would make now, and some of you will not be happy with it, which means I would hear some more unpleasant comments. But it does seem to me that we need to perhaps actually organize a conference that is simply called self-criticism in order to really raise the difficult questions. I can only tell you that recently, and this is quite common, and I know many of us have ran into it, but I have been to a meeting where someone said to me: Look John, what did Hasan Turabi say ten years ago and what are they doing in the Sudan? What did he write in your book, and what are they doing in the Sudan? We need to, when we have these conversations, be very specific about specific experiences, specific events, and really discuss them. Let me bring this to a conclusion by saying that my teacher many years ago, Ismail al-Faruqi, taught me in class something that has always saved me, when he said that in Islam, it was not enough to know the truth, but one has to do, to actualize, in American slang we would say one has to be proactive. And I think our last speaker

raised this question. Unless one can translate ideas into actions, then we will be simply like generations before us and generations that will come after, and we will simply be talking about an academic discussion (I use the word 'academic' here in a very limited sense) rather than talking about the fact that ideas have to be operationalized, have to be actualized in order to make a difference. It seems to me that Zaki Badawi yesterday said that the West is suspicious of us. Well many Muslims are suspicious of the West. But increasingly there is no West. Zaki Badawi is saying the West is suspicious of us? He is a man of the West, as well as of the Muslim world. In fact the West is increasingly part of the Muslim world. As one of my colleagues likes to say, the capitals of the Muslim world are no longer Cairo or Damascus, or cities in – as it were, the traditional Muslim world. They are now New York, London, etc. Fathi Osman is a perfect example of a man who has stood in two civilizations or cultures. He has lived in Cairo, he has lived all over the more traditional 'Muslim world', or what was referred to as 'the Muslim world' in the past. But he has also lived in the West for so many years, and he is sitting very close to the West, and part of his problem sometimes finding difficulty in walking is that he's trying to be in two parts of the world at the same time for too long.

We need, it seems to me, to realize that real issues remain and will continue, but we have to move beyond our suspicions and threats. We have to move beyond, what an Iranian scholar talking about Iran and the West said. 'Iran and the US engage in mutual satanization', and they still do that. Both sides really refer to the other as 'shaytan'. It seems to me that part of our mission is to move beyond that to understand and respect. Not to do so is to betray reality. This is not an academic question. It is to betray the realities, the demands of God, and the demands of the world in which we live; the demands of religion and politics. For it is not only true that increasingly we need to recognize that we are all children of Abraham, but we also do live in a global village. We are interdependent. Everyone recognizes that. There can be no survival unless we recognize that interdependence, religious, economic, political, cultural, civilizational. It seems to me that we are responsible to move beyond this. We are responsible. We cannot keep

Rethinking Islam and Modernity

blaming the other side. The West cannot explain everything, simply because it says that it is simply trying to defend its national interest. And many Muslims cannot simply continue to say the same old things. Well let me put it this way. When I was a young scholar, I had to catch a plane from a conference. The person who was chairing that conference was Professor Fazlur Rahman, and he said: 'we have a young professor here. He has to catch his plane. Can I ask the other panellists, all of whom were Muslim, to please move quickly beyond condemning the Crusades, and British colonialism, and get to the subject of their topic?' Each side has that body of historic memory that we have to move beyond. That is our challenge. If you will excuse me for promoting something that I represent, this is precisely what the Center for Muslim-Christian Understanding at Georgetown University was established to do. This is precisely what we do, both with our permanent scholars and our visiting scholars like Fathi Osman.

It seems to me that the man that we honour today represents everything that we need to do. He is indeed, from my point of view, a scholar activist. He is indeed a man who has attempted to bridge, if you will, the worlds of Islam and the West. He has done it intellectually by studying at the best institutions on both sides. He has done it by teaching at the best institutions on both sides. He has done it by living, by writing, by speaking, by engaging both sides. And if we wish to really honour him, then we move beyond our words to embodying this, it seems to me, in our lives, in our work. Thank you all for coming.

List of Contributors

Tarek al-Bechri is a prominent intellectual, legal expert and a prolific writer. His last post was the first vice-chairman of the Council of State, Egypt's highest constitutional court. His published works include: *Al-Ḥarakah al-Siyāsiyyah fī Miṣr* (The Political Movement in Egypt), *Al-Muslimūn wa'l-ʿAqbāṭ fī Itār al-Jamʿīyah al-Waṭaniyyah* (Muslims and Copts within the Framework of National Community), *Bayna al-Jamʿīyah al-Dīniyyah wa'l-Jamʿīyah al-Waṭaniyyah fī'l-Fikr al-Siyāsī* (Religious Community and National Community in Political Thought), *Al-Ḥiwār al-Islāmī al-ʿIlmānī* (The Islam-Secularist Dialogue), *Bayna al-Islām wa'l-ʿUrūbah* (Between Islam and Arabism) and *Ṭabīʿat al-Ḥadāthah* (The Nature of Modernity).

Rafik Bouchlaka is Director of the London-based Maghreb Center for Research and Translation and is also a researcher at the University of Westminster where he is currently preparing a Ph.D thesis on Islam, Secularity and Modernity. He has contributed to such journals as *Islāmiyyah al-Maʿrifah* and *Maraṣid* and published articles in Arabic papers and magazines including *Al-Ḥayāt* and *Al-ʿĀlam*.

Abdelwahab El-Affendi is a Senior Research Fellow at the Centre for the Study of Democracy, University of Westminster, London. Educated at the Universities of Khartoum, Wales and Reading, he is Co-ordinator of the Project on Democracy in the Muslim world at CSD. He is author of *Turabi's Revolution: Islam and Power in Sudan*, *Who Needs an Islamic State?* and *Al-Thawrah wa'l-Iṣlāḥ al-Siyāsī fī'l-Sūdān* (Revolution and Political Reform in Sudan). He has contributed to many leading journals, including *African Affairs* and the *International*

Journal of Middle Eastern Studies, and *The Routledge Encyclopaedia of Philosophy, Social Science and Conflict Analysis*, and *Islam and Justice*. Having previously worked as a diplomat in the Sudanese Foreign Service, and as a professional pilot, El-Affendi has also taught or undertaken research at the Universities of Khartoum, Oxford (St. Anthony's College) and The Chr. Michelsen Institute in Bergen, Norway. El-Affendi also contributes regularly to a number of publications, including *Al-Quds Al-ᶜArabī* and *Middle East International* and was Managing Editor of *Arabia: The Islamic World Review*.

Abdelwahab M. Elmessiri is Professor Emeritus of English and Comparative Literature at Ein Shams University in Cairo. He has authored several books in both Arabic and English. The Arabic publications include: *Epistemological Bias; Zionist Ideology: A Case Study in the Sociology of Knowledge; The Earthly Paradise: Studies in American Culture; The Princess and the Poet: A story for Children; Secrets of the Zionist Mind; Zionism, Nazism and the End of History: A New Cultural Outlook; The Encyclopedia of the Jews, Judaism and Zionism: A New Explanatory Paradigm* (8 vols). His publication in English include: *The Land of Promise, A Critique of Political Zionism; Israel and South Africa: The Progression of the Relationship; The Palestinian Wedding: A Bilingual Anthology of Palestinian Resistance Poetry; A Land of Stone and Thyme, A Collection of Palestinian Short Stories*.

John L. Esposito is the Founding Director of the Center for Muslim-Christian Understanding: History and International Affairs at Georgetown University and is Professor of Religion and International Affairs and of Islamic Studies at Georgetown University. Esposito is also Editor-in-Chief of *The Oxford Encyclopaedia of the Modern Islamic World* and *The Oxford History of Islam*. He is also author of: *Islam: The Straight Path; The Islamic Threat: Myth or Reality?; Islam and Democracy* (with John O. Voll); *Islam and Politics; Political Islam: Revolution, Radicalism or Reform?; Islam and Secularism in the Middle East* (with Azzam Tamimi); *Islam, Gender and Social Change* and *Muslims on the Americanization Path* (with Y. Haddad); *Voices of Resurgent Islam; Islam in Asia: Religion, Politics, and Society*; and *Women in Muslim Family Law*.

List of Contributors

Rashid al-Ghannoushi is leader of the Ennahda Party in Tunisia and is renowned as an original and very prominent Islamic thinker. Educated in philosophy in Damascus and Paris, he became active in Tunisian politics with the launch of the Islamic Trend Movement in 1981 (later the Ennahda Party). He was imprisoned several times for his political views before being forced into exile. He now lives in London. His publications include *Al-Ḥurriyyah al-ʿĀmmah fi'l-Dawlah al-Islāmiyyah* (Public Liberties in the Islamic State), *Ḥuqūq al-Muwāṭanah: Ḥuqūq ghayr al-Muslimīn fi'l-Mujtamaʿ al-Islāmī* (Rights of Citizenship: The Rights of Non-Muslims in Muslim Society), *Ḥuqūq al-Mar'ah bayna al-Qur'ān wa Wāqiʿ al-Muslimīn* (Women's Rights Between the Qur'ān and the Reality of Muslims), *Fi'l-ʿIlmāniyyah wa'l-Mujtamaʿ al-Madanī* (Approaches to Secularity and Civil Society). He has also contributed to a number of edited works, journals and newspapers.

Fahmi Huweidi is a leading writer on Islamic issues whose famous column in the Egyptian daily *Al-Ahram* is syndicated in publications in a number of Arab countries. He has worked as Managing Editor of *Al-ʿArabī* monthly magazine in Kuwait and Deputy Editor of the monthly *Arabia: The Islamic World Review* in London. His published works include *Muwāṭinūn lā Dhimmīyūn* (Citizens Not Dhimmīs), *Al-Maqālāt al-Maḥẓūrah* (The Banned Articles), *Al-Islām fi'l-Ṣīn* (Islam in China), *Azmat al-Waʿī al-Dīnī* (The Crisis of Religious Consciousness) and *al-Tadayyun al-Manqūṣ* (Defective Religiosity).

Fathi Osman is a well-known writer and a leading Muslim thinker and educator, currently residing in Southern California where he is engaged in teaching and writing. Educated at the Universities of Cairo, Alexandria and Princeton, he has distinguished himself as a pioneer advocate of reform of Islamic thought based on the values of democracy and human rights within a genuine Islamic perspective. He joined the renowned Islamic reformer Shaikh Muhammad al-Bahi in the latter's efforts to reform al-Azhar in the 1960s and later went to teach at the Universities of Oran (Algeria), Riyadh (Saudi Arabia) and Princeton before moving to London in 1981 to edit the monthly magazine

Arabia: The Islamic World Review (London, 1981–87). His numerous published works on Islamic history, law and doctrine, include: *Al-Fikr al-Islāmī wa'l-Taṭawwur* (Islamic Thought and Change), *Ḥuqūq al-Insān bayna Sharīʿat al-Islām wa'l-Fikr al-Gharbī* (Human Rights in Islamic Law and Western Thought), *The Children of Adam, Jihād: A Legitimate Struggle for Human Rights*, and *Muslim Women in the Family and Society*.

Munir Shafiq is a prominent writer and political analyst, formerly Director of the Palestinian Research Center in Tunisia. After a celebrated career as a Marxist theoretician, he embraced Islam and published a number of important works from his new perspective. These include *Al-Islām fī Maʿrakat al-Ḥaḍārah* (Islam in the Battle of Civilization), *Al-Islām wa Naẓariyyat al-Dawlah al-Ḥadīthah* (Islam and the Theory of the Modern State), and *Al-Ḥarakah al-Islāmiyyah: Ittijāhāt wa Tayyārāt* (The Islamic Movement: Trends and Tendencies). Shafiq also contributes regularly to a number of leading Arabic newspapers such as *Al-Ḥayāt* and *Al-Mujtamaʿ*.

Index

A

Abbasid(s), 32, 38, 40, 51, 74, 92, 158
ʿAbd al-Raḥmān ibn al-Qāsim, 80
ʿAbduh, Muhammad, 24, 135
ʿAbdul Malik, 76
ABIM, 144, 155
Abraham, 181
Abū Isḥāq, 78
Abul Aʿlā Mawdūdī, 114
Abū Shuqqah, Muḥammad Abdul Halim, 117
Abū ʿUbaid ibn Sallām, 76, 77
Abū Yūsuf, 31, 48
Abū Zayd, Nasr Hamid, 154
Adam, 29, 42, 56
El-Affendi, Abdelwahab, 123, 170, 180
Al-Afghānī, Jamāl Al-Dīn, 24, 170
Afghanistan, 81, 174
Africa, 53, 71, 94, 101, 120, 145
Alexandria University, 125
Algeria, 25, 81, 124, 174
Algiers, 127
ʿAlī ibn Abī Ṭālib, 50, 51, 84
Allah, *see* God
American Declaration of Independence, 66, 68
El-Ammoudi, S., 171, 176
Amnesty International, 29
Anderson, Perry, 12, 13
Anṣār, 50
Ansari, Javed, 133, 134, 135, 136, 138

Arabia/Arab(s), 25, 35, 43, 45, 68, 71, 72, 74, 85, 86, 94, 97, 101, 105, 111, 114, 128, 159, 169
Arabian Peninsula, 111
ʿArafāt, 68
Arendt, Hannah, 16, 17, 18, 19, 20
Aristotle, 10, 11, 12, 13, 14, 173
'Article 19', 29
Asad, Muhammad, 129
Al-Asāwirah, 50
Asia(n), 11, 13, 14, 20, 53, 71, 81, 94, 101, 145, 150, 151, 154
Aswan, 125
Australia, 106
Al-Awzāʿī, 32, 35
Azad, Abuʾl-Kalam, 37, 160
Al-Azhar University, 75, 125, 126, 127
Al-ʿAzīz, ʿUmar ibn ʿAbd, 32

B

Badawi, Zaki, 87, 147, 153, 181
Al-Bahi, Muhammad, 126, 127
Baghdad, 21, 39
Al-Balādhurī, 32, 50
Balkans, 71
Al-Bannā, Ḥasan, 114, 116, 124, 125
Al-Bechri, Tarek, 66, 89, 144, 160, 163, 174, 175, 179
Beijing, 46, 56
Beirut, 84
Berques, Jaques, 23

Index

Bible, the, 7
Bill of Rights, 27
Bodin, Jean, 11, 12
Boers, 20
Bouchlaka, Rafik, 9, 159, 161
Britain/British, 20, 66, 81, 124, 163, 182
Bukhara, 39
Bulgaria, 71
Burgat, François, 144, 179
Burke, Edmund, 18, 148
Burma, 47
Bush, George, 134
Al-Buti, Ramadan, 118, 119
Byzantium, 13, 32, 34, 53, 125

C
Cairo, 21, 39, 86, 124, 125, 181
Cairo University, 124, 125
Canada, 106
Canovan, Margaret, 18, 19
Cantori, Louis, 144, 147, 151
Cape of Good Hope, 81
Center for Muslim-Christian Understanding, 141, 182
Center for Strategic and International Studies, 55
China/Chinese, 13, 28, 46, 53, 58, 101, 102, 105, 170
Christian(s), 13, 49, 51, 81, 85, 86, 101, 129, 137, 147, 152, 154
Colonialism, 22, 94, 128, 131, 152, 182
Communications Decency Act, 59
Communism, 128, 129, 130, 131, 134, 137
Confucius, 150
Convention on the Rights of the Child, 56
Copts, 31, 86
Cordova, 39

Council of the League of Arab States, 28
Crusades, 85, 86, 128, 131, 169, 182
Cyprus, 76, 77, 78, 79, 80

D
Damascus, 21, 39, 181
Darwin, 1, 4
David, 111
Daʿwah, 119
Day of Judgement, 88
Declaration of Independence of the United States, 27
Declaration of the Rights of the Child, 28
Declaration of the Rights of Man and the Citizen, 27, 56
Degobineau, 18
Democracy, 9, 15, 26, 61, 161, 163
Derrida, 152
Despot(ism), 9, 11, 12, 13, 14, 15, 16, 26, 35, 110
Dhimmīs, 47, 48, 49, 50, 51, 52, 55, 66, 67, 76, 80, 81, 82, 83, 84, 85, 86, 87, 88, 89, 90, 91, 97, 98, 99, 100, 101, 146, 170, 179, 180; denigration of, 90; Islam's attitude towards, 86; participation in government, 66, 82; rights, 84; status of, 49, 85
Document of Human Rights in Islam, 28
Dracula, 7

E
Economic(s), 3, 17, 117, 122, 151, 161; loans, 58; market, 4; values, 138; Western, 21
Economies, 106, 107
Education, 1, 21, 67, 69, 75, 87, 92, 101, 106, 113, 114, 117, 158
Eichmann, 6

Index

Egypt(ian), 31, 35, 39, 40, 41, 67, 72, 74, 81, 86, 101, 116, 124, 126, 127, 133, 151, 155, 158, 163, 164, 171
Elmessiri, Abdelwahab M., 1, 153
England/English, 27, 43, 75, 139, 155, 165
Enlightenment, the, 7, 13, 148, 149, 166
Ennahda Party, 155, 184
Eritrea, 104
Esposito, John, 144, 154, 157, 180
Europe(an), 11, 12, 14, 16, 18, 20, 28, 29, 35, 70, 71, 72, 85, 86, 92, 101, 106, 130, 152, 164, 169, 175
European Convention on the Rights of Man, 28
European Council, 28

F
Fahmi, Ahmed, 176
Faisal (King), 129, 130, 137
Al-Faisal al-Saud, Muhammad (Prince), 130
Al-Faruqi, Ismail Raji, 127, 130, 180
Fatwā, 76, 81
Faustus, 7
Fez, 39
Fiqh, 80, 153, 166, 168
Foucault, 4, 152
France, 18, 66, 150, 165, 179; Declaration of the Rights of Man and Citizen, 27; law, 163; Revolution, 71, 159, 177
Frankenstein, 7
Freud, 4
Fuqahā', 167, 168, 174

G
Galtung, John, 21, 22
Georgetown University, 144, 145, 182

George Washington University, 141
Germany, 16, 59, 150, 151, 162, 165, 168, 169
Al-Ghannoushi, Rashid, 50, 100, 109, 144, 147, 153, 158, 160, 164, 173, 176, 177, 179
Al-Ghāzalī, Muhammad, 88, 100, 168, 174
Gibb, H.A.R., 24
God (Allah), 2, 4, 28, 29, 30, 31, 32, 34, 35, 37, 42, 56, 65, 68, 77, 88, 89, 90, 109, 110, 111, 117, 118, 120, 122, 169, 173, 175, 176, 181; blessings, 110; 'chosen people', 87; commands, 121; consciousness, of, 31; guidance, 33, 48, 109; law, 30, 33, 34, 43; message, 31, 37, 65; rebellion against, 110; word of, 34
Gorbachev, Mikhail, 136, 178
Greece/Greeks, 9, 10, 11, 12, 158, 161, 172
Grosrichard, Alain, 11

H
Al-Hamrā', 50
Hanafi school, 40
Hasan, Dusuqi, 116
Hegel, 148, 156
Hereafter, 37, 121
Hindus, 102
Hirah, 31
Hitler, 6
Hobbes, 3
Al-Hodaybi, Hasan, 125
Hoffman, Abdel-Halim, 144, 162, 168, 173
Hourani, Albert, 23
Human Rights, 27, 29, 32, 36, 56, 60, 64, 66, 67, 70, 71, 123, 141; concept of, 56, 72; enforcement, 63; modern, 27; monitoring, 29;

Index

Muslim side, 55; universal, 42, 67; Western conception, 36, 58
Human Rights Watch, 29
Husein, Adel, 100
Hussein, Saddam, 177
Huweidi, Fahmi, 84, 100, 153, 158

I

Ibn ʿAbd al-Ḥakam, 31
Ibn al-Jarīr al-Tabarī, 31, 50
Ibn Kathīr, 156
Ibn al-Khaṭṭāb, ʿUmar, 31, 34, 35, 67, 83
Ibn al-Muqaffaʿ, 40
Ibn al-Qayyim, 85, 86
Ibn Taymiyyah, 174
Ibn al-Walīd, 31
Ijtihād, 37, 38, 64, 154, 160, 161
Imam Muhammad ibn Saud University, 127
Imperialism, 9, 16, 17, 18, 21
India/Indian, 13, 101, 102, 105, 161
Indian Ocean, 81
Indonesia, 139
International Covenant on Civil and Political Rights, 56, 63, 67
International Covenant on Economic, Social and Cultural Rights, 28, 56, 67
International Monetary Fund, 93, 104, 151
International Year of the Child, 28
Iqbal, Muhammad, 37, 160
Iran, 116, 123, 133, 137, 139, 158, 181
Iraq, 50, 82, 133
Al-Islām (Shaikh), 40
Islam(ic), 22, 27, 28, 30, 31, 33, 35, 36, 37, 43, 46, 51, 65, 74, 80, 82, 83, 84, 88, 89, 96, 100, 115, 118, 120, 129, 130, 132, 134, 137, 138, 139, 146, 147, 148, 150, 153, 154, 156, 158, 159, 160, 161, 164, 166, 167, 169, 170, 171, 172, 173, 174, 177, 178, 179, 180, 181, 182; civilization, 85; confrontation, with, 13; converts to, 83; criteria of, 32; culture, 23, 24, 33; despotic, 14; divine sources, 33; economics, 150, 161, 167, 168; hermeneutics, 23; history, 23, 80, 112, 126; human rights, 27; imposition of, 39; jurisprudence, 36, 38, 76, 168; law, 33, 39, 41, 75, 113, 166; legal obligation, 33; media, 132; message, 38, 44, 109; mission, 110; modern, 22, 24; movement(s), 104, 109, 115, 116, 117, 122, 130, 134, 147, 173, 174, 176, 177, 178; organization(s), 54; propaganda against, 100; reform(ist), 115, 118, 127; revival(ism), 102, 129, 136, 139, 143; societies, 23, 24, 111, 149, 166, 167; state(s), 9, 116, 141, 176, 177; teachings, 47, 90; values, 54, 109, 128, 158, 172, 173
Islamic Center of Southern California, 141
Islamic University of Malaysia, 141
Ismāʿil ibn ʿAbbās, 78
Isphahan, 14
Israel, 111, 139
Istanbul, 21, 81
Italy, 12

J

Jaballah, Ahmed, 178
Jabbar, Saad, 147
Jackson, Michael, 7
Japan, 149
Jew(s), 31, 49, 81, 85, 88, 154
Jihād, 123, 143
Jizyah, 50, 90
Jordan, 133
Al-Juwaynī, 120

Index

K
Kashmir, 102
Keane, John, 15, 16, 25
Khallaf, Abdul-Wahhab, 80
Khawārīj, 113
Khedive, 67
Khilāfah, 81
Khomeini, 120
Kissinger, Henry, 136, 137
Koebner, R., 10
Kom Ambo, 125
Korea, 58

L
Laroui, 168
Latin America, 94, 101
Al-Layth ibn Saʿd, 77
Lebanon, 32, 81, 90, 139
Lefort, Claud, 15
Lewis, Bernard, 127
Libya, 81, 133
Locke, John, 4, 30
London, 21, 29, 123, 128, 131, 171, 180, 181
Los Angeles, 46
Luttwak, Edward, 55

M
Machiavelli, 3, 12
Madinah, 38, 50, 89, 111, 158
Madinah Document, 89
Madonna, 7
Magians, 85
Magna Carta, 27
Al-Mahdī ibn Tumart, 120
Makkah, 50, 77
Malaysia, 59, 143, 149
Mālik ibn Anas, 77, 78
Mālikī school, 80
Mammon, 3
Mansfield, Peter, 138

Marcuse, 5
Marx, 28, 39, 56, 136, 162
Al-Māwardī, 49
Messaoudi, Michèle, 165, 179
Michelangelo, 7
Middle Ages, 49
Middle East, 9, 16, 21, 23, 26, 97, 138, 149, 151, 158, 171
Al-Minya, 124
Mitchell, Richard, P., 138
Mitwalli, Abdulhameed, 80
Mohammed, Mahathir, 59
Moosa, Ibrahim, 154, 161, 162, 174
Montesquieu, 10, 11, 12, 13, 14
Morocco, 81, 133, 139, 151
Moses, 110
Muʿawiyah, 76, 84
Muḥammad, the Prophet, 31, 42, 50, 51, 68, 77, 84, 86, 88, 89, 90, 110, 111, 112, 119, 121; Companions, 36, 88; farewell sermon, 68; message, 45; *Sunnah*, 33, 43, 44, 49, 64, 87, 90, 174
Mukhallad ibn Ḥusain, 78
Mūsā ibn Ayman, 78
Muslim(s), 13, 27, 29, 30, 32, 33, 34, 37, 40, 42, 45, 46, 47, 49, 51, 52, 53, 61, 62, 64, 65, 67, 72, 75, 77, 78, 80, 82, 83, 85, 86, 88, 89, 92, 96, 101, 102, 103, 104, 105, 107, 115, 116, 129, 130, 131, 132, 135, 136, 137, 138, 140, 142, 148, 154, 156, 157, 161, 163, 165, 166, 169, 170, 171, 174, 176, 177, 179, 180, 181, 182; activists, 55, 143; animal slaughter, 58; civilization, 38, 85; communities, 24, 30, 32, 46, 80, 81, 102, 112, 178; conquests, 80; countries, 33, 39, 40, 52, 94, 96, 99, 134, 165; culture, 170; heritage, 32, 34, 35, 40; history, 38, 39, 85;

Index

intellectual(s), 123, 127, 130, 148, 155; jurists, 53, 80, 90, 92; minorities, 33, 49, 97, 98, 99, 100, 101, 105; minorities in the West and in other countries, 49, 51, 53, 54, 72, 97, 101, 102, 103, 104, 105, 106, 107, 108, 115, 136; organization(s), 54, 55, 176; policy-makers, 92; revival, 104; scholars, 104, 158; societies, 26, 37, 39, 40, 43, 66, 81, 83, 85, 86, 90, 120, 131; solidarity, 31; state(s), 30, 50, 80, 81, 104, 120; strategy, 53; *'ulamā'*, 113, 158; *Ummah*, 53, 92, 94, 96, 98, 99, 110, 113, 114, 116, 120, 130, 131, 178; women, 44; world, 21, 24, 81, 86, 90, 92, 94, 95, 96, 105, 123, 127, 128, 131, 134, 136, 139, 142, 145, 148, 158, 160, 164, 171, 172, 181; younger generations, 32

Muslim Brotherhood, 100, 116, 124, 125, 142

Muslim Women's League, 46, 47

N

Nadha Party, [see Ennahda]
Nafiʿ, Bashir, 157, 161
Napoleon, 86, 159
Nasser, Gamal Abdel, 125
Nationalist Progressive Front, 118
Nepal, 47
Newton, 4
New York, 29, 181
New Zealand, 106
Nietzsche, 5, 6
Nimeiri, 134
Al-Nuqrashi, Mahmoud, 124

O

Orabi, Ahmad, 67, 68
Oran University, 127

Organization of Islamic Conference, 28
Orient(al), 14, 20, 24
Orientalist(s), 20, 95, 127, 152
Osman, Fathi, 27, 84, 90, 123, 124, 125, 126, 127, 128, 130, 131, 134, 135, 136, 139, 140, 141, 142, 143, 144, 145, 146, 147, 153, 157, 160, 165, 169, 170, 171, 176, 181, 182
Ottoman(s), 12, 13, 21, 40, 71, 74, 81, 86, 90

P

Pact of the Nobles, 31
Pakistan, 101, 133, 135, 139
Palestine, 82, 94, 124, 128
Panza, Sancho, 6, 7
Paris, 14, 21
Pasha, Qadri, 110
Permanent Regional Arab Committee for Human Rights, 28
Persia(n), 11, 13, 14, 31, 50, 74, 81, 90, 111
Political asylum, 61, 62, 63
Polytheism, 109, 110
Princeton University, 127
Prometheus, 3, 6, 7

Q

Qaradawi, Yusuf, 100
Al-Qāsim ibn Sallām, 32
Qayrawan, 39
Quixote, Don, 7
Qur'ān(ic), 29, 30, 31, 33, 34, 35, 36, 37, 38, 41, 42, 43, 44, 45, 47, 48, 51, 53, 56, 60, 61, 62, 64, 65, 68, 77, 78, 79, 87, 88, 89, 103, 109, 110, 111, 116, 117, 119, 121, 122, 142, 173, 174; laws of, 48; perspective, 30; principles, 41
Qutaybah ibn Muslim, 32

Index

Qutb, 114, 125

R
Rabīʿ ibn ʿĀmir, 31
Rahman, Fazlur, 182
Rawls, John, 25, 26
Renaissance, the, 7, 11, 13
Receher, Nicholas, 52
Ribā, 167
Richter, Melvin, 10, 12
Riyadh University, 127, 128
Robinson, Jeffrey, 129
Romans, 76, 77, 78, 111, 158
Rome, 28
Rosenthal, Franz, 35
Rousseau, 3, 4, 13, 30, 157
Russia, 81, 101, 102, 105, 106, 164
Russian Revolution, 28
Rustam, 31

S
Sabaens, 88
Sahara, 53
Said, Edward, 138
Salahuddin, Muhammad, 133
Salvator, Armando, 22
Samarqand, 32, 39
Sandel, Michael, 25, 26
Sassanid(s), 34
Scandinavia, 53
School of Judiciary Training, 41
Secular(ism), 1, 2, 3, 6, 9, 16, 20, 25, 26, 108, 137, 149, 153, 160, 168, 171, 172, 173; Èlite, 23, 24; in the Muslim world, 21; in Turkey, 23; project of, 22; state, 115
Al-Shāfiʿī, 39, 49, 52
Shafiq, Munir, 92
Sharīʿah, 30, 33, 34, 40, 41, 47, 54, 75, 78, 79, 88, 98, 99, 103, 105, 139, 158; codified laws, 40, 79, 81;

Courts, 41; duties, 98; educational institutions, 39; implementation, 38, 55; principles and objectives, 38, 41, 64; scholars, 79
Sharif, Hashem, 139
Shattuck, John, 56
Shelly, Mary, 7
Shīʿah, 51, 113, 120, 174
Shūrā, 54, 113, 149, 156, 160, 161, 162, 163, 175
Slavery, 14, 35, 67
Smith, Adam, 4
Socrates, 173
Solomon, 111
Sonn, Tamara, 144, 151, 155, 158, 165
Soroush, Abdolkarim, 144, 165, 166, 172
South Africa, 20
Soviet Union, 28, 137
Sparks, C. Stephen, 10
Spinoza, 4
Saudi Arabia, 28, 124, 127, 128, 132, 137, 139
Sudan, 81, 133, 139, 180
Sufyān ibn ʿUyainah, 77
Sunnī, 119, 120, 137, 174
Syria, 35, 50, 81, 118, 133, 150

T
Al-Ṭabarī, 32
Tawḥīd, 109, 110, 111, 116
Temple University, 127, 130
Thailand, 149
Thatcher, Margaret, 178
Tibi, Bassam, 13, 14, 21
Al-Tirmidhī, 31
Tocqueville, Alexis de, 14, 15, 16
Tunisia, 81, 117, 133, 143, 177
Turabi, Hasan, 100, 134, 180
Turkey/Turkish, 12, 13, 23, 25, 74, 114, 169

193

Index

U

Umayyad(s), 38, 51, 72, 92, 111, 112, 158
United Nations, 27, 29, 59, 60, 61, 62, 63, 66; charter, 59, 64; Committee of Human Rights, 63; General Assembly, 27, 28, 29, 32, 56, 66; Security Council, 29
United Nations Commission on Human Rights, 66
United Nations Fourth World Conference on Women, 46
United States of America, 21, 29, 35, 57, 58, 59, 70, 71, 75, 86, 92, 101, 106, 124, 127, 128, 130, 134, 137, 139, 141, 145, 151, 152, 156, 170, 180, 181; Bill of Rights, 27; Constitution, 27; Declaration of Independence, 27; Revolution, 71, 177
Universal Declaration of Human Rights, 27, 32, 33, 40, 56, 59, 63, 66, 67, 68, 69, 70, 75, 157
University of Southern California, 141
UN World Conference on Women and Non-Governmental Organizations Forum, 57

V

Vienna, 21, 56, 58, 135, 169
Vienna Declaration and Program of Action, 56
Volga basin, 53
Voll, John Obert, 37

W

Wafd Party, 124
Washington, 55
Weber, Max, 5, 8, 18, 19, 160
West(ern), 8, 14, 18, 22, 24, 27, 35, 39, 60, 66, 86, 87, 92, 93, 94, 96, 97, 98, 107, 123, 125, 128, 131, 134, 135, 137, 138, 139, 142, 145, 147, 150, 154, 159, 161, 163, 165, 166, 171, 172, 173, 174, 175, 176, 177, 178, 181, 182; academia, 25, 26, 151, 152, 159, 160; challenge, 24; civilization, 6, 95, 108, 129, 138, 164; colonialism, 9; concept of the state, 71; culture, 130; domination, 104; economics, 21; education system, 21; hegemony, 93, 94, 95; hermeneutics, 22; initiatives, 27; intellectuals, 135, 152, 164; laws, 41; legal practice, 33, 40; media, 131, 135; modernity, 1, 2, 4, 6, 37; Muslim minorities in, 49, 51, 53, 54, 72, 97, 101, 102, 103, 104, 105, 106, 107, 108, 115, 136; outlook, 3, 165; philosophy, 4; political thought, 9, 12, 13, 66, 72; powers, 81; scholars, 49, 135; societies, 107, 135, 136, 160, 165; technology, 128; values, 129
Will, 45
World Bank, 93, 104, 149, 151
World War I, 81, 164
World War II, 28, 101, 106
Women, 43, 44, 47; equality for, 43; Muslim, 44; rights, 46, 57; right to inheritance, 45

Y

Yaḥyā ibn Ḥamzah, 78
Yamani, Ahmad Zaki, 128, 129, 130, 136, 137, 138
Year of Human Rights, 28
Yemen, 133

Z

Zaidan, Abdul Karim, 50, 100
Zakāt, 48, 83, 90
Zia-ul-Haq, 133
Zionism, 94, 95, 111, 128, 131